THE GREAT FLAP OF 1942

ADVANCE PRAISE FOR THE BOOK

'A superbly well-researched, tightly constructed and beautifully written exploration of an almost forgotten chapter in the history of the Second World War. *The Great Flap of 1942* is a brilliant recreation of a particular time and place, effortlessly pinned to the page in stylish, witty and evocative prose. Mukund Padmanabhan, long regarded as one of India's most admired journalists and editors, has now emerged from that chrysalis to reveal himself as a new superstar of Indian narrative non-fiction'—William Dalrymple

'A magnet of a masterpiece, Padmanabhan's book pulls into its field the filings of veracious history, the bewitchment of a great story and the lure of the finest prose. I have rarely been so gripped, so totally captivated by any book on war and its mine-clogged realms of human folly'—Gopalkrishna Gandhi

'In *The Great Flap of 1942*, Mukund Padmanabhan has produced a gem of a book, telling not only a little-known story but packing it with the most astonishing details. Briskly paced, always interesting, and—despite its fraught settings—capable of inspiring more than a few chuckles, *The Great Flap of 1942* is both a page-turner and a well-researched slice of history. I enjoyed the book thoroughly, from the first page to the last'—Manu S. Pillai

THE GREAT FLAP OF 1942

HOW THE RAJ PANICKED OVER A JAPANESE NON-INVASION

MUKUND PADMANABHAN

VINTAGE
An imprint of Penguin Random House

VINTAGE

USA | Canada | UK | Ireland | Australia
New Zealand | India | South Africa | China | Singapore

Vintage is part of the Penguin Random House group of companies
whose addresses can be found at global.penguinrandomhouse.com

Published by Penguin Random House India Pvt. Ltd
4th Floor, Capital Tower 1, MG Road,
Gurugram 122 002, Haryana, India

Penguin Random House India

First published in Vintage by Penguin Random House India 2024

10 9 8 7 6 5 4 3 2

The views and opinions expressed in this book are the author's own and the facts are as reported by him which have been verified to the extent possible, and the publishers are not in any way liable for the same.

ISBN 9780670098477

For sale in the Indian Subcontinent only

Typeset in Garamond by MAP Systems, Bengaluru, India
Printed at Thomson Press India Ltd, New Delhi

www.penguin.co.in

Contents

For Amma, naturally

And ye shall hear of wars and rumours of wars: see that ye be not troubled . . .

—Matthew 24:6

Author's note

The names of places, cities, towns and villages used in this book are those that were used at the time. Since this is how they were referred to in the sources, the retention of the old names has been done for the sake of convenience and ease of reading.

Foreword

The childhood stories my mother told me were the sparks that kindled my interest in The Great Flap of 1942. She had finished high school when her family fled Madras in the last wave of the exodus that all but emptied the city. Despite the official advisories to leave and the fear of Japanese air raids and invasion, her father had decided to stay put—until it was impossible to remain any longer. In a rumour-fuelled, panicky Madras, provisions were low, transport was hard to come by, domestic help had vanished and restaurants had shuttered. The tipping point for her family arrived when the milkman stopped coming.

She moved with her parents and siblings to Coimbatore, well away from the coastline and less threatened by Japanese bombs. They spent a whole year there, where my mother completed the first year of the two-year Intermediate degree—a requirement in those days to enrol for a graduate course. When the family returned to Madras, well after the threat had blown over, she was very upset at being refused permission to register for the second year of the Intermediate course. She was told by Miss Myers, the Principal of Queen Mary's College, somewhat flatly, that she needed to do the first year all over again.

Refusing to accept what she regarded as an injustice, she scouted around to find a college that would have her. This led her some 250 km away to Besant Theosophical College in Madanapalle, the institution where the Indian national anthem 'Jana Gana Mana' was set to music during Rabindranath Tagore's brief stay in 1919. It was a bold decision for a sixteen-year-old girl to make in those days, but it made her stronger, exposed her to new friends and changed her life in significant ways.

As I grew up, I became aware that there was not a single person I knew whose family hadn't fled Madras in 1942. There was a dim recognition then that there was a story crying out to be written about the panic and the flight of people. And there is a painful recognition now that almost everyone who remembers The Great Flap is either no more or unable to remember the events as they unfolded in accurate detail.

When my mother's family returned to Madras, they found their house stripped bare. Thieves, who had the run of an empty city, had made off with anything that could be removed—doors, doorknobs, windows and grills. It was the senseless absurdity of it all that fascinated me about my mother's stories. That an entire city could have fled because of an invasion that never happened is a story with an irresistible twist of dystopian futility.

What began as a book mainly about Madras morphed into something much larger. It soon became apparent that writing about the Flap demanded a broader narrative arc, starting with Japan's attack and conquest of South-East Asia and its forays into the Indian Ocean and the Bay of Bengal. At the same time, my research made it clear that it wasn't just Madras, but pretty much all of India that was caught in the Flap. People fled from other coastal towns on both sides of the seaboard and from many places in the interior. Government departments—not only in Madras but in places such as Cuttack and Cochin—were hurriedly moved to 'safer' places.

The exodus from towns and cities across India disrupted many hundred thousand lives—of rich and poor alike. Quite remarkably, and there is enough evidence to establish this, the flight of people was encouraged by the colonial administration. The men who ruled India then believed that it was much better, from a military and administrative point of view, if there were fewer people in towns and cities that Japan was likely to target. As a result, 'non-essentials', 'non-effectives' or 'useless mouths' in the so-called threatened areas were either actively persuaded to leave or not discouraged from fleeing. It is a myth that Indians fled because they were timorous. 'Europeans' (the term generally used to describe white folk) fled in fright as well in a Flap that was very much of British making.

The book addresses how World War II, specifically the Japanese threat, impacted Britain's attitude to the question of India's freedom. At the same time, the war influenced the course of the nationalist movement. It may be impossible to determine exactly how much the threat of Japan, or the possibility of an Axis victory, which seemed very real in the first few months of 1942, influenced the two momentous events that year: the failure of the Cripps Mission and the launch of the Quit India Movement. But these events, at the very least, deserve to be examined against the looming backdrop of war.

While writing this, I was painfully aware that I am not formally trained in history. Apart from primary sources, the book owes a lot to many accomplished works written by those who have been schooled in the subject. Two are foremost in my mind. There is my dear friend Indivar Kamtekar's sharp and formative essay, 'The Shiver of 1942', the obvious starting point for anyone with an interest in the Flap. Srinath Raghavan's proficient and illuminating *India's War: World War II and the Making of Modern South Asia* is the other.

I owe a lot to the many friends who read a chapter or two of the manuscript and encouraged me to complete it. My interest was also kept alive by the surprised reactions of those who heard my replies to their questions about the Flap. For instance, while many people in Madras were aware of the wartime exodus, most were astonished to learn that something between 75 and 90 per cent of the city's population fled. Hardly anyone knew that the panic had also gripped the interior, leave alone the story of how British and American folk took fright and bolted from the sequestered hill station of Kodaikanal. That Orissa's capital Cuttack, a town the British regarded as especially vulnerable, shifted most of its government departments to interior Sambalpur is an event that seems to have all but vanished from historical memory.

I would be lying if I denied the occasional rush of delight on finding such stories in the archival material and newspaper columns I pored over. Whether this is something of a hidden history is up to the reader to decide. I hope, at the very least, it is a narrative of events that have been somewhat neglected, of stories that have been lost.

Introduction

In the early hours of 7 April 1942, three Japanese aircraft were spotted over the Bay of Bengal by an ageing Atalanta on a routine reconnaissance mission from Madras. The hulking plane was fondly referred to as the 'Victory Bus' (because it was used for patrols every day) or the 'Lazy Susan' (because it chuntered along at a genial pace). Essentially a passenger aircraft that served the British Empire's colonies in Africa, it could carry up to nine passengers. Some Atalantas found their way into the British Overseas Airways Corporation (BOAC) in India. From there, they made their way into the Royal Air Force, each fitted with a single .303 machine gun.

So long in the tooth, the Atalanta could have been easily extracted out of the sky by the three Japanese aircraft, whatever their make or type. But oddly enough, it was the Japanese pilots who veered away after studying the aircraft intently, apparently frightened by the four-engined plane's size. The story that made the rounds in Madras was that the Japanese turned and fled in terror, suspecting it was some sort of new secret British weapon. If true, this was possibly the only instance until then of the British scaring off the Japanese in World War II. It was invariably the other way around, with British India cowering in fear over an impending Japanese attack, a dread that had set in when Japan entered the war a few months earlier.

The world over, Japan's entry into the war in December 1941 was headlined as the savaging of Pearl Harbour. In India, the real worry was over a synchronous operation—the invasion of Malaya. This invasion brought the war closer home, not only geographically, but also because of the large number of Indians who worked and lived there. Japan left no one in any doubt that Malaya was part of a bigger military game plan, with simultaneous attacks in other parts of South-East and East Asia, such as Hong Kong, Singapore and the Philippines. The Indian reaction may have been driven by self-interest, but from Japan's strategic point of view, the attack on Malaya was no less important than that on Pearl Harbour. The latter was aimed at destroying the United States' Pacific Fleet, at preventing it from impeding Japan's plan of occupying a vast number of countries, including Malaya, Singapore, Burma and the Dutch East Indies.

Pearl Harbour was insurance. South-East Asia the prize.

Over the next few months, Japan advanced with a speed that stunned the world, ripping apart like muslin an Empire that was woven purposefully over centuries. Having landed troops in southern Thailand and at Kota Bharu in northern Malaya, the Japanese swept southwards, deterred neither by the myth of impenetrable jungles nor the large numbers of British, Indian and Australian troops that were massed there. From Johor in Malaya, it was just a short hop across the Straits to force the British, holed up in a Singapore already battered from the air, to submit to a humiliating surrender.

The fall of Singapore on 15 February 1942 meant much more than the loss of an important island. Singapore symbolized the tight grip exercised by the British Empire on South-East Asia and South Asia, a place from where it controlled the trade that flowed through the Indian Ocean. It was also mythologized by the British, without any foundation as we now know, as an unbreachable fortress. The 'worst disaster and the largest capitulation in British history', lamented a devastated Prime Minister Winston Churchill of the surrender of 1,36,000 men, which included British, Indian, Australian and Malay soldiers, after just a week of fighting.

The attack and fall of Malaya and the humiliation at Singapore, which was perceived as a bulwark against Japanese designs on India, sent frissons of fear through the subcontinent. A stream of people began leaving cities on both sides of the seaboard. They fled from coastal towns as far-flung as Calcutta, Cochin, Cuttack, Chittagong and Bombay. Villages on the coast, too, emptied out. And there was flight from unlikely places deep in the interior such as Delhi, Ahmedabad, the industrial township of Jamshedpur and the coalfields of Bihar. From Calcutta, between 13 and 30 December 1941, about 17 per cent of the population left by train from Howrah and Sealdah stations. This doesn't factor in the many tens of thousands that hurried out in steady streams via the roads. All over the country, the British rulers, tacitly or otherwise, encouraged people they regarded as 'non-essential', or irrelevant to the war effort, to flee. At the same time, they attributed the rushed departures to the fearful and faint-hearted nature of Indians.

The panic only grew as the Japanese got closer to the Indian mainland, intensifying the speculation that a full-fledged invasion was imminent. In March 1942, Japan entered the lovely archipelagic waters of the Andaman and Nicobar Islands and took its capital Port Blair without so much as a cheep of resistance. On 5 April, a sizeable Japanese fleet, led by Admiral Chuichi Nagumo, the man who commanded the main carrier that attacked Pearl Harbour, sailed into the Indian Ocean. Waves of aircraft bombed Colombo and, a few days later, the port town of Trincomalee. Off Ceylon's eastern coast, the venerable British aircraft carrier *Hermes*, and its companion, the destroyer *Vampire*, were sunk, killing over 300 men.

Meanwhile, on 6 April, the coastal towns north of Madras, Vizagapatam and Cocanada (now Visakhapatnam and Kakinada), were raided from the air. Although the damage was not great, it was inflicted by planes that lifted off from the decks of a second Japanese fleet, the Malay Force, that was prowling in the Bay of Bengal. The targets were merchant ships that the fleet picked off with an almost cavalier abandon. As many as twenty of them were dispatched to the bottom of the sea.

Of course, there was no invasion of the Indian mainland, full-fledged or otherwise. In fact, the Japanese had no such plan at all. The air raids on Ceylon were aimed at destroying the British Eastern Fleet, which had regrouped in the island nation after the fiasco at Singapore. And the objective in the Bay of Bengal was to disrupt Allied shipping, which was suspended for a while after the attack.

Yes, Japanese soldiers did make a foray into Indian territory two years later, in 1944, entering the north-eastern region from their bases in Burma. Alongside them were members of the Indian National Army (INA), the formation led by Indian nationalists committed to securing independence by the use of armed force. But by then, the balance in the war had shifted considerably. Japan had lost its naval and air superiority in crucial battles with the US, and British India was much better placed in terms of men and armaments. The Japanese would not only be pushed back to the border, but forced to retreat much further into Burma by counter-attacking Indian troops.

In late 1941 and early 1942, the story was very different. The run of continuous successes after it entered the war made Japan seem invincible. Questions had begun to be raised about whether the British were even capable of defending India, heightening the sense of insecurity. Rumours swirled, widening in eddies, their increasingly fantastic nature doing nothing to either reduce their credibility or impede their spread all over the country. Surely you know that the Tatas, the country's biggest industrial group, have done a deal with the Japanese to prevent their steelworks in Jamshedpur from being bombed? Heard about the machine guns dropped in the Prisoner of War (PoW) camp near Dehradun to enable them to capture the town? Is Archibald Wavell, India's Commander-in-Chief, even alive?

Raj officials were dismayed about the proliferation of wild rumours and their inability to defuse them. But unwittingly, they played a role in contributing to their spread. The attempt to play down or obscure casualties in places such as Malaya and Singapore with descriptions such as 'slight' or 'moderate', and the unwillingness to reveal numbers of dead and injured, was counter-productive. Such obfuscation was defended on the grounds that it was done to prevent people from panicking, but it only reinforced the scepticism about official statements and figures, providing another trigger for rumours.

Similarly, officials of the Raj played down the level of anxiety and disruption in the lives of people as a result of the Japanese scare. In British circles, the period was often informally referred to as 'The Great Flap of 1942'. But the magnitude of this flap and the extent of the disruption have not received the attention they deserve. The historian Indivar Kamtekar suggests that the obsession with independence and the end of Empire led historians, nationalist and imperialist, to push what he calls the shiver of 1942 into the margins. They did this because the Japanese scare didn't fit into the grand narratives of either the freedom struggle or that of decolonization.

Nevertheless, the outbreak of war in the West and Japan's entry into it changed the contours of Indian politics. Viceroy and Governor-General Lord Linlithgow's unilateral declaration that India was at war in September 1939, just hours after Britain made a similar announcement, laid the ground for a tactical game. The British wanted Indian support for and participation in the war effort and were prepared to make minor concessions for the same. In response, the Congress Party linked such support to the ultimate goal—independence. As concessions were made and rejected and more concessions sought, different schools of thought emerged within the Congress. Subhash Chandra Bose, ousted from the Congress, threw in his lot with the Axis powers and eventually assumed control of the INA, which was formed in 1942 by Indian PoWs captured by the Japanese in Malaya and Singapore. But other differences remained among the top leadership over how the Congress' position on the war should be aligned with the quest for freedom. The virtue of pacifism, the imperative to fight against fascism and the best course to fashion national unity were among the issues that divided leaders such as Mahatma Gandhi, Jawaharlal Nehru and C. Rajagopalachari.

Memories of 1942 largely revolve around events such as the announcement of the Cripps Mission, its eventual failure, the launch of the Quit India Movement, the arrests of top Congress leaders and so on. These are regarded by nationalists as an integral part of the chronicle of India's struggle for freedom. In British eyes, they were events in a comforting story about the peaceable transfer of power. In contrast, The Great Flap of 1942 is bereft of an ending, and wanting of a historical climax. The Japanese didn't show up after all. The tizzy over the invasion was much ado about nothing. Maybe it was. But there is no reason why histories, like fiction, cannot be stories without ends. Open-endedness may have relegated this story to being largely ignored, but it is this very character that lends it a fascinatingly fictional feel.

That so much fear, disruption and upheaval could have happened because of a non-event is best reflected by the madness that gripped Madras, the first Indian city of the British Empire. A couple of days after the lumbering Atalanta sighted the Japanese aircraft off the coastline, the British government received military 'intelligence' of a large-scale Japanese invasion south of the city. On the following day, the Madras Presidency's Governor, Arthur Hope, issued a communiqué asking all those whose presence was not essential to leave. Already in a dither over rumours that

Madras would be the next Japanese target, the evacuation order only compounded the chaos. Roads were jammed with people fleeing with their belongings on foot, in cars and bullock carts. The railways were overrun. By the middle of April, something between 75 and 90 per cent of the city's population had evacuated.

The government's decision to move most of its departments to a scattering of inland towns made things even worse. The bulk of British officials and European residents left. These included judges of the Madras High Court, which was split and transferred to two towns. Food was in very short supply, prices rose steeply and empty houses were routinely ransacked by thieves.

In the welter of confusion and chaos, the government ordered that all 'dangerous' animals in the Madras Zoo be shot dead. The fear was that Japanese bombs could destroy zoo enclosures and free animals such as lions, tigers, bears and snakes and turn them perilously loose on what remained of the citizenry. The Commissioner of the Madras Corporation, O. Pulla Reddi, one of the few senior officials ordered to stay behind, was tasked with organizing the murders at the zoo. Reddi, who believed that an imminent Japanese invasion was highly unlikely, tried to reason with the Commissioner of Police, Lionel Gasson, that shooting the animals dead would be 'hasty and premature'. But to no avail. The Malabar Police carried out the operation with cold and clinical efficiency, finishing the job in a few blood-splattered minutes.

On this day of madness, Reddi recalled in disbelief, 'Everybody seemed to have lost his head.'

1

The Conquest of Malaya

Just before 8 a.m. on 7 December 1941, the first wave of 183 aircraft swept over Oahu island in Hawaii. The second wave of Japanese planes followed shortly. Together they sank or damaged eighteen ships, killed a little over 2400 Americans and injured about a thousand others. The surprise attack on Pearl Harbour, which led the US to declare war on Japan the following day, is one of the watershed events of World War II. But in Japanese eyes, the objective of the attack—the stuff of countless books and movies—was, in a way, somewhat limited. It was to incapacitate the US Navy and prevent American interference in Japan's grand design—the subjugation and control of South-East Asia.

Almost simultaneously, the Japanese conducted air raids on US-held Philippines, Guam and Wake Island. They also pounded a poorly fortified British Hong Kong from the air, as their troops rained down from across the frontier in China. It was the third prong of this coordinated assault that had the greatest strategic significance for India and the Raj—the invasion of Malaya. While Britain appeared to have written off Hong Kong, having already conceded that it was indefensible against a full-fledged Japanese assault, the attack on Malaya hugely unsettled it. Malaya, with its reserves of tin and acres of rubber plantations, was an important economic asset. And then, there was the big question:

Could Malaya be a staging post for the big prize, the proverbial fortress of Singapore?

Japan answered the question by unequivocally signalling that the island fell within its sphere of hegemonic interest. Within hours of making landfall in Kota Bharu in north-west Malaya, a fleet of seventeen Japanese bombers hit two airfields as well as Raffles Place, Singapore's commercial hub. Bad weather forced a reduction in the scale of the operation. By the ruinous standards of World War II, there was relatively 'little damage'. However, about five dozen people were killed, most of them Gurkhas from the 2/2 Regiment.

There was a popular belief within the British armed forces that Singapore could not be assaulted from the north, via Malaya. To begin with, Malaya, unlike Hong Kong, was thought to be well defended. Earlier in the year, the 9th Indian Infantry Division was sent to augment the Malaya Command. Two days after Kota Bharu, the *Times of India* editorialized self-assuredly: 'It is indeed fortunate for India that Malaya, our eastern outpost, is strongly garrisoned with British, Indian and Australian forces.'[1] The British also thought poorly of Japan's army, as being made up of men who were fearful, bandy-legged and far-sighted with their squinty eyes. It was this kind of racially tinged conceit that led Harbakhsh Singh, then a young Indian Army officer posted in Ipoh, to conclude, 'The Peninsula of Malaya was lost because of the poor opinion that the British held of Japanese soldiers.'[2]

There was another reason for this false sense of composure and confidence—geography. A rain-forested mountain range, about 650 km from north to south, ran like a thick green spine down the middle of the peninsula. Streams that grew into swiftly flowing rivers emerged from it like tendrils that emptied out on both sides—the Straits of Malacca on the east and the South China Sea westwards. The coastal plains were made up of a mix of mudflats, sandy beaches and mangrove forests. Throw in jungle swamps, rainfall and venomous snakes, and it seemed like there was a case to support the prevalent view that it would be difficult, if not well-nigh impossible, to overrun Malaya and take Singapore from the north.

It was a view amplified by the Raj's propagandists soon after the Japanese made landfall at Kota Bharu. Reports in Indian newspapers took the 'impenetrable jungle' theory a step further, citing an Indian Army observer as saying: 'The Indian troops, who form the majority of the garrison of Malaya, together with the British, Australian and Malay comrades are barring the way on every possible invasion route.' Declaring that Singapore was 'the vital bastion for India's eastern defence', he went on to claim that jungle warfare was an Indian speciality and that the morale of the troops was very high at the prospect of action.[3]

He was, of course, hopelessly wrong on the last two counts. There was nothing to support the view that Indian troops were more acclimatized to or more adept at jungle warfare; a sizeable number of them lacked even general training.[4] The fear of snakes, as one might expect, was 'universal', Indians being no exception to the rule. When there were air raids, members of the 5th Battalion of the Sikh Regiment would rush to their rain-filled slit trenches only to get bitten by snakes trapped in them.[5] Those from the 4th/19th Hyderabad were mortified to find themselves covered in shiny brown and black leeches.[6]

As for morale, it was low for a number of reasons—ordinary communication being one of them. The war had forced the rapid expansion of the Indian Army, which ballooned to 9,00,000 by December 1941; of them, 2,64,000 were serving abroad by early 1942.[7] The urgent need to augment troops dismantled the old British myth, reinforced by the 1857 uprising, that only martial races in India were loyal and fit enough to fight. The Indian Army now spoke a babel of tongues, making it even more difficult for

British officers to communicate with the men, let alone win their trust. The officers were completely dependent on reports prepared by men under their command, who often tailored them to please their superiors.[8]

By the advent of World War II, the Raj had also been forced to give in, if only in an agonizingly slow and piecemeal way, to having more Indian commissioned officers in the army. The future Prime Minister of India, Jawaharlal Nehru, saw this reluctance as a cynical attempt to isolate the Indian Army from its people. 'All key positions were kept in the hands of Englishmen and no Indian could hold the King's Commission. A raw English subaltern was senior to the oldest and most experienced Indian Non-Commissioned Officer . . . No Indian could be employed at army headquarters except as a petty clerk in the accounts department.'[9] But as it was in many ways during the Raj, the more things changed, the more they remained the same. In January 1942, there were 596 Indian commissioned officers, a figure that had risen sharply since 1939 and would balloon to 8340 at the end of the war in September 1945.[10] But inequalities persisted in at least two ways. The British paid themselves more than Indians—a British lieutenant received 50 per cent more than his Indian counterpart.[11] Much worse for preserving the esprit de corps was the undisguised racism in Malaya.

There were clubs, swimming pools, railway carriages and buses for the exclusive use of white people. At Ipoh railway station, Captain Ranjit Rai found himself allotted a seat in a red carriage, while two British officers, junior to him, were allotted places in a white carriage. Rai insisted on getting the seat allotments reversed, sending his British subordinates to the red carriage, but the local stationmaster, a South Indian, maintained it was against the rules and refused to flag off the train. The matter had to be referred all the way to Singapore before orders were relayed down to the stationmaster to allow the train to depart.[12]

Harbakhsh Singh was extremely upset by an invitation extended by the Raja of Perak for drinks and dinner. It was extended only to British officers and nurses, and Harbakhsh was horrified by his Commanding Officer Lt Col Perkins' acceptance of it. In an army where Indians held similar positions, Singh justifiably felt that Perkins should have either refused the invitation or insisted it was extended to Indian officers. 'What a disappointment!' he recalled, of someone he regarded as physically brave, but 'a bit of an imperialist'.[13]

In Malaya, Prem Sahgal, who captained a Baluch regiment, was aghast at how colour-conscious the British were. In Kelantan, the club was off bounds for him, a policy the British rationalized by saying, 'How can we take Indian officers, when we don't take senior Malays?' Sahgal refused to allow the battalion's band to play at the club. He told the British colonel that he had disallowed this because three Indian officers who contributed to the maintenance of the band were ineligible to become club members. Sahgal, of course, had suffered discrimination before. In Singapore, a year or so earlier, he was given a temporary membership by mistake to a Europeans-only club, which was revoked. Even earlier, in Peshawar, Prem had conceived of a cheeky but successful tactic to send a message to the wives of British officers, who would scramble out of the pool every time an Indian officer went for a dip.

> I collected my chaps and we got beer and lashings of sandwiches and lay on the edge. When an English girl went in, we went in. And when she got out, we got out. So after a while, she got tired of all this going in and getting out, and there was no more problem.[14]

Sahgal would go on to become one of the leading lights of the INA, which was formed with active Japanese aid and encouragement to liberate India with the help of those who lived outside it. He was something of a reluctant recruit. But once he enrolled, he rose quickly to serve as military secretary to

Subhash Chandra Bose, the rebel Congressman who would go on to lead the INA and declare himself head of the Provisional Government of Azad Hind (Free India). The charismatic woman Sahgal married, Lakshmi Swaminathan, would be appointed the Minister for Women's Affairs. Raised in Madras and born in a distinguished family, she would lead a trained squad of women, the Rani Jhansi Regiment, named after the queen who became a symbol of courage and resistance during the Indian uprising of 1857.

* * *

There are numerous other stories of Indian Army officers feeling slighted by the British in South-East Asia. How much such racial discrimination contributed to the formation of the INA is a matter of debate.* But there is no doubt it contributed to the hardening of anti-British sentiment and encouraged Indian officers to be more open to Japanese overtures. This sense of disaffection was, of course, not a post-invasion phenomenon, having existed well before the Japanese bombed Hong Kong or landed at Kota Bharu. Discrimination, a growing nationalist sentiment and the nagging feeling that Britain could end up losing the war had together stoked both anger and estrangement. In May 1940, a company of Ahirs in Malaya agitated for the reinstatement of an officer with anti-British views; their protests spread to a company of Jats.[15] In early 1941, Sikh troops as well as the Sikh community in Hong Kong were disaffected, leading the general officer in command (GOC) to complain that Japanese subversive activity

---

* Hugh Toye, 'The First Indian National Army, 1941–42', *Journal of Southeast Asian Studies*, Vol. 15, September 1984. Toye suggests the impact of racism on the accession of officers to the INA was probably exaggerated and that other reasons played a role, such as the British defeat in Malaya and Japanese efforts to befriend Indian soldiers.

against Indian troops remained unabated.[16] In May 1941, the 4th/19th Hyderabad Regiment in Singapore was close to mutiny, protesting against the sending home of an officer with nationalist views. His 'crime'? Living with a white woman.[17]

All in all, the inequitable and prejudiced climate in South-East Asia was ideal for subverting Indian Army men. And the groundwork for this was laid before the Japanese made landfall at Kota Bharu. Japan, of course, was not looking to merely build an army. It was casting its strategic net much wider, expanding its influence by cooperating with and supporting resistance in the region. By September 1941, Japan's Supreme War Council had established Fujiwara Kikan (F-Kikan), which was tasked with working with independence movements in Malaya, Thailand, Indonesia and Burma. Named after the man who headed it, Major Fujiwara Iwaichi, this military intelligence operation worked hand in hand with Indian nationalists in the region. In time, the local Indian organizations would be knit together to form the Indian Independence League, headed by Rash Behari Bose, the Indian revolutionary who went into hiding in Japan after he was accused of planning the assassination of Viceroy and Governor-General Lord Hardinge in 1912.

In Malaya, F-Kikan had an interest in two other ethnic groups: the overseas Chinese, who were potentially hostile, but critical for their economic muscle and business acumen, and the Malay Sultans, who were regarded as necessary to win the confidence of the people. F-Kikan went as far as 'rescuing' the Sultan of Kedah's family members, who were in hiding to escape the looting by locals and Japanese soldiers, and returning them to the town of Alor Setar. Fujiwara Iwaichi personally disciplined the Japanese soldiers who were involved in the looting.[18] But it was the Indians, soldiers and civilians, who probably mattered most to F-Kikan's aims in South-East Asia. There were about 2 million Indians at the time, 8,00,000 in Malaya, more than a million in Burma and the rest in Thailand, Indonesia, Hong Kong, the Philippines and Indochina. Some were politically active; most of those who weren't were supporters of the Congress Party.[19] Indians also made up the bulk of the British Army in the region. While Indian soldiers could be employed in the defence of the region, civilians could be co-opted in working to remove the British from India as a part of Japan's professed aim to keep 'Asia for the Asians'.

Fujiwara's work in Malaya began days before the Japanese made landfall at Kota Bharu. He met up with Giani Pritam Singh, who was active in an organization working for Indian independence in Bangkok. The Sikh missionary was a key member of the Ghadar movement, formed by expatriates to overthrow British rule. He fled to Bangkok after the movement failed to pull off the mutiny it had planned in 1915 against the British Army in India. Pritam Singh, who was already in touch with other Japanese Army officers, agreed that he and his men would accompany Fujiwara and his officials into Malaya. As the Imperial Japanese Army advanced southwards, its job was to secure the support of the Indian population and persuade captured soldiers to sign up to fight for Indian independence.

Fujiwara and Pritam Singh would taste their first success quickly, one that laid the ground for the creation of the INA. After the disastrous Battle of Jitra, Mohan Singh, a commissioned officer, and a few of his men of the 1st/14th Punjab negotiated their surrender with the Japanese. Devastated by Japanese tanks and flanking attacks, it was 'Every man for himself' as the battalion disintegrated and dispersed. Mohan Singh and his men were treated well. On 14 December, in a small town in the jungles near Alor Setar, Fujiwara and Pritam Singh, accompanied by two interpreters, came to see Mohan Singh. Fujiwara's striking ability to win the trust of Indians and create an atmosphere of genuine friendship and cooperation was very much in play on the day. 'It was as if we had already known each other and were great friends,' gushed Mohan Singh, who would go on to hold political discussions for days with Fujiwara. But it was their first meeting he regarded as 'auspicious' as it took place on the very day that he got married a year earlier. Both events were turning points that 'completely changed the course' of his life.[20]

Mohan Singh and fifty of his men were adopted by F-Kikan, given armbands with the letter 'F' and made to work closely with the Japanese Army. They were sent out to mop up stragglers around Alor Setar who were trying to find their own regiments. Within three days, the numbers had swollen to 1000. At the end of December, General Yamashita, who saw potential in Fujiwara's recruitment drive, ordered that all captured Indian Army men be handed over to Mohan Singh. In early February, Fujiwara arranged for Mohan Singh to meet Yamashita over tea. Without waiting to be introduced, the General gave him a fatherly hug and promised that Japan's government would help in his noble cause of liberating India.

Mohan Singh would have his moment in the sun when Singapore was 'liberated' a few days later, on 15 February 1942. By then, the number of troops under his command had expanded to 10,000.

* * *

India reacted to the coordinated assaults on 7–8 December in its own way. Pearl Harbour may have been the international headline, but it was Malaya that actualized the threat in Indian minds. There were a number of reasons for this. Geographically, the war had come closer. Then, there was the threat to Singapore, which Indians living under the Raj were taught stood unassailably between them and Japan's hegemonic designs. There was also a sizeable Indian population in Malaya which, by late 1938, had swollen to almost

7.5 lakh,[21] the majority of them Tamils who were sent either as indentured labour or hired on cheap contractual terms to work the sugar, coffee and rubber plantations. There were communities from other regions as well, prominent among them the Sikhs who were engaged in a variety of professions, including policing and money-lending. By October 1941, there were 56,000 Indian troops in Malaya,[22] of which there were about 31,000 ground forces, the others engaged in work such as administration, signals and mechanical transport. Both civilians and soldiers had relatives at home, and Indian leaders were concerned about their plight. From mid-1938, Indian emigration of labour to Malaya was banned in response to the falling rates paid to plantation labour. In November 1941, Hriday Nath Kunzru moved a resolution in the Council of States, the Upper House of the legislature, seeking the Governor-General's full support to improve living conditions and secure higher wages for Indian workers in rubber plantations. It rankled him that these workers were paid less than Chinese ones, by as much as 50 per cent or more. Eventually, Kunzru withdrew his resolution,[23] although reluctantly, to avoid embarrassing the government.[24] There was arguably also a more remote and transcendent connection. Malaya was very much part of the ancient sphere of India's cultural and religious influence. Hinduism and Buddhism had made their presence felt over 2000 years ago. Recent archaeological digs in the Bujang Valley in the north-west of the peninsula have unearthed a kingdom dating back to the fourth or fifth centuries CE, probably the oldest in the South-East Asian region.

'[Japan's] attack on Malaya and Pearl Harbour recalls Germany's onslaught of Russia and the diplomatic pourparlers that preceded it,' editorialized *The Hindu* wordily. The hyphenation of the two attacks reflected the importance attached to Malaya. If this wasn't enough, it went on to clearly spell out what really mattered at home: 'The immediate interest in India is the struggle in Malaya . . .' However, the newspaper discounted any cause for 'serious apprehension' given the mangrove swamps and long stretches of sandy beach that made up Malaya's coastline. The narrow approaches to the south, it reckoned, were heavily protected and the only other conduits were 'footpaths made up of deep ravines and dense forests'.[25]

The newspaper was probably only echoing what the military establishment believed, a sense of security that the Japanese shattered within days of their assault. The invasion of Malaya, which took place in the dead of night, a little before the attack on Pearl Harbour, had two prongs. Troops from one Japanese division landed at Kota Bharu in the north-eastern state of Kelantan. At the same time, troops from another division landed at two points slightly to the north in Thailand and pushed towards the western coast. Together they would sweep down the peninsula with a speed and ferocity that shook the Empire.

The operation was led by Commander Yamashita Tomoyuki, the 'Tiger of Malaya', who was given the job despite a history of rivalry with Prime Minister Hideki Tojo.[26] He sought fewer divisions than his superiors were willing to give him, and felt 60,000 men were enough for the job. He would have liked to be in Singapore in a matter of three weeks, or before the new year was rung in. It would take a little longer, but his confidence was not misplaced.

The attack on the coast of Kota Bharu was the first ground battle fought between Japan and the Allied forces in World War II. It was Indian soldiers of the 8th Infantry Brigade who manned the pillboxes strung along the beach and tried to fend off the amphibious landing. A battalion of Dogras put up a strong defence, killing about 1500 enemy troops and sending ripples of anxiety among Japan's military top brass.[27] But the Japanese ground forces succeeded in first creating and then widening the breach; eventually, they would push forward and capture the airstrip, leaving the Allied forces to fall back and take up positions further south.

As this pattern of resistance and retreat kept repeating itself over the next month, India watched the progress of the war keenly. There was hardly any news about the fate of Indian civilians, which worried relatives at home. As for the fighting, it was Indian soldiers of the III Corps, made up of the 9th and 11th Infantry Divisions, that saw much of it in the early days, having been posted in the northern and central regions of Malaya. But well before this, and just two days after the invasion, news that shattered the confidence of the British, and in turn, their belief in sustaining an Empire, had come from an unexpected quarter. Britain's naval prestige took a brutal hit with the sinking of the battleship *Prince of Wales* and its accompanying cruiser *Repulse*. The two capital ships had arrived in Singapore only a week earlier in the hope they would serve as a deterrent against possible Japanese aggression in the region. They were sent up the eastern coast of Malaya towards Kota Bharu to attack Japanese warships in the mistaken belief the Allied vessels were immune from air attack. The battleship and the cruiser made a detour towards Kuantan, south of Kota Bharu, on receiving a false report of a Japanese landing. Shadowed by a submarine and spotted by reconnaissance aircraft, the two vessels were exposed without air cover to waves of Japanese aircraft, which crippled and then eventually sank them. Eight hundred and forty lives were lost. A shaken Prime Minister Winston Churchill would write:

> In all the war, I never received a more direct shock . . . As I turned over and twisted in bed the full horror of the news sank in upon me. There were no British or American capital ships in the Indian Ocean or the

> Pacific except the American survivors of Pearl Harbour . . . Over all this vast expanse of waters Japan was supreme, and we everywhere were weak and naked.[28]

The sinking of the ships was a military fiasco, but the British would shortly suffer another more significant, at any rate, more irreparable, kind of loss—that of character. In Penang, then ruled directly by the Crown as a part of the Straits Settlements,* Britons and other Europeans slipped out surreptitiously soon after the island came under attack. It was decided to withdraw Allied troops as well, leaving Malay, Chinese and Indian residents at the mercy of Japanese planes and, later, Japanese troops. Together, they would reduce the capital Georgetown to a litter of bodies and a waste of rubble.

Japanese reconnaissance planes arrived first, scouting the island almost leisurely for a couple of days. People turned out to watch as if it were an aeronautical show, but on 11 December, the bombers arrived to pound the capital, killing unsuspecting people who came out on the streets, watching skywards with a mix of fear and fascination.

The decision to withdraw troops from Penang, which the British regarded as a fortress and vital gateway to the Indian Ocean, was defended on strategic grounds. The abandonment, it was claimed, was undertaken to consolidate troops on the mainland. As the Japanese advanced down the Malayan peninsula, there was already a feeling that it was important to

* British Malaya was then made up of three entities: the Straits Settlements (which included Singapore, Malacca and Penang), the Federated States (Selangor, Perak, Pahang and Negri Sembilan, all British protectorates) and the Unfederated States, which were nominally run by independent Sultans (such as Johor, Kelantan and Kedah).

protect the biggest asset in the region—Singapore. In an editorial on 21 December, *The Hindu* described the evacuation of Penang as a 'surprise' and a blow to the Indian community (which was 53,000-strong, according to the 1931 census), but went on to rationalize it as a not-so-serious loss from the strategic point of view. Suggesting that the withdrawal was to provide Singapore additional protection, it said: 'If Singapore is lost, the position of the Allies will become untenable; the loss of the hinterland of the Peninsula may therefore be risked in order to make Singapore impregnable.'[29]

But it was not so much the troops, but the selective and surreptitious evacuation of white civilians that damaged British prestige. They were ferried to the mainland and then put on trains at Butterworth. When they spilled out on the platform at Kuala Lumpur, the ladies gathered there to offer them tea and commiseration were surprised to find they were all white.[30] In one stroke, the evacuation exposed the old colonial lie that British rule was for the benefit of the natives. 'The moral collapse of British rule in South-East Asia came not at Singapore, but at Penang,' wrote historians Chris Bayly and Tim Harper in what has become a much-quoted sentence.[31]

The abandonment of Penang had its echoes in India. In a widely reported address to the Rotary Club in Bombay, a Mr Mallal, an evacuee from Singapore, pointed out that while the whole white administration of Penang was evacuated (with the exception of a doctor and two Salvation Army members, who chose to stay behind), Asiatics were not allowed to leave by the same boats, not even women and children. Describing it as disgraceful, he added: 'I do not think the British people will ever live it down.'[32] At a Federation of Indian Chambers of Commerce and Industry (FICCI) meeting in Delhi, Rajabali Jumabhoy, president of the Singapore chapter, pointed out that no Indian was allowed to leave after Penang suddenly fell into Japanese hands.

When they eventually could, they were made to pay (unlike Europeans who had free passage), were provided inferior boats and, unlike Chinese and Jews, were allowed to evacuate only to India. A string of questions based on Jumabhoy's charges of racial discrimination was raised in the Council of States, only to be stonewalled with a response that the issue was already under inquiry.[33]

There were anxieties in the Madras Presidency as a large number of the Indians in Penang, as indeed elsewhere in Malaya, were Tamil. In an attempt to address this, the Madras government put out a communiqué in early January explaining that the facilities to evacuate the entire population were inadequate. It attempted to allay apprehensions through a couple of lies. The statement claimed that the Japanese were observing international conventions in the territories they occupied, which was far from true. It also attempted to rationalize the limited evacuation by stating that 'many people did not want to abandon their homes and possessions'.[34] Interestingly, around the same time, the Madras Presidency's Governor, Arthur Hope, privately admitted that evacuating Europeans from Penang and leaving Indians behind 'has done a great deal of harm'. Yes, the presence of so many Indians presented 'obvious transport difficulties'. But even so, he made bold to tell Viceroy Linlithgow, 'there is a pretty bitter feeling about it'.[35]

Back in Britain, Harold Macmillan, the newly appointed Undersecretary of State for the Colonies, would tell the House of Commons that arrangements for evacuation were limited by the amount of shipping available and the need to conduct it in secrecy. 'No discrimination of any kind was made in connection with opportunities for evacuation,' said the man who would go on to become prime minister.[36]

With the ruling class having vanished and the Japanese continuing to pound the island, Penang was witness to looting and a complete breakdown of law and order. It was a Tamil of Sri Lankan origin, Manicasothy Saravanamuttu, the Editor of the Penang-based *Straits Echo*, who led the effort to restore some semblance of normalcy by constituting a volunteer force that did everything from preventing theft to preserving food and disposing of dead bodies. 'Uncle Sara', as he was known to friends, was convinced that the continued bombing was the result of a lack of information about the withdrawal of troops and the evacuation of the white ruling class. The committee that ran the town believed that hauling down the Union Jack that flew atop Fort Cornwallis could signal the evacuation. But there were no volunteers, and Sara had to commandeer a sub-editor at his newspaper, another Tamil called R.S. Gopal, for the job. Passing dead bodies and burning buildings, Gopal managed to clamber up the flagpole to remove the Union Jack that was tightly sewn to the pole.[37]

But this didn't stop the bombings. It was only on 18 December that Japan's ground forces on the mainland became aware that the British had evacuated the town.[38] The troops marched in that afternoon. They took the island without so much as a bullet, but those who remained in Penang lived in sheer terror, having to put up with all manner of horrors, including mass beheadings and rape. As the Editor of a newspaper that had earlier published unfavourable reports about the Japanese, Sara was thrown into a cell on Boxing Day. He slept with his face against the iron bars to avoid the stench from his bucket. He was in prison when a fake story made the rounds that he had been nominated by the Japanese as the Governor of Penang. A report was widely published, including in India, that the Japanese had selected him for the job to avoid the mistake Hitler made of failing to set up civil administrations in conquered territories.[39]

By mid-January, the Japanese had forced the Allied troops to their last defensive position in Malaya, southernmost Johor. And by the end of the month, they had fallen back to Singapore, blowing a big gap in the Causeway that linked Malaya and Singapore. But the fright in India took root much earlier. The attack on Malaya convinced many people that India would be the next target of aerial attack or, perish the thought, even an invasion. This triggered an exodus from Indian cities and coastal towns within days of the landing at Kota Bharu. Between 13 and 30 December, Bengal reported that 'something like 4,00,000 people' left by train from Calcutta and Howrah, in excess of what was normal during this period. Added to this was the 'steady stream of traffic leaving Calcutta and the industrial areas by road'.[40] In other words, more than 17 per cent of the city fled in about seventeen days! Of course, many more would leave as the Japanese pushed forward. People had started to flee Madras, Cochin, Cuttack, Bombay and far-flung places such as the coalfields of Bihar. Many made their way back from Ceylon to Chettinad and Ramnad in the Madras Presidency. As we shall see, the exodus was widespread and would spike sharply as the months wore on. People streamed out of 'vulnerable' cities, towns and even villages along the coastline. The panic, a word that the Raj administrators were averse to using, was much more widespread and ran much deeper than is commonly believed.

One reason for this is that the British had talked up Malaya's so-called invulnerability. Apart from increasing nervousness and alarm, this generated a deep sense of distrust in British propaganda. 'There is also a good deal of annoyance that we had repeated ad nauseam that we were ready and prepared for all eventualities and that Malaya was so strongly fortified that no attack could succeed. The result has had a bad effect on public opinion and there is great criticism of our propaganda and lack of belief in our initial statements,' wrote Governor Arthur Hope in a complaining tone to Viceroy Linlithgow.[41]

The attack and fall of Malaya set many things in motion in India. The tongue of rumour wagged wildly as people fled cities, spreading stories of fantastic Japanese prowess and contemptible British cowardice. Such chinwag suited the Japanese, and the British tried hard, though unsuccessfully, to arrest the rumour-fuelled alarm. At the same time, the Raj administration intensified Air Raid Precaution (ARP) activity. These measures stoked the panic, as they convinced many Indians that an attack was imminent. A sizeable section within the Congress Party became convinced that a weakening Britain presented the opportunity for a bolder push towards freedom. The defeat in Malaya also prepared the ground for the birth of the INA, midwifed by the Japanese on a football field in a Singapore park. There, a pledge was made to work for the liberation of India through war and armed resistance.

As for Britain, it finally signalled it was prepared to revise its old and scorned offer, that of Dominion Status in the indefinite future and set up a body after the war to devise a constitution. A reluctant Churchill, under some pressure from US President Franklin Roosevelt, was coerced into offering, or at least signalling that he was prepared to confer, some kind of freedom on India in exchange for its loyalty to the war effort.

In Malaya, the Japanese continued to advance speedily southwards, a good part of it on bicycles, which gave them greater mobility and helped to effectively outflank Allied troops. The town of Jitra and the airbase at Alor Setar succumbed quickly, and by 17 December, Lieutenant General Arthur Percival had fallen back to establish a line along the Perak River. When this couldn't hold, there were other attempts to hunker down along the Slim and Muar rivers, but these defensive lines were forced to give way as well. By 11 January, Kuala Lumpur had also fallen, and by the end of the month, the Allied forces had retreated from Malaya to hold the city that Churchill ordered to 'be converted into a citadel and defended unto the death'.[42]

Singapore.

2

The Fortress Crumbles

On the morning of 31 January 1942, Arthur Percival's army was hunkered down in defensive positions north of the island overlooking the Causeway, the only link between Malaya and Singapore. Soldiers in his multinational force watched in awe as Indian sappers set charges to the Causeway and triggered a series of massive explosions. As the waters hurried to repossess the gap, Singapore was detached from the peninsula. The Causeway was destroyed almost immediately after the last of the troops crossed over. They were Australians and Scotsmen from the Gordon Highlanders and the Argyll and Sutherland Highlanders. With that special British flair for crafting a ceremony in defeat, these men were bagpiped over to tunes such as 'Bonnets over the Border' and 'Hielan' Laddie'.[1]

The troops had begun journeying back to Singapore from 25 January onwards, when Percival, as GOC Malaya, had ordered them to retreat. In Singapore, he had 85,000 troops under his command, Indian, British, Australian and a few Malay and Chinese units. Of these, a little less than half were Indian; of the thirty-eight infantry battalions under his command, as many as seventeen were from India.[2]

Singapore was reinforced with troops arriving from Australia and India weeks before it was attacked, even as the Japanese were making their way southwards in Malaya. On paper, the balance was very much against Japan. The somewhat portly and poker-faced Yamashita had a little less than a third of what Percival had under his command. But his troops were trained well in the China Sea, where they practised amphibious landings, coped with humid conditions and learnt to travel quick and light, unencumbered by the inessential accoutrements of warfare. In contrast, most of Percival's troops were not conditioned to fight in the tropics.

Moreover, Singapore was not prepared for an attack from the north. If anything, it was primed for a raid from the sea. A number of its fabled big guns were fixed, capable of firing only southwards. Worse, even those that could be trained northwards were principally equipped with armour-piercing ammunition, effective against ships, but of little use against infantry. Whether Percival should have spent more time shoring up the northern defences and whether this would have slowed down the Japanese are questions debated by military historians. But as the untruths about Singapore's unassailability started to unravel, it became clear to a flabbergasted Churchill that there were no fortifications in the north. He admitted: 'The possibility of Singapore having no landward defences no more entered into my mind than that of a battleship being launched without a bottom.'[3]

The Causeway between Singapore and Malaya was 1 km long, but there were areas towards the west where the distance between the two coastlines was about half this length. It was around here that Yamashita decided to launch his offensive on the night of 8 February. His artillery resounded and then rained across the Straits as his men crossed over in armoured crafts and plywood-sheet boats made from Completely Knocked Down (CKD) kits. Those who couldn't find a place on either simply swam over. The Australian brigade manning the coastline was forced to withdraw within a matter of hours. The grip on Singapore quickly tightened with more troops pouring in, some wading across the 70-foot gap in the Causeway created by the explosion. Japanese aircraft destroyed oil storage tanks, incapacitated airfields and terrorized the city by the indiscriminate use of anti-personnel bombs.

Yamashita was desperate to extract a quick surrender, driven by the force of compulsion and a taste for the ceremonial. He hoped Singapore would fall by 11 February, the day that Japan's first Emperor, the probably mythical Jimmu, is said to have been crowned in 660 BCE. It is also the day the new constitution was promulgated by Emperor Meiji in 1889 and continues to be celebrated as Japan's National Foundation Day. However, the leaflets that were dropped from planes urging surrender fetched no response. So, on 11 February, Yamashita had a reconnaissance plane drop a cardboard tube with a detailed letter in English that he signed and addressed to the British Commander. Resistance was futile, he said. Continuing down this path would only expose Singapore civilians to 'infliction by fire and sword' and would do nothing to 'increase the fame of the British Army . . .' He suggested that Percival send a messenger up the Bukit Timah Road carrying a white flag as well as the Union Jack, adding helpfully that he could be escorted by a bunch of soldiers for protection.[4]

Unknown to the British, Yamashita was low on ammunition and couldn't afford to engage in a protracted war. Rations were low as well, forcing soldiers to seize them at gunpoint from villagers. But he never let up on the heavy barrage, convincing the British that the Japanese ground forces had received fresh ammunition supplies. He would recall that his attack on Singapore was 'a bluff that worked', recording in his diary: 'I knew that if I had to fight long for Singapore, I would be beaten. That is why the surrender had to be at once. I was very frightened all the time that the British would discover our numerical weakness and lack of supplies and force me into disastrous street fighting.'[5]

However, Churchill knew that Percival's men outnumbered Yamashita's by roughly three to one; as a result, he was unwilling to accept surrender and the fighting continued for a few more days. But broken sewers, littered bodies, destroyed water conduits and the looming threat of an epidemic eventually forced the British hand. On 15 February, in a building of the Ford Motor Company outside Bukit Timah village, Yamashita demanded and secured Percival's unconditional surrender. A scrum of Japanese reporters, newsreel cameramen and still photographers were present to record the moment that Churchill would describe as the 'worst disaster and the largest capitulation in British history'.

* * *

Surrender played out very differently for Indian soldiers in Singapore. Similarly, defeat meant something very different for Indian residents, of which there were some 20,000.[6] Indian soldiers were treated with kid gloves unlike their British and Australian counterparts. And Indian residents were generally spared the horrors wreaked on a section of the Chinese population, whose loyalties were questioned.

The booklet that Yamashita had ordered his ground forces to pore over, titled 'Read this Alone and the War Can Be Won',[7] had prepared his men for such differential treatment. Japan's next great mission, the booklet declared, was to assist in the independence of various people such as the Thais, the Annamese (Vietnamese) and the Filipinos, and 'to bring the blessing of freedom to the natives of South Asia and the Indian people'. In dealing with Indians, men like Yamashita and Fujiwara Iwaichi were working to a plan, one that had Tokyo's larger geopolitical interests in mind and directed at seating Japan at the head of the table of the Asian family of nations. As we shall see later, even though Japan had no intention of invading British India, it was very much in its strategic focus.

Nothing illustrates the discriminatory treatment meted out to PoWs more dramatically than the incident involving Prem Sahgal. The day before Percival formally surrendered, Sahgal found himself arrested by the Japanese and led away. A little later, he found the rest of his battalion trooping in, led by his second in command, a young English lieutenant. Their hands tied, both Sahgal and the British officer were asked to sit under two trees.

> A Japanese non-commissioned officer came up, worked the bolt of his rifle, and shook his head, meaning a bullet was too good for me. Then he took out his sword. I looked around and saw that they made this young Britisher kneel and chopped off his head.[8]

Sahgal assumed his turn was next, but the identity disc on his wrist saved him. In reply to a question, he answered that while he was an Indian (*Indoka*), he was not a *Ganjika.* This earned him a tremendous wallop on the head. On realizing that the questioner wanted to know whether Sahgal was a friend of Gandhi's, he quickly replied that his father knew the Mahatma personally. It soon became clear that the Japanese would not kill him. Sahgal asked them why they beheaded his second in command. 'We kill all English and Australian officers,' he took their reply to mean. As for Indians, they were all friends. The soldiers took Sahgal to a Japanese colonel, who was sitting at a table with an omelette and a bottle of cognac before him.

> I was introduced, and after a bit, he said, 'have a drink.' I picked up a glass and poured one that big, and drank it. And then, for the first time, it struck me just what had happened. Until that moment, I'd been paralyzed.[9]

Two days later, the INA was born in a Singapore park.* Sahgal was not present at this historic moment. But two other senior INA

---

* The INA would be formally established more than a year later on 1 September 1942. But as an organization, its date of birth is debatable, having been born and reborn more than once. It could be argued that it really came to life in Malaya, or at the moment Mohan Singh and his band of surrendered men signed up.

officers tried for treason along with him three years later—Captain Shah Nawaz Khan and Lieutenant Gurbaksh Singh Dhillon—were there. They were the first to be tried in the infamous Red Fort trials, which persuaded no less than Nehru to sign up to be a member of the team to defend INA officers. The three were found guilty of waging war against the State and dismissed from service, only to be released a couple of years later in independent India as heroes who fought to liberate the country.

On the evening of 16 February, orders were issued that Indian soldiers were to march to Farrer Park the following day. Not every unit received the message, but the soldiers began to arrive in the morning; by noon, some 40,000 of them had gathered in an open space by the stadium. A few Japanese and Indians positioned themselves on the stadium balcony with microphones and loudspeakers. But it was an Englishman who kicked off proceedings with Colonel Cecil Hunt making a summary announcement that all Indian soldiers were prisoners of war and that they were being handed over to the Japanese.

Fujiwara was up next. The founder of F-Kikan urged the Indians to consider themselves as friends rather than prisoners, stressing that India deserved to be free and that Japan would help put together an army of liberation. It was left to Mohan Singh to sew things up, which he did rather nicely, leaving many of the men cheering and weeping. Were they willing to join the INA, he asked. By the time he was finished, it was clear that most of them were.

Not everyone, however, bought into the pitch. These included some officers who joined the INA later. Gurbaksh Singh Dhillon and Shah Nawaz Khan were among those who refused to sign up, upset that Indian soldiers were being handed over by the British to the Japanese like heads of cattle.[10] The men at Farrer Park were divvied up. Those who refused to sign up were dispatched to PoW camps in different parts of the island. The others were absorbed into the INA, the supreme command that was housed in a northern suburb of the island, where Mohan Singh was comfortably lodged.

Claims of Japanese atrocities against some of those who refused to join the INA surfaced during the Red Fort trials. But, by and large, Indian PoWs did not suffer the kind of horrors inflicted on others. As someone who didn't think much of either Mohan Singh (whom he had met briefly in Penang) or the idea of a liberation army, Sahgal became a PoW and was placed in Neesoon, the largest of the PoW camps. Being potential INA recruits, the Japanese made a show of treating the prisoners well, sometimes going to comical lengths to demonstrate good faith. When the prisoners demanded milk, their captors promised to make it available. At a ceremony near another PoW camp, to which senior officers at Neesoon were invited, fifty bulls were paraded and presented. It took a lot of explaining to convince the Japanese that 'he-cows give no milk'. But the Indians went through with the ceremony, with 'terrific bowing . . . and Mohan Singh bowing back looking very grave'. After the Japanese left, the gates were opened and the bulls released.[11]

Sahgal was sent to the airfield at Tengah where his men were put to work to extend the runway and construct underground shelters. He could afford a couple of bottles of beer every week on his allowance and was 'quite happy'. Gradually, his reservations about joining the INA softened. The Bidadari resolution, which was drafted on Mohan Singh's return from Tokyo in April 1942 and which declared that independence was every Indian's birthright, contained a rider that Sahgal claimed was included on his insistence.[12] It said vaguely that the INA would 'take action for India as demanded by the people of India in India',[13] leaving Mohan Singh with the latitude that he wanted.

The INA was a reality that the prisoners could not ignore and a recruitment drive saw its ranks swelling over the months.

There were those like Harbakhsh Singh, lodged in the Bidadari camp, who refused to sign. He and other PoWs would be frequently asked to assemble in the open to listen to Mohan Singh's 'harangues' about freeing India from the grip of the British. It didn't help that as Mohan Singh spoke, Fujiwara stood behind him like a 'menacing poker'.[14]

The INA offered far better living standards than a PoW camp did, something the Japanese hung out there as a temptation. Outside the Bidadari camp, for instance, they placed an INA unit in barracks. As the prisoners were lined up and packed off to work with a handful of boiled rice as the day's ration, their counterparts in the INA would be engaged in a round of physical training, while hot puris and tea were being readied for them.[15]

Another lure for Indian officers was that the INA gave them far more power than they would have enjoyed under the British. But the reasons for the success of Mohan Singh's recruitment drive went beyond the selfish or self-serving. What swung Sahgal eventually was his friend R.M. Arshad with whom he had detailed discussions about the merits of signing up. Arshad would recall at Sahgal's trial: 'We discussed all the pros and cons and we unanimously decided that under the circumstances we owed our allegiance to the country.'[16] In June 1942, Mohan Singh had enlisted some 25,000 volunteers. By the end of August, with great excitement in South-East Asia after Gandhi's rousing 'Quit India' call and the mass arrests of Congress leaders, this number had swelled to 40,000.[17]

The INA would go through a lot of churning, with a disillusioned Mohan Singh falling out with the Japanese and 'disbanding' the INA in December 1942. The Japanese refused to accept its dissolution and kept it alive with the help of Rash Behari Bose, who was a part of the revolutionary Ghadar movement and hiding in Japan after the assassination attempt on Lord Hardinge. A year later, in July 1943, another Bose, Subhash Chandra, would arrive in Singapore and be handed over formal charge of the INA. A few months later, the work he did from his sea-fronted Singapore villa to collect funds and recruit volunteers to put a government in exile in place would come to fruition. On 21 October, he would stand on stage before a packed Cathay cinema hall to proclaim the formation of the Provisional Government of Free India. A couple of days later, he would declare war against Britain and the United States.

* * *

The collapse of Singapore echoed all over the world. 'The defence of the British crescent in Asia, as every schoolboy knew, rested on the "fortress" at Singapore,' wrote Bayly and Harper.* It was delusionary to believe that Singapore was some kind of unimpregnable bastion, but the shock of its surrender was so much greater because the British not only bought into this myth but led people in its colonies to believe it. In India, and elsewhere, what was perceived as a smug certainty was called out. 'The news of the fall of Singapore wears the aspect of a disaster only because it has come against this background of over-confidence and reassurance,' wrote Bombay's *Free Press Journal.*[18]

For India and other colonies, the defeat in Malaya had spawned the idea that the British were not stayers. The shocking abandonment of Penang raised questions about commitment. So, for that matter, did the eventual retreat to Singapore, even though this was arguably a military necessity. Did the British really care about the places which they ruled and protected? Could they, if push came to shove, up and leave from India? The fall of

---

* Christopher Bayly and Tim Harper, *Forgotten Armies*, p. 106. They define the crescent as that stretch of land that sweeps from Bengal in eastern India, going along Burma and Malaya, with Singapore at the end of the arc.

Singapore raised a related question. Being too preoccupied with the war in the West, wasn't there a lack of commitment to protect Asian colonies?

Such questions were raised not only in India and its neighbourhood but also in far-flung Australia and New Zealand. The Australian Prime Minister, John Curtin, who exchanged a series of cablegrams with Churchill, was deeply resentful about what he saw as Britain's failure to provide adequate air cover to Malaya and Singapore. The defence of the latter was vital to Australian interests; by 1930, about 60 per cent of Australia's trade passed through Singapore.[19] As it did in India, Singapore's surrender sparked off fears of a Japanese invasion of the Antipodes. Soon after the surrender, New Zealand's Prime Minister Peter Fraser declared, 'It would be idle and wrong to pretend that the fall of Singapore has not brought danger nearer to our shores.'[20] In Australia, the danger came more quickly than expected when, only four days after Singapore surrendered, almost 200 Japanese planes pounded Darwin. This would be the first of a series of aerial attacks on the Northern Territory aimed at neutralizing or at least weakening Australian/Allied retaliation to Japan's invasion of Timor.

Within days of Pearl Harbour/Kota Bharu, Australia issued an order for the evacuation of the tiny population of Darwin, making it compulsory for all women and children to leave. While no such order was issued in India at this time, the 'voluntary' exodus of people from cities, as we shall see in some detail later, began soon after the Japanese assault on Malaya. People began fleeing from places believed vulnerable to air strikes over a period of five months, from December 1941 to April 1942. The loss of Singapore contributed to a spike, which grew bigger when there was an increase in the number of refugees arriving in India from Burma. The last surge occurred in April, when a big Japanese fleet suddenly turned up in the Indian Ocean.

The set of fortnightly reports for the first half of December 1941 received by Home Secretary Eric Conran-Smith from administrators of presidencies and provinces noted that the attack of Malaya had generated a sense of 'nervousness', 'uneasiness' and 'dismay'. But some of them took care to stress that none of this could be characterized as 'panic', an expression they evidently felt should be used only to reflect a much greater degree of anxiety. Even so, the 'outbreak of the war with Japan had overshadowed all other matters', reported Bombay. Delhi revealed that refugees had started arriving from Calcutta. Orissa said there was a realization, for the first time, that the danger of war was approaching India and that newspapers were speculating about air raids on the country's eastern seaboard. The Madras Presidency's Chief Secretary, Sir Sonti Venkata Ramamurthy, the first Indian to occupy this position, reported that people in Vizagapatam and Cocanada felt that they were 'rapidly coming within range of at least aerial attack'.[21] Quite extraordinarily, it was these very towns—and not Madras, which was widely believed to be under serious threat—that would be bombed by the Japanese three months later.

Hoarding and speculation, very much a part of the 'skill sets' of Indian merchants and businessmen even today, sprang instantly to life. In Madras, speculation in yarn resulted in what the *Times of India* described as an 'orgy of buying', resulting in a sharp but very temporary spike in prices.[22] Riots in Madurai ensued as a result of the speculation. There was an artificial 'firewood famine' with dealers shuttering down to compel the government to raise the maximum price fixed for the commodity.[23] There was also 'a good deal of discontent among the poor at the high price of rice and other foodstuffs', Chief Secretary Ramamurthy noted.[24]

Sundry Japanese nationals all over India were picked up under the Defence of India Rules almost immediately after Japan entered the war. Calcutta took fifty-eight Japanese people (including nineteen women) into custody, shut down the offices of the consulate-general, and sealed the premises of all Japanese godowns and business concerns. A Romanian woman and two Japanese nationals were held in Nagpur. In Patna, a Japanese dentist who had been practising for the last two and a half years was detained.[25] The Central Provinces reported the internment of a well-known Buddhist priest, Noburu Tenzaki, living at Sewagram. All the fifteen or so Japanese nationals in the Madras Presidency had left after the Indian government, taking a cue from the United States and Britain, froze Japanese assets in July 1941. By December 1941, the number of Japanese in India had reduced considerably. There were 691 of them when Britain declared war on Germany in September 1939, a number that dwindled after the freeze order was issued, and reciprocal arrangements made for Indians in Japan and Japanese in India to return home.[26]

If the assault and eventual loss of Malaya felt like the war had entered its neighbourhood, the surrender at Singapore left India feeling undefended. There was a strategic basis for this since, despite the naval base in Ceylon, the nearest British one eastwards of it was in Australia. Japan had made big and worrying advances elsewhere in South-East Asia by the time Singapore surrendered. A day earlier, on 14 February, it invaded Dutch Sumatra, dropping hundreds of paratroopers after a wave of sustained bombing. By then, Malaya was totally under Japanese control, Hong Kong had surrendered, British North Borneo had fallen, the Dutch-controlled South was under pressure, the invasion of Burma was underway, Java was under attack, and the US was engaged in fending off the assault in the Philippines. Referring to the staggering advances Japan had made, Maulana Zafar Ali Khan—poet, politician, key member of Tahrik-e-Pakistan (the Pakistan Movement) and a man regarded as the father of Urdu journalism—would warn the Indian government that the war was at its door. 'What prevents Japan from landing in Madras? Nothing. Japan can invade India tomorrow.'[27]

That India could be the next target was discussed in a number of newspapers. For instance, the *Statesman* described the danger as 'real and immediate', including among the risks the possibility of a land attack through Burma, an amphibious attack on Ceylon and landings at various places on the Indian coastline.[28] Raj officials felt that cities on the eastern coast such as Calcutta, Madras, Vizagapatam and Cuttack could be in the crosshairs.

The administration did its share to further the sense of alarm. Having created and routinely reinforced the myth that Singapore was unimpregnable and would never be allowed to fall, its assurances that India remained safe post-surrender rang false. Congress leader C. Rajagopalachari squarely laid the blame for the fright in Madras at Arthur Hope's door. Criticizing him for suggesting that Madras was safe as long as Singapore was secure, Rajagopalachari said the Governor, having surveyed the situation in Malaya, ought to have known that Singapore's fall was inevitable. The surrender didn't surprise him at all, said the former Premier of the Madras Presidency, who resigned along with his ministry after British India declared war on Germany without so much as consulting the Congress. If he was Premier, 'the Governor would not have made a speech stating there would be no danger to Madras till Singapore fell', he told a cheering audience.[29] He was also scathing about the Madras government's extremely muddled communiqué issued two days after Percival capitulated to Yamashita which, as we shall see, triggered another round of panic and a second wave of departures from the city.

The shock of losing Singapore reverberated all over India. But there was at least one place where it was met with celebration—in Purana Qila, or Old Fort, in Delhi, where more than 2000 Japanese civilians, including women and children, were interned in makeshift tents. Many of them were picked up on 8 December, soon after the attack on Pearl Harbour, and most were from

Malaya and Singapore. They were a motley lot, one that included corporate executives from companies such as Mitsubishi and Mitsui, Okinawan fishermen from Singapore, planters, traders, engineers, teachers, tailors, dentists, confectioners, hairdressers and a maker of bean paste.[30] They lived in makeshift shelters in very poor conditions, while they waited to be moved to a more permanent camp in Deoli, Ajmer. They were given a poor diet, which they complained about more than once. A total of 106, including women and children, died from malaria, dysentery and beriberi. The survivors marked the fall of Singapore with a feast: '. . . fishermen from the Andamans, the shopkeeper from Singapore and the dentist from Kuala Lumpur all joined in the festivities.'[31]

The mood would change at the end of the war in 1945, with the Deoli camp splitting in two between the *kachi-gumi* (victory group) and the *make-gumi* (a group that accepted the defeat). Refusing to believe that Japan had lost the war, the kachi-gumi attacked members of the make-gumi, dunking urine over them, soiling their doors with faeces and dragging them out for fierce hidings. There were injuries but mercifully no one died.[32]

3

Before the Fall

While the fall of Singapore triggered a huge wave of panic, strong ripples of unease about Japan's expansionism existed well before its formal entry into the war. Soon after Pearl Harbour, Japan declared, in the name of Emperor Hirohito, that it was compelled—unavoidably, against its wishes, for the sake of its existence and self-defence—to 'cross swords with America and Britain'.[1] But by then, the conflict in Asia was already well underway.*

In 1931, Japan orchestrated an incident to invade Manchuria to feed its increasing industrial demand for raw materials, which it arranged through the puppet state it established there. Six years later, another minor occurrence became the pretext to launch a massive invasion of China. Despite scoring victories and capturing major Chinese cities, the Japanese met with strong resistance from China's armed forces, particularly in the countryside.

The defeat of France after just weeks of fighting in June 1940 presented Japan with an opportunity in South-East Asia. Days before the Armistice was signed between France and Germany, Japan forced Indochina's Governor-General Georges Catroux

* There are those who believe that World War II really began in July 1937 when Japan invaded China rather than 1939, when Britain declared war after Germany's invasion of Poland.

to close supply routes to China. Fresh demands coupled with aggressive threats were made, including the right to have airbases and station troops, leading the government to yield in September. However, the government continued administering the region, which made Indochina uniquely placed as a French colony under Japanese control.

Meanwhile, the US, which had been supporting Chinese nationalists in their war against Japan, was getting increasingly concerned. The speed at which Japan was arming itself, its advance into Indochina and its suspected designs in South-East Asia pointed to an increased danger of a full-fledged war in the Western Pacific region. The signing of the Tripartite Pact in September 1940 only strengthened this apprehension. The Pact, inked in Berlin with much fanfare by Germany, Italy and Japan, was specifically targeted at the US. In Article 3, the three countries pledged to 'assist one another with all political, economic and military means' when one of the three was attacked by a nation 'not involved in the European war or in the Chinese–Japanese conflict'.

The US was the only major power that fit the bill, the Soviet Union being excepted as it was involved in both spheres. Having signed a non-aggression pact with Germany in August 1939, along with a secret codicil divvying up Europe, Stalin had already occupied the eastern half of Poland and invaded Finland, forcing it to concede a part of its territory. China was provided arms, aircraft, aid and military advice by the Soviet Union until it got caught up with Germany's shock attack in June 1941. The Pact provided some reassurance that Germany would not threaten Japan's pre-eminence in East and South-East Asia. Japan hoped that it would deter the US from getting into a confrontation, which post-Pact would mean fighting on two fronts (a two-ocean war).

By this time, the US was already asserting economic pressure on Japan; in 1938, it notified manufacturers that the government was against the export of aircraft and aeronautical equipment, applying so-called 'moral embargoes'. A string of other sanctions followed, and by the summer of 1941, in response to Japan's moves on Indochina, it froze all Japanese assets in the US. Britain and its colonies quickly followed suit. Around the same time, the US went even further by embargoing the two items essential for conducting any war—steel and petroleum. Coming at a time when four-fifths of Japan's oil requirement was sourced from the US, Tokyo's options were limited: to either appease the US and withdraw from China, or look towards the Dutch East Indies as an alternative source of supply and to draw up the sea lanes that led to Pearl Harbour.[2]

Not surprisingly, perhaps, Japan chose the latter. It was a path aligned to its objective of creating a Greater East Asia Co-Prosperity Sphere, its own version of a *Lebensraum*, a place where a number of nations would acknowledge the pre-eminence of a Japan that was called upon by divine right to unite the 'eight corners of the world' (*hakko ichiu*). The idea of a Co-Prosperity Sphere made the Japanese feel that the war had a greater purpose and that its objective went well beyond punishing the recalcitrant Chinese nationalist leader Chiang Kai-shek.[3] The people who fell within this Sphere needed to recognize it was in their own interest.

It was in August 1940, just before Japan signed the Tripartite Pact, that Foreign Minister Yosuke Matsuoka announced the creation of a Greater East Asia Co-Prosperity Sphere. Apart from promoting a pan-Asian vision and its interest in the region, the timing of the declaration could have been aimed not merely at the inimical Allied powers but also at Germany. Jeremy A. Yellen has argued: 'Japanese leaders sought to deny Germany a hegemonic position in Japan's backyard. Japanese pre-eminence in East and South-East Asia served as a precondition for joining the Axis Pact.' In other words, Japan's propaganda about creating a Co-Prosperity Sphere was aimed at deterring all 'competitor colonial regimes from Asia'.[4]

There was some ambiguity about the boundaries of this Sphere, but initially, it included at least China, Manchuria (Manchuko), the Philippines, the Dutch Indies, French Indochina, Thailand, Malaya and Burma.[5] But even before Matsuoka's announcement of the Sphere, internal reports had begun to stress that the Indian subcontinent was integral to Japan's sphere of interest; in July 1940, Prime Minister Fumimaro Konoe's Cabinet declared that Japan would build a new order in 'Greater East Asia', the 'Greater' implying the inclusion of the Indian subcontinent.[6] A month earlier, a ministerial conference he presided over on national policy suggested that Japan's *seikatsuken* (living space) would eventually include India, Australia and New Zealand.[7] In British eyes, such moves only confirmed the long-standing hypothesis about Japan's designs on India.

By 1936, Britain had drawn up a 'Memorandum on Japanese Aggression Against India'. Stating that Japan's long-term ambition was to control East Asia and the Southern Pacific, it went on to imply that any power with such aims could well have 'designs on the rich prize of India' if the opportunity offered itself. The acquisition of English and Dutch possessions in South-East Asia would be 'essential preliminaries' for executing operations against India, it predicted.[8] Linlithgow's anxieties about Japan also emerged in 1936, soon after his arrival in India. He was not persuaded by the 'traditional obsession' with India's north-west frontier and urged more attention be directed at the threat from the south-east. His son Charlie is said to have found him lying on the floor in his New Delhi study in the winter of 1936–37 with a map spread out before him. 'I believe our guns in Singapore are facing the wrong way,' he is reported as having said, prophetically.[9]

Even so, the Indian subcontinent may never have, as Bayly and Harper suggest, 'loomed large in Japan's imperial vision'.[10] But the absence of a plan for a full-scale invasion didn't imply a lack of strategic intent. And this lay in 'freeing' India from the British and perhaps ultimately in dealing 'a death blow to Western influence by linking up with a German thrust to the Middle East'.[11] But an India that was schooled to look at South-East Asia as a stronghold for its own security was bound to be alarmed. A couple of days after Japan attacked Malaya, the *Times of India* warned: 'Burma and India, particularly the provinces of Assam and Bengal, must prepare for enemy aircraft, and our coastal shipping routes for raiders', adding for good measure that 'the war is on our doorstep'.[12] The sense of alarm was also partly because British India was unprepared for an attack from what it regarded as a ramparted East. Until then, it was generally believed that any threat would develop from the country's north-western frontiers.

* * *

While India shivered in 1942, there were chills about Japan's imperial intent much earlier. An extremely compelling illustration of this is contained in the proceedings of the Council of the Madras Corporation, which reveal the city's representatives obsessing about the danger Japan posed to India well before Pearl Harbour. Of particular concern was the threat Japan posed to Singapore and what this meant for Madras.

In February 1941, the Council unanimously resolved to donate a sum of Rs 7500 for strengthening the defences of Singapore. Quite remarkably, this was more than eight months before Pearl Harbour/Malaya and more than three months before Japan's muscle flexing in Indochina. A resolution to contribute this sum (along with another Rs 2500 for the Royal Indian Navy) was moved and carried after Mayor C. Basu Dev circulated a note in its favour. 'Our very existence is in peril,' it said. 'We must now make a gesture and set an example to other cities and towns of India to follow.'[13]

Two developments led Basu Dev to conclude there was a 'grave and urgent menace'—the concentration of Japanese forces at Hainan and Tokyo's moves to ink a neutrality or non-aggression pact with the Soviet Union. Basu Dev was probably alarmed that the 'feverish military preparations' on Hainan island, off the southern Chinese coast, were in preparation for an attack on Malaya. This is exactly what happened. As for the Russo-Japanese neutrality pact, it would be signed only a couple of months later, but it was already, as Basu Dev recognized, a fait accompli. Like others, he is likely to have believed that Japan would benefit from the pact by insuring itself against a Soviet invasion and freeing up its soldiers to concentrate on its expansionist agenda elsewhere. 'The Eastern gateway of India, Singapore, is now in imminent danger and its defences will have to be strengthened . . . Madras particularly with its long coast line is one of the most vulnerable parts of India for attack by Sea and Air from the East,' read his note.

By this time, there were those such as V. Chakkarai Chettiar, the future Mayor of Madras, who were 'beginning to feel the pulsation of this invasion'. He was convinced that an invasion would happen sooner or later, given that 'it is the declared policy in the inner circles of the Military Authorities in Japan that somehow or other they should hold sway over India'. At a time when Britain was spending as much as Rs 18 to 19 crore (180 to 190 million rupees) on the war every day, Chettiar admitted Rs 10,000 was 'a mere flea bite'. But it was important to signal to the governments both in India and Britain that the people were interested in the defence of their own land.[14] Linlithgow conveyed Secretary of State Leo Amery's thanks to the Corporation of Madras. The Viceroy described the contribution as 'a valuable and imaginative gift', adding that it was 'a right instinct on the part of Madras to look to the soundness of the Eastern bastion of our defences'.[15]

The threat to Singapore and ipso facto to Madras was a theme that played out even earlier than this. As early as March 1938, the Council of the Madras Corporation passed a resolution, in the face of an 'impending world conflagration', asking the Madras government for at least three months' military training for all physically fit adults.[16] To put this in perspective, this resolution about a world edging closer to war was passed soon after Germany incorporated Austria into the Reich (*Anschluss*). It was a year and a half before Britain declared war on Germany and two years before Japan's moves on Indochina. That councillors of a municipal corporation discussed and worried about a world war just weeks after Germany's first major act of aggression—the annexation of Austria—is remarkable. Even more so are the references to Japan, which figured more than once in the debates. The resolution's mover, G. Rajamannar Chetty, described Japan, which he claimed spent 60 per cent of its revenues on 'military armaments', as an 'ever-increasing danger to India'. Despite the presence of the naval base at Singapore and the proposed defence measures to be taken in the foreshore of north Madras, the city would be helpless to ward off attacks from the air, he said. Four years later, it was exactly this fear of Japanese bombs that spread panic in the city. It is something of an irony, of course, that Rajamannar Chetty, a Congressman who was devoted to Subhash Chandra Bose, saw Japan in such a menacing light. Years later, his leader would actively collaborate with the Japanese in trying to rid India of the British through an armed struggle.

Unlike Rajamannar Chetty, some other councillors struggled to square up the need for military training with the Congress Party's adoption of the Gandhian creed that non-violence was the only legitimate form of resistance. For instance, P.S. Bashyam Chetty, who seconded Rajamannar's resolution, made a distinction between the struggle for freedom, where the path of non-violence would be adhered to, and building 'a virile and strong nation' for which military training was absolutely essential. S. Venkatachalam Chetti stressed that the army sought by Indians was not to attack but to defend itself against aggression. M. Damodaran Naidu said if India was attacked by Japan or some other power, he was certain that 'lying down before them as we did in the civil disobedience days will not be any avail to us'. Referring to Gandhi's plan of constituting a non-violent army of volunteers, the Justice Party's T.R. Kothandarama Mudaliar was caustic. Stressing that all armies need to be violent to the degree necessary when defending a country, he quipped: 'A non-violent army cannot keep back the invader by black magic.'

* * *

In 1938, the Corporations of Bombay and Calcutta[17] passed similar resolutions demanding military training, the last supported by no less than Subhash Chandra Bose. Such resolutions tacitly recognized that in a world consumed by war, India could only depend on itself, as opposed to Britain or America, to defend itself. They also reflected the widespread feeling of vulnerability, which only increased as the war clouds thickened. The advances made by the Japanese raised a natural question: Where would India stand if Britain lost the war? This sense of susceptibility was also partly on account of the fact that most Indian soldiers were fighting Britain's wars in Europe, Africa and South-East Asia; they were not defending home.

The feeling of defencelessness was aggravated by the marked British reluctance to set up units in India that manufactured armaments. An old policy that went back to the days of the East India Company, it served at least two purposes. It kept India continually dependent on British arms. And it addressed colonial fears that creating an industrial capacity in the manufacture of armaments would threaten Britain's hold on India.[18]

As the war intensified, there was increasing frustration that demands for armaments manufacture—in particular, aircraft and armoured vehicles—were falling on deaf ears. In 1940, the

Council of States, the Upper House of the legislature comprising representatives of the provinces and the princely states, recommended immediate steps to build aircraft and automobiles in India at the earliest possible date. 'We are exceedingly weak from the point of view of defence, and should Britain fail to defeat the totalitarian powers, we shall be left absolutely defenceless,' said the resolution's mover Hriday Nath Kunzru. A moderate Congressman, Kunzru had left the party with others who preferred gradual constitutional reform over what they regarded as revolutionary methods to join the Indian National Liberal Federation, formed in 1919. The production of war material is no longer a political question, but one of interest to Indian nationalists, he argued. India's defence was vital to British interests as well.[19]

Before Britain entered the war, an expert committee chaired by Ernle Chatfield was set up to make recommendations on the defence of India; among the things it suggested was modernizing and re-equipping the armed forces and a sharing scheme between Britain and India to finance this. The onset of war and the threat of Japan forced a change in British attitudes to armaments manufacture. In September 1940, the Roger Mission visited India to explore how to ramp this up. On the recommendations of the Mission, twenty projects, a mix of new factories and expansions of existing ones, were approved at a capital outlay of Rs 12 crore.[20] But the appointment of the Mission came too late and its recommendations were modest. This was partly because of the belief that American assistance would be forthcoming, obviating the need for long-term measures to expand armaments production. The men who manned the Mission also probably knew that the British government would not accept any recommendation that involved major supplies of plant equipment, skilled labour or materials.*

* The *Statesman* highlighted how the Mission was conditioned by these negative factors in a persuasive editorial, 'Planning Now', 2 March 1942, p. 4.

In December 1940, the far-sighted Indian industrialist Walchand Hirachand set up Hindustan Aeronautics Limited in association with the Maharaja of Mysore, Sri Jayachamaraja Wadiyar. A couple of years later, the Indian government took control of the company by forcibly buying out the industrialist's stake. The first aircraft produced by the company, now among the biggest in the aerospace and defence sector in the world, was the modest two-seater training aircraft, the Harlow PC-5.

Complaints about India's lack of defence preparedness only became sharper after Singapore's fall. Another resolution was moved in the Council of States asking the Viceroy to expedite the manufacture of war materials. It was rejected, but the discussion dwelled on the government's allegedly obstructionist attitude to creating industrial capacity. While huge strides were made in armaments manufacture in countries such as Australia and Canada, India languished. Kunzru, who supported the defeated resolution, would lament that India was unable to even provide rifles to the people it had trained. 'Isn't this a scandalous state of things?' the moderate asked.[21]

The feeling that Britain was focused on defending its own turf rather than some corners of its foreign fields intensified. Interestingly, this criticism was levelled not only by nationalists but very forcefully by the *Statesman*, the venerable British-owned newspaper that, although far from nationalist, pushed for a greater role for Indians in managing their own affairs. It championed for some years the modernization of the Indian Army and the creation of an indigenous aircraft industry and regretted that these had not come to pass.[22] The newspaper held Lord Beaverbrook, the charismatic, philandering newspaper baron who was appointed Minister for War Production by his friend Churchill, at least partly responsible for this insular outlook, portraying him as if he were a yesteryear Brexiteer. On the very day Singapore capitulated, the newspaper's Editor, Arthur Moore, wrote a brutal signed article, calling him a 'defeatist' and an 'evil genius', a man 'almost solely concerned with . . . the invasion of England'.

> In the end, he would make Britain into a lone little island like Singapore, for which there would be nothing left but surrender. He is losing us the oil, tin, and rubber of the British and Dutch Empires while he piles up tens of thousands of aircraft and takes in England behind his Maginot Line of the Channel . . . make him a Duke, or anything. But in heaven's name, let him resign quick.[23]

Not content with this, the newspaper also penned an editorial blaming the 'little mind that hoarded its munitions like a miser sitting at home counting his gold that has gone ill with a great Empire'. Calling for self-reliance in arms and declaring that India could produce rifles and ammunition in vast quantities, it ended on an uncharacteristically tabloid-ish note: 'With rifles and men we can shoot Japs. Japshooters are what we want. Form, riflemen, Form.'[24]

Not surprisingly, Moore's article came to the attention of the British authorities.[25] In a few months, Viceroy Linlithgow is said to have forced the *Statesman* to dismiss Moore. Although Linlithgow is believed to have personally agreed with some of Moore's views and even praised him as a journalist, the *Statesman*'s Editor had probably become too controversial for his liking.

The conquest of Singapore raised the inevitable question: Where would Japan go next? Some believed it would be Australia, a view that seemed to be strengthened by the bombing of Darwin within days of the surrender. Others maintained, and correctly, that its attention would turn to Ceylon and the Indian Ocean. In early March, an aircraft carrier strike force sailed towards Ceylon under no less than Vice Admiral Chuichi Nagumo. The hero of Pearl Harbour was given two tasks: destroy the British Eastern Naval Fleet at Colombo and Trincomalee, and disrupt merchant shipping in the Bay of Bengal.

4

Ceylon and the Bay of Bengal

At 6 a.m. on 4 April 1942, Squadron Leader Leonard J. Birchall lifted his Catalina off the freshwater as the viridescence waxed around him on the fringes of the lovely Koggala Lagoon. An officer of the Royal Canadian Air Force, he had arrived in Ceylon only a couple of days earlier from the Shetland Islands in Scotland, where he flew patrols over the North Sea. There was no time to lose given the pressing demand for reconnaissance in the Indian Ocean. The intelligence about a Japanese fleet headed for Ceylon needed urgent corroboration.

As he ascended from the water runway at the Royal Air Force's flying boat base near Galle in southern Ceylon, Birchall set a south-easterly course. He had a full tank, enough to keep him in the air until the following morning. Having flown for some ten hours with nothing to report but vast expanses of empty sea, Birchall was 360 miles from Dondra Head, Ceylon's southernmost tip, when he prepared to return to base. It was then that a speckle in the southern horizon caught his attention.

As he brought the Catalina lower and closer, the innocuous dot disaggregated into a threatening flotilla of aircraft carriers, cruisers, destroyers and supply ships. Birchall tried to turn back, but his Catalina was spotted and taken down by a bunch of Zeros, which scrambled from one of the aircraft carriers. The speedy

Mitsubishi-made fighter planes, which the Japanese used to menacing effect during the war, caught up with the flying boat easily, forcing Birchall to take the Catalina down to the sea. But importantly, he was able to send a message back only moments before a shell destroyed the radio and shattered the leg of the wireless operator. 'Due to our flying at a low altitude, it was impossible to bail out but I managed to get the aircraft down on the water before the tail fell off,' recalled Birchall.[1]

The Zeros wouldn't let up on the strafing. Two men, one of them the wireless operator Lucien Colarossi, went down with the plane. Another was killed in the water. Birchall and five others, of whom three were badly injured, were picked up by a Japanese destroyer and transferred to the aircraft carrier *Akagi*. They were beaten up to find out whether a radio message had been sent, which they denied. They would end up spending three years in captivity in various Japanese internment camps. After the war was over, Churchill would refer to Birchall as the 'Saviour of Ceylon' and applaud him for making 'one of the most important single contributions to victory'.[2] Released after Japan's defeat, Birchall was awarded an OBE, received several other American and Canadian awards and retired as Air Commodore. He made many trips that he called 'pilgrimages' to Ceylon (now Sri Lanka). On one such visit, at the age of eighty-six, he told a Sri Lankan newspaper: 'It was only after the war ended that I knew it hadn't been in vain. That Ceylon had been saved.'[3] The Japanese fleet never intended to invade and occupy Ceylon, and so 'saved' is perhaps something of an overstatement. But his warning over the radio robbed the Japanese of some element of surprise. RAF units in Ceylon and the garrison in Colombo were placed on alert from 3 a.m. on 5 April, and the harbour emptied of warships and merchant vessels.

Even so, the British underestimated how quickly the Japanese planes could attack, and thereby failed to take full advantage of

Birchall's warning. Their calculations about the range of Zeros, which they didn't know enough about, were way off the mark. So, when Colombo was bombed and strafed at 8 a.m. the following morning, most of their fighters were on the ground and some of the pilots engaged in that extravagant English ritual—breakfast.[4] But if Nagumo hoped he could catch Ceylon napping as he did the US in Pearl Harbour, he was mistaken. Intelligence had already tipped the British off about a Japanese fleet heading Ceylon's way. What Birchall did was help by pinpointing its position.

Following Pearl Harbour, the Allies had achieved considerable success in breaking Japan's codes and ciphers, much of it done by the Americans. By the end of March, Vice Admiral James Somerville had received a communication from the US Navy of a Pearl Harbour-type attack on Ceylon. But for this, there may well have been a catastrophic disaster. Days before the attack, orders were issued to move the British fleet away from Colombo to the safety of Addu Atoll, in the southernmost tip of the Maldives, a base unknown to the Japanese. On the morning of 5 April, Easter Sunday, a swarm of 122 planes, Zero fighter aircraft accompanied by bombers and dive-bombers, swept over to raid Colombo. The Easter Sunday bombings was how it came to be known, but in Sri Lanka, the expression acquired a different meaning almost six decades later. On 21 April 2019, the day Christians gathered to commemorate the resurrection of Jesus, Islamist suicide bombers set off explosions in three churches and three high-end hotels, killing over 260 people, more than forty of them foreigners.

* * *

The strategic importance of Ceylon had grown in the Admiralty's eyes after the sinking of *Repulse* and the *Prince of Wales* on 10 December 1941. It began looking further westwards for a naval base. The Eastern Fleet (or East Indies Fleet) withdrew from the

Sembawang base in Singapore. After the surrender, the fleet was moved to Trincomalee in Ceylon. Just five days after the sinking of the two ships, Vice Admiral Somerville was told he would be appointed Commander-in-Chief of the Eastern Fleet.* He would arrive in Ceylon only three months later though, less than ten days before the Japanese attacked. He chose the slower and more leisurely route from Britain by an aircraft carrier allocated to his fleet, the HMS *Formidable.* Before the journey, he spent some time studying the situation and availed of some 'well-earned' leave.

The news, as the *Formidable* made its slow loop around the Cape of Good Hope and approached Ceylon, was anything but encouraging. By then, Japan had quickly dominated the waters east of Singapore. By the time Somerville arrived in Colombo on 26 March, it had also advanced westwards, overrunning the Andaman Islands. Somerville kept his cheer up during the voyage, reporting back to the Lordships at the Admiralty even 'events of minor importance' such as the birth of five kittens and how a rat caught in a trap fell on the Captain's head. ('With the exception of the rat, all are doing well.'[5]) But he was aware of the difficult task he had been given, made even trickier by the fact that a large part of the Eastern Fleet was old and unfit. He wrote to his wife:

> I hear a lot of blah about how everything now depends on our maintaining control of the Indian Ocean . . . That's poor bloody me and I wonder how the devil it is to be accomplished. My own battle-boats are in various states of disrepair and there is not a ship at present that approaches what I call a proper standard of fighting efficiency.[6]

Somerville's flagship was the reconditioned *Warspite.* The fleet was made up of three venerable aircraft carriers (including the ill-fated *Hermes*), four ancient battleships and about two dozen

---

* He would be promoted to Admiral a day after the Easter Sunday raid on 5 April 1942.

cruisers and destroyers. Somerville's main task was to protect the sea lanes to the Middle East for ships that rounded the Cape of Good Hope and travelled along the east coast of Africa. He and his deputy, Algernon Willis, had realized that they would be unable to withstand a full-scale assault and invasion of Ceylon. The best counter to even a less ambitious attack, they reckoned, was to avoid losses by attrition and refrain from operations that did not have reasonable chances of success. In short, keep the fleet 'in being'; afloat and in readiness. The defence of Ceylon was important but neither he nor the Admiralty wanted to take 'excessive chances' with the Eastern Fleet for the sake of it.

Somerville informed the Admiralty and Archibald Wavell, by then the Commander-in-Chief of India, that he was not prepared to use his fleet 'offensively' and that there was nothing he could do until it was properly trained. 'Damned if I am going to fritter it away in penny numbers . . .' he noted, as he complained about the lack of war experience among his staff officers. 'It was all the most amateur party I ever heard of.'[7]

Even so, Somerville, who saw himself as something of a fighting admiral, was not averse to having 'a good crack' at the enemy. On 30 March, two days after he received intelligence about an approaching Japanese fleet, he set sail south-east of Colombo on the *Warspite,* accompanied by two aircraft carriers and his mix of cruisers and destroyers. The idea was to head towards the probable launch point of Nagumo's fleet at night and initiate an unexpected torpedo attack while withdrawing from detection during the day.

But all he encountered over the next few days was a 'flat calm' and a scorching sun that left his 'face and arms like raw beetroot'. When nothing turned up, Somerville may have concluded that either the intelligence about the fleet was mistaken or that the Japanese were playing a waiting game.[8] The thought that they had abandoned all plans to attack Colombo also crossed his mind. 'I fear they have taken fright which is a pity because if

I could have given them a good crack now it would have been very timely.'[9] By 2 April, there were far more pressing reasons to abort the mission—his fleet was running out of fuel and water. The aircraft carrier *Hermes,* its escort, the destroyer *Vampire,* and two cruisers (*Cornwall* and *Dorsetshire*) were sent back to Ceylon. He took the rest of the fleet to Addu Atoll in the Maldives. He would write to his wife: 'Now I am off to one of my ruddy Atolls which I understand is the last word in beastliness.'[10]

* * *

On the same day that Somerville arrived in Colombo, the last 90 miles in a plane from the deck of *Formidable,* Chuichi Nagumo, the hero of Pearl Harbour, left Staring Bay in the Dutch East Indies for Ceylon. His fleet was fashioned around a nucleus of five aircraft carriers, all of which had taken part in the Pearl Harbour raid. His orders for what was called Operation C were clear: destroy Britain's sea power, which had been reorganized in Ceylon. In tandem with Nagumo, Vice Admiral Jisaburo Ozawa set sail with his Malay Force from southern Burma. His fleet comprised the light carrier *Ryujo,* accompanied by a mix of cruisers and destroyers. His task was simpler, at least one that was likely to meet with little or no resistance—sink merchant ships in the Bay of Bengal and create additional panic by attacking a couple of installations on India's east coast.

Nagumo's plan was always to attack on Easter Sunday. It was Somerville who was led to believe on the basis of intelligence received that it would happen earlier. When the Japanese planes showed up over Colombo on 5 April, Somerville was already in his 'beastly' atoll. The beautiful ring-like coral islands didn't impress his Commodore Ralph Edwards much either, whose diary recorded it as 'the most horrible place I have ever visited'. 'Damn and *blast* it looks as if I have been had,' exclaimed Somerville when he learnt that a Catalina had spotted the Japanese fleet,

'... here I am miles away and unable to strike ... it is maddening to think they've slipped me this time.'[11]

Just before 8 a.m., the first wave of Japanese planes that took off from the five aircraft carriers appeared over Colombo. Their principal targets were warships in the harbour area, but there were hardly any of them there. The secondary targets were infrastructural facilities such as the rail yard and the oil depot at Kollonawa. To the surprise of the Japanese, the British Hurricanes were on the ground as they swept over the airport at Ratmalana. The aircraft at the racecourse, where a temporary airstrip had been built, were alerted and able to put up some resistance. But both places were bombed and there were civilian casualties when wayward bombs killed seven at a military hospital in Angoda and some others at the Maradana railway station. Altogether eighty-five people, including seventeen airmen, were killed and an almost similar number injured. The British would claim to have fought off the Japanese, downing as many as twenty-seven planes, a vast exaggeration. One estimate put it at six.[12] The British, who feared Ceylon would be invaded, declared victory for 'beating back' the Japanese. But Nagumo lacked the men and the material to effect even a temporary occupation, let alone carry out a full-fledged invasion.[13]

The public in Colombo was taken by surprise. There was no prior information about the approaching Japanese fleet or a clear warning about a possible aerial attack. There were air raid alerts though, one of which was sounded on 2 April. Comprehensive orders for Air Raid Precautions were issued, which suggested that something was brewing. This included advice about what should be done in the event of 'enemy agents' landing in parachutes or coming in via the sea. A sum of Rs 5000 was offered for their capture![14]

The bombing of Colombo lasted barely twenty minutes; it was still underway when Admiral Nagumo received a message that one of his reconnaissance planes had spotted two ships south-west of Colombo. They were the *Cornwall* and the *Dorsetshire.* The two cruisers had been sent back to Colombo after Somerville abandoned his plan to ambush Nagumo during the night; the former returned to escort a convoy of troops and the latter for a refit. Following Birchall's warning, they were ordered to sail out to Addu Atoll to which Somerville had set off earlier. It took Lieutenant Commander Takashige Egusa's Type 99 ('Val') dive-bombers just under twenty minutes to send the two cruisers to the sea bed. Asked how his planes had sunk the British warships, Egusa shrugged, saying it was simpler than bombing the *Settsu*, the battleship that Japanese aircraft used as target practice. Over 400 were killed and it took two whole days for the 1112 survivors, many of whom were adrift on floats, rafts and sundry bits of wreckage, to be rescued by Somerville's ships.

Having done with Colombo, Nagumo turned his attention to Trincomalee. Once again, the British, who had advance information of the attack, were bested. A merchant ship and some other vessels were damaged in the attack on Trincomalee harbour, but Nagumo was disappointed in finding no sign of Somerville's warships. Once again, though, he got lucky. A reconnaissance plane spotted the aircraft carrier *Hermes* along with the destroyer *Vampire* some 65 miles south of the harbour and close to the coast.

The plan to sail away from the danger and return to the harbour was dead in the water. To the surprise of the Japanese, the two ships had no aircraft cover. Egusa's Val dive-bombers made short work of the aircraft carrier, sinking it in under thirty minutes, and then proceeded to do the same for the *Vampire*. Sixty years after it went down, a local diver would find the resting place of the *Hermes*, now a popular dive site. Over 300 seamen were killed in the two attacks. Not so long after, Nagumo set off eastwards. There was speculation and warnings about the possibility of a second attack, but Ceylon's brief tryst with the war was over.

* * *

On 1 April, Vice Admiral Jisaburo Ozawa led his fleet out from Mergui in southern Burma westwards into the Bay of Bengal. His Malay Force fleet was smaller than Nagumo's, built around the light carrier *Ryujo*, six cruisers and four destroyers. Ozawa lingered near the channel that separates the Andaman and Nicobar Islands for a couple of days, probably waiting to synchronize his attack with Nagumo's. On the morning of 4 April, he headed in the general direction of Orissa on India's north-eastern coast.

By then, the Andamans were already under Japanese control. It was a foregone conclusion that the Bay islands could not be defended; as a result, a number of British families evacuated soon after Japan entered the war. On 12 March, the last four British officers—the Deputy Commissioner, the Superintendent of Police, the Harbour Master and the Jailor—left Chatham Island in secret for the Indian mainland. Ten days later, Japanese ships were sighted close to Port Blair, the capital, as the sun went down. By midnight, the advance companies had landed and Japan was in control by the morning of 23 March. The few Europeans and Anglo-Indians who had chosen to remain were arrested and confined at Ross Island.[15]

At the crack of dawn on 5 April, bombers lifted off the *Ryujo* on search and destroy missions, sinking one ship, disabling another and damaging a third.[16] Before sunset that evening, Ozawa divided his naval force into three groups, which headed towards different points of the Indian coastline. Ozawa himself was a part of the central group, which was made up of the *Ryujo* and five other ships. The three groups were fairly spread out, the distance between the southern and northern ones as much as 400 miles.

It was easy pickings. The following day, the northern group sank seven ships in a little over three hours, starting with the Norwegian tanker *Elsa*, which was on its way from Madras to Calcutta with a bellyful of kerosene. Not long afterwards, a Japanese biplane located six merchant ships sailing close to the coastline. There was an attempt to scatter but the Japanese warships caught up with the group and all six—the *Malda, Autolycus, Indra, Exmoor, Silkworth* and *Shinkuang*—were speedily sunk.

Together, the three groups sank at least twenty ships and damaged three more in the space of two days.[17] It was an attack of international dimensions. Eleven flew UK flags. Three each of the remaining nine were of the Netherlands, Norway and the United States. The merchant ships were completely helpless against the might of Ozawa's force, as the ordeal of Stanley Salt graphically reveals. The handsome radio operator, all of nineteen, was on the SS *Sinkiang*, with a mixed crew of Chinese seamen, Indian stewards and British officers. Having set off from Calcutta and bound for Colombo, the *Sinkiang* was part of a convoy. On the afternoon of 5 April, distress calls from some 40 miles away from a ship that was bombed, the *Harpasa,* triggered the order that all ships break convoy at sunset. The ships dispersed and the distances between them grew as they continued to sail southwards. Salt received further distress calls early the following morning. One after another, the four ships that were part of the same convoy reported attacks by Japanese aircraft. The pattern of each attack was the same: one plane would 'zoom in, drop one bomb and beat it'.[18]

Soon enough, the *Sinkiang* was attacked as well, the bomb exploding harmlessly in the water. But more trouble loomed on the eastern horizon in the enlarging form of an aircraft carrier (the *Ryujo*) and a cruiser. The *Sinkiang* attempted to change course towards the coast which lay some 25 miles away, but it was no match for the Japanese ships, which began to shell it.

The radio room was hit and Salt found that 'blood was pouring out of gaping holes' in his legs. He tried to jump into a boat that was being lowered, but the bow of the merchant vessel swung down, pitching him into the sea. From the water, he became a spectator to the 'drama's final act', watching as 'salvo after salvo was pumped into the *Sinkiang*' until she reared in the air and went down perpendicularly.[19]

There was, of course, more drama as Salt, after floating in his life jacket for what seemed an eternity, found an empty lifeboat, which he managed to haul himself into. Within minutes, he found that his companion Len, the gunner, had also clambered aboard despite a nasty thigh wound. Together, the two were desperately bailing the waterlogged boat, when they saw a destroyer coming towards them. It came close enough for the two to see the leering grins on the faces of the Japanese crew as they lined the railing. But it left them alone, an experience that survivors from other merchant ships also recounted with a mix of relief and gratitude. The Japanese, despite their reputation among the British for gunning down survivors, were clearly tasked only with sinking ships. Orissa's Governor Hawthorne Lewis would write to Linlithgow that although survivors were sometimes only 20 or 30 yards away from the warships, the Japanese 'did not deliberately interfere with them when in boats, nor machine-gun them, nor fire on them'.[20]

Within a few hours, the numbers on the lifeboat had risen to twenty-one. Many were in a pitiful state. The second engineer's spine protruded through a gaping hole in his back. One of the gunners was badly scalded and had to keep being restrained from jumping into the sea to cool his wounds. Two died on the lifeboat, which slowly made its way to the Orissa coast, where fishermen rushed to drag it through the surf and carry the wounded to safety.

The damage done by Ozawa's rampaging warships in the Bay of Bengal was not insignificant. Almost 1,00,000 tonnes of cargo bound for far-flung places such as Colombo, Karachi, Madras and Mauritius were sunk with the ships. Around the same time, there was some Japanese action on the western seaboard as well. A single submarine patrolling the Indian Ocean sank two merchant ships. Eleven died in the torpedo attack on the *Clan Ross*, which was loaded with general cargo and explosives, en route from Liverpool to Cochin. The crew in the *Bahadur*, headed from Bombay to Basra, had already taken to their boats when it was taken down.[21]

The attacks didn't receive much publicity, possibly because there was nothing even remotely positive that could be spun out of the incidents, little to show by way of retaliation against the rampage in the Bay of Bengal. Or could it have also been because attacks at sea lack that chilling sense of propinquity that those on land possess? Whatever the truth, it was Vizagapatam and Cocanada, the first towns on the Indian mainland to be raided from the air, that dominated newspaper headlines.

For those in Orissa though, it was Ozawa's warships that caused the most anxiety. Salt was only one of about 500 survivors, many badly injured, who found their way to the coast. On 5 April, the Orissa government received a message from Calcutta of a freighter sunk off Puri, whose crew had taken to rafts. But RAF planes failed to trace either vessel or crew. However, on the following day, they reported sighting two Japanese warships. There were explosions and firing heard by people on the coastline of Cuttack district. Two teams, headed by Inspector-General of Police E.A.O. Parkin and the Collector, headed out to investigate. Travelling along the river Devi, a distributary of the Mahanadi, Parkin and others located different parties of shipwrecked sailors—Indian, British, American, Norwegian and Chinese. Most of them had spent two or three nights in the care of hospitable villagers. They were gathered together and put on the eighteen buses that had been sent out. The survivors arrived in Cuttack on the afternoon of 8 April. A couple of crew who died on shore were buried in the sand. Some others trickled into Cuttack later, including some seventy Royal Marines from the *Malda,* which was on its way to Colombo.

In Cuttack, the panic set in by 6 April. Fuelled by rumours of firing in the village of Kujang, people fled the town by train that evening and the following morning. The military authorities viewed the incidents seriously, believing—or at least willing to consider—that the attacks could be a precursor to a full-fledged invasion. The Calcutta-headquartered Eastern Command pressed the Orissa government to move all forms of road transport 20 miles inland. Significantly, even bicycles were covered by the order, raising the question of whether this was to safeguard against the kind of 'bicycle blitzkrieg' the Japanese carried out in Malaya. Also, all boats on navigable rivers were to be pulled back above the anicuts. The military advised the Orissa government not to delay any further and immediately move all its departments further inland from Cuttack. Such a move was already in 'operation'. Governor Lewis believed that Cuttack, located on a delta formed by the Mahanadi, was particularly vulnerable. A few days earlier, after much cogitation, he had publicly declared that the government's headquarters would be shifted to Sambalpur.[22]

The hostel at Cuttack's Ravenshaw College (now a university) was commandeered for survivors and served as a makeshift hospital. Food, bedding and clothing were made available. Most of the operations were performed by a Major Hicks of the Indian Medical Service, who received Rs 500 from grateful shipping agents in Calcutta as a mark of appreciation. The survivors were from eight ships sunk by the raiding mission's northern group and from other vessels destroyed by the central and southern groups. The *Sinkiang,* which carried Stanley Salt, was a victim of the central group, its survivors making landfall further to the south, a little north of Vizagapatam. Having been helped to safety by fishermen, he and other survivors were given sips of a 'native brew' that boosted their 'flagging spirits', and provided shelter in huts after the beach was hit by a torrent of rain. One fisherman helped himself to Salt's wallet, but any misgivings vanished when he and the others were fed by the womenfolk. As for the wallet, Salt rationalized he was but the victim of an opportunist.

An Indian doctor appeared the following morning. He estimated nine men needed morphine, but was carrying only eight shots. Salt's companion, Len the gunner, gamely agreed to sit out. The doctor told the survivors that the nearest hospital, a small one that performed no surgeries, was at Chicacole (now Srikakulam), north of Vizagapatam. The crew got on to three ox carts provided by the villagers and travelled for two hours till they reached a road, after which they took a decrepit bus that headed at a dizzying and dangerous speed to the small hospital. One doctor and two nurses were all this hospital had. Right through the night, other survivors from destroyed vessels kept trickling in. By the following day, as many as 200 were accommodated in Chicacole, many of them wounded. Vizagapatam was only 70 miles away. However, the exodus following the 6 April bombing had carried away many hospital staff. The town was not equipped to handle 200 patients in any case. Arrangements were made for them to go to Calcutta, where Salt spent a year, seven months in hospital and the remainder in convalescence.

5

The Bombings

At 5.40 a.m. on 6 April 1942, a Wapiti with Flight Lieutenant David Small and Pilot Officer Maurice Barker took off from the airfield at Vizagapatam.[1] Two days earlier, Small had received orders to patrol the area north and south of the port at first light. He was given no information about what vessels, enemy or other, were likely to be there.

Only days before, Small was ordered to take charge of the Coastal Defence Flight (CDF) at Vizagapatam, the sixth CDF established following the outbreak of war. A former employee of the famous coffee trading firm, Peirce Leslie and Co., Small had earlier signed up for the Indian Air Force Volunteer Force (IAFVF). The Vizagapatam CDF was constituted only in February 1942; the others—Madras, Bombay, Calcutta, Karachi and Cochin—were formed earlier. Tasked with helping in the defence of India's principal ports, the CDFs were manned by a mix of regular IAF men and volunteers with civilian licences to fly. The CDFs were poorly equipped in terms of aircraft, relying largely on Wapitis, single-engine biplanes, for their patrols. 'Should we be flying Wapitis and converted un-armed airliners of pre-war vintage if there had been any strength in the country?' lamented W.W. Russell, another IAFVF volunteer, based at Kochi.*

As the only available navigator at the CDF in Vizagapatam was ill, Small chose to play the role, ordering Maurice Barker† to pilot the two-seater. Fifteen minutes into the flight, Small spotted smoke at a distance which, a little later, showed itself as a smouldering ship. Climbing and altering course, he saw gun flashes and a cluster of ships in a confusing formation. Soon they revealed themselves as an aircraft carrier, a battleship, a cruiser, two destroyers and a merchant ship in flames. An even closer look confirmed the naval vessels were Japanese. They were 'belching fire' at the merchant vessel 'like hounds around a fox at bay'.[2] The hounds were a part of the pack of Ozawa's central group. As for the fox, it was probably either the *Ganges* or the *Bienville*, going by the time, the position, survivors' accounts and Small's estimate of tonnage.

Small and Barker would make history of sorts by being the first two men to witness Japan's assault on the mainland. They continued to shadow the Japanese naval force and were luckily not spotted by the three Zeros that flew below them. Returning to the aerodrome in Vizagapatam, which lacked communication facilities, Small had to go to Naval Headquarters to file his report. He took off again for another patrol but this time found nothing. A third scouting expedition was not possible. In the early afternoon, as his Wapiti was being refuelled, Japanese aircraft were already over Vizagapatam.

---

* W.W. Russell, *Forgotten Skies: The Story of the Air Forces in India and Burma* (London: Hutchinson and Co., 1945). The converted airliners were commandeered from Tata Airlines, India's first domestic carrier, which was later rebranded Air India.

† Maurice Barker would go on to become the IAF's first Anglo-Indian Air Marshal.

Earlier that morning, Cocanada, south of Vizagapatam, was bombed by a lone single-engine aircraft, becoming the first town in India to be raided from the air. A ship and a launch belonging to a private company were machine-gunned as they approached the roadstead. The Indian captain was killed and the wireless operator wounded. Later that afternoon, about a dozen bombs were dropped on oil installations from another aircraft. The damage was minimal. Only one oil tank suffered a direct hit, but fortunately, it was empty. Another tank was struck a glancing blow, which failed to pierce it.[3]

Vizagapatam, which was attacked thrice on the same day, suffered much more damage. In the morning, the attacks were at sea, directed at the ships entering the harbour. The port was hit in the early afternoon by the first wave of five Type 97 bombers that took off from the *Ryujo*. Another attack on the port followed at dusk. Reports of how many planes took part and how many bombs were dropped vary. The damage to the workshop at the shipyard was minimal, but one bomb fell squarely on a shelter, killing five and injuring about forty. Fortunately, the bombs narrowly missed a ship carrying about 350 kg of explosives that was berthed in the harbour.[4] At least eight people died in the attack, all memorialized in a plaque at the city's museum. It also displays the shell of a 250 kg unexploded bomb, which is something of a tourist attraction.

The exodus from Vizagapatam, as we shall see later, began months earlier. But the bombing created a huge fright and the town emptied out. After his two-day sinking-bombing spree, Ozawa's fleet withdrew to the area between the Andaman and Nicobar Islands. A little later, Nagumo would remove his fleet to Singapore to prepare for the assault on Port Moresby. His success as well as that of the Imperial Japanese Navy would be short-lived. In early June, Nagumo's fleet would lose four aircraft carriers in the Battle of Midway in the Pacific Ocean. A major turning point in the war, it led him to seriously contemplate suicide. Ozawa would succeed him as Commander of the Navy's 3rd Fleet and take part in operations with a depleted force until the end of the war.

In the Indian Ocean, Ozawa's limited objective of disrupting Allied shipping and creating panic was more than achieved. Together with Nagumo, he succeeded in creating the impression that the operation was part of a larger plan to invade and occupy Ceylon and India. They were able to do this despite the fact that they didn't have the necessary resources, in terms of men, ships or land-based aircraft, to carry out even a temporary occupation.[5]

* * *

The threat of a full-fledged invasion had blown over by mid-April 1942. But over the next two years, the Japanese continued to episodically bomb Indian cities, strikes intended to disrupt shipping, harass the administration, spread panic and undermine Indian confidence in Britain's capacity to defend the country.

After Vizagapatam and Cocanada, there were two raids on the aerodrome at Chittagong on 8 and 9 May. The town was not hit, but the casualties were considerable as the bombs fell on labourers working on the runway. Of the 300 workers, more than 100 were killed and seventy injured.[6] In the town, about 10 miles away, almost all the shopkeepers left; so did the middle classes. Chittagong would be raided many more times over the next few months.

It was the princely state of Manipur, which was under the command of the Governor of Assam, that bore the brunt of the next round of Japanese bombs. Imphal in Manipur was hit twice, on 10 and 16 May, assaults that have almost vanished from historical memory. The lack of anti-aircraft guns allowed the Japanese planes the luxury of a leisurely dummy run, after which they let their bombs fall 'in one shattering crump'.[7]

The intensity of the bombing and the scale of the damage was no less severe than that inflicted later on Calcutta and other parts of Bengal. That they don't earn much mention in accounts of this period is apiece with the Indian tendency to neglect the North-east.

Manipur was then nominally ruled by Maharaja Bodhchandra, who succeeded his father in September 1941. In a state that was largely peaceful, the most difficult moment that Christopher Gimson, the British political agent, probably faced was the *nupi lan* or women's war over the high price of rice, which was mopped up by Marwari merchants for export to other areas.[8] His red-bricked Residency was fronted by a scimitar-shaped lotus pool that 'caught the sun or was battered by the monsoon shafts'. It also boasted six grass tennis courts that were 'among the finest in the world', kept in careful shape by twenty-four gardeners. On Sunday evenings, his friends would come over to dine and listen to his expansive collection of some 2000 records, the gramophone attended by a man in scarlet and gold livery who changed and turned over the vinyl discs.[9]

The possibility of war reaching this idyll seemed remote to people, Europeans and Manipuris alike, even after Japan invaded Malaya. The sense of complacency didn't last very long. Within weeks of the Malaya invasion, the Japanese attacked Burma from Thailand. They took Rangoon with the help of the Burmese Independence Army days after British troops withdrew on 1 March. Imphal would gradually go from being a secluded town fringed by impermeable hills to becoming a hotbed of activity. Soon, it was receiving a flood of Indian refugees from Burma, an exodus set off by the fear that there would be attacks by local Burmese and the Japanese in the absence of protection from the Indian Army. Over time, Imphal would transform itself into a forward post with reinforcement of arms and men.

The two bombing attacks in May 1942 disrupted communication services and led to a 'complete breakdown' in

Manipur's civil administration. Almost all officials abandoned their posts and fled the town; the number of people that remained in most departments after the second raid was at best 'exiguous'.[10] Eyewitnesses recorded labourers and demoralized subordinate officials streaming down the roads. Poignantly, at the same time, refugees from Burma were flowing into Imphal via Tamu, one of the two routes into India.

Almost the entire population fled Imphal, which raged with fires from incendiary bombs and was subject to a 'good deal of looting'. The military was forced to commandeer whatever stocks remained in the bazaar. It also had to manage the railway line after the departure of staff in places such as Tinsukia, Digboi and Manipur Road. The main target of the attacks was the Residency (now the Raj Bhavan), where twenty-five craters were counted on the grounds. At Imphal, the quarters of the 4th Assam Rifles was bombed. The damage was slight, but the direct hit on the canteen stores destroyed whatever remained of the rum, provoking 'much humorous comment among the jawans'.[11] The main gate of the jail was demolished, freeing criminals who engaged in looting and dacoity.

Initial government assessments, based on varying reports, said that eighty died in the two raids. But it was learnt to have been considerably higher. It was estimated that almost 100 died in the first raid and something under thirty in the second.[12] A number of those killed on the road were refugees streaming into Imphal. This was unusual insomuch as Japan's air raids during the period were largely directed at military camps and infrastructure such as ports and airfields. The collapse of the civil administration and the depopulation of Imphal meant that there was no one to bury or cremate the corpses of men and cattle for days. Plaques of the three British Army men who were killed in the second bombing are in the town's war cemetery.

There was a third raid on 18 May over Derby Tea Estate, located near Silchar in Assam, not far from Manipur's eastern border.[13] It appears that the existence of a trolley line and a silver-painted factory roof led the Japanese bombers, eighteen of them flying very high, to mistake the tea estate for a railway station—probably Badarpur junction, which Tokyo radio claimed had been bombed. As a result of this mistake, about forty-three estate labourers were killed, most of them in their houses.[14] The survivors fled into the neighbouring forest to return later. The Derby Tea Estate, a property developed by a British jockey with the prize money he had won at the Calcutta Derby, still wears the scars, though they exist now in the agreeable form of craterous waterbodies.

* * *

From mid-1942 onwards, many other places were bombed in the north-eastern region, the attacks continuing well into 1943. Most of the attacks were aimed at infrastructure, many of them in smaller places with airfields and aircraft maintenance facilities. Among the raided places were Feni, Cox's Bazar, Noakhali (in Bengal), Lakhimpur (Assam) and Agartala (Tripura). Between 1 January and 4 April 1943 alone, military intelligence estimated that 252 bombers and 160 fighters were deployed to raid fourteen places in Bengal, Assam and Tripura; of the 599 civilians injured in these raids, 180 died.[15]

Of course, it was the two principal and strategic port cities in the Bengal Presidency, Calcutta and Chittagong, that were subject to the most raids. It was the latter, now in Bangladesh, that could claim the title of being the most bombed, as many as fourteen times between May 1942 and January 1943. The first raids on 8 and 9 May prompted large numbers of people to leave Chittagong, followed as they were by rumours of a Japanese invasion. As there was no air raid for the next few months, the townspeople began to slowly trickle back. But the city was bombed on 25 October and once again on 5 December. However, it was a more severe raid on 10 December that led people to believe that Chittagong would be subject to indiscriminate bombing, triggering a second exodus.[16] The last raid on Chittagong occurred on 29 May 1943, when fifteen bombers hit its airfield from a great height, killing six workers.

The war correspondent of the British-owned the *Statesman* visited Chittagong in February 1943, not long after the two January raids. He reported that he did not see a single wreckage of a house. In fairness, he wrote, the Japanese tried to confine themselves to military targets. As for the 5 December bombing of Lama Bazar, the business quarter, this was probably because the Japanese were forced to hastily dump their bombs to make a quick escape while being chased by British fighters.

Written in the form of a propagandist diary, the report was all praise for the civil administration and fortitude of Chittagonians, who have learnt to 'take it'. British soldiers also came in for effusive praise. 'Nowhere in India perhaps has Tommy Atkins* filled so successfully the role of protector and friend.'[17] But the war correspondent did acknowledge the acute situation with respect to food, a problem encountered all over the country in the face of the looming threat of war. Rice, dal and cooking oil were available only at 'fantastic' prices. As for wheat flour, sugar and ghee, they were virtually unobtainable.

Apart from Chittagong and Calcutta, Feni and Cox's Bazar also witnessed multiple raids, which continued into 1943. In strategically located Feni, close to Burma's border, the two raids on 21 March and 4 April killed twenty-one and sixty-six people, respectively.[18]

* * *

Calcutta had its first raid much later, on 20 December 1942. The *Statesman* led with news of the attack on its front page, but made

---

* Tommy Atkins is British slang for a common soldier in the British Army.

light of it editorially, as did the British authorities. The fact that bombers from airfields in Burma came at night and dropped their loads from a great height only reflected the strength of Calcutta's defences, the paper suggested. It also said that there was no military damage, that injury to civilian property was slight, and that many people were not even aware that a raid had occurred. 'Gentle crumps in the distance, if heard, might have meant anything. The general attitude on hearing the news that bombs were dropped may, therefore, vary. Some may ask: "Is that all?"'[19]

The air raid, which killed two people and injured fourteen others, was by no means a major one. But the claim that public morale was unaffected ('Well done, Calcutta!' exuded Linlithgow[20]) was a falsehood, even if very much in keeping with the British practice of playing down the extent of the panic triggered by bombing and the general threat of invasion. In Calcutta, the air raids would follow thick and fast (on 21, 22, 24 and 28 December) triggering a second exodus, the first of which took place soon after the Japanese invaded distant Malaya. When the first bombs fell on 20 December, the *Statesman*'s Assistant Editor Ian Stephens was away in Bombay. He took a train back to Calcutta, and as it neared his destination two days later, he noticed 'strings of people carrying packages with bundles on their heads' leaving the city along the path by the railway line. At Howrah station, the scene was chaotic: 'Halls and platforms were choked with people awaiting trains. And when we got out, crossing the bridge proved to be quite a tussle with a mass of traffic pressing Westwards; every imaginable form of vehicle appeared to be in use.'*[21]

The fact that civilian areas were not spared exacerbated the sense of fear. After the third successive day of bombing, Bengal's

* Stephens was appointed Editor of the *Statesman* in August 1942, after his predecessor Arthur Moore was sacked.

Premier or Chief Minister A.K. Fazlul Huq went on All India Radio to say that the first victims of the 22 December raid were a Bengali woman and her two children. How can a small city market, where other ordinary folk were killed as a result of indiscriminate bombing, be regarded as a military objective, he asked. 'So much for these worthless professions that will not deceive anybody.'[22]

A joint war communiqué issued in New Delhi, which boasted of providing 'a comprehensive picture' of the first three raids, said that twenty-five people were killed and 100 injured.[23] Controversially, the communiqué claimed that Calcutta was given enough warning for all three raids and that there was no evacuation from the city. This provoked a snarky response from the *Statesman*, which said that while it did not know what the term 'evacuation' officially meant, large numbers of people could be seen leaving the city on 23 December (after the second raid); moreover, there were others who had left earlier. It also complained that the interval between the sirens and the bomb-dropping was much too short.[24] The newspaper blamed the administration for failing to put out reliable information promptly, leading to rumours gaining currency. If there were fewer rumours, the population would have been 'less suddenly depleted'.[25] To deal with the exodus, the government set up relief centres for the homeless and kitchens that could feed as many as 22,000 people for a fortnight. A large number of camps 'with medical comforts' were established along the main roads heading out of the city.[26]

The Christmas week raids left the city feeling weak and vulnerable. The Hurricanes in Calcutta were largely ineffective against the Japanese night raiders.* But by January, this shortcoming had prompted the British to divert a few Beaufighters

---

* The Japanese used only bombers, Mitsubishi Type 97s, which the British called Sallys.

from Malta to Calcutta. These radar-equipped night fighters started arriving in Calcutta on 12 January to become the core of a new squadron deployed to defend the city.[27] As a result, the sixth and seventh Japanese raids on Calcutta, on 15 and 19 January, were greeted by a robust aerial response. On 15 January, twenty-one-year-old Maurice Pring, who had arrived in Calcutta only weeks earlier, scrambled into a Beaufighter to meet three Sallys on a clear and luminous moonlit night, taking them down in a matter of minutes. His valour earned him a couple of medals and instantly turned him into a celebrity and hero. He would become the face of the Air Force's poster for recruitment, an honour he shared with Harjinder Singh, who rose from the ranks to become one of India's first commissioned Pilot Officers. 'This is . . . Pring and this is . . . Singh', the poster declared as if to suggest that the playing field was level and that there was plenty of room for career growth.

Tragically, Pring would be killed later that year during a Japanese raid on Calcutta, by far the most damaging one. This occurred on 5 December 1943, at a time when Calcutta and other parts of Bengal were reeling from a devastating famine. It was also a time when it was believed that the threat to the city had somewhat receded. When the planes struck, Calcutta was defended only by old and ineffective Hurricanes. The best fighter squadrons had been temporarily moved to Chittagong and other places in East Bengal. If they were tricked into moving by the Japanese, as Ian Stephens suggested, then it worked.[28] This time, the bombers, accompanied by fighters, were unafraid to come in the light of day. The main target was the dockyard and warehouses at Kidderpore, an important trade hub from where supplies reached other places, including China. A communiqué issued from New Delhi on the day of the bombing said the damage was 'slight'. The following day, another press communiqué clarified that it was damage to targets of military importance that was 'slight'. There were 500 casualties, about a third of them fatal,[29] which Stephens noted was 'a considerable figure from one raid even by 1940 London standards'.[30] The 250 planes that came in two waves left the docks in ruins; set fifteen of twenty-nine storage sheds afire; destroyed fifty wagons and one engine in the nearby railway yard; and left three ships, one dredger, four tugboats and eleven barges smouldering in the water.[31]

> The area was also strewn with hundreds of corpses—human and animal—untended and unclaimed, that had already begun to rot in the afternoon sun. To make matters worse, the gates of the docks remained unmanned and hundreds of curious on-lookers entered the area to survey the damage and collect souvenirs, with crowds . . . allowed to collect around the [dead] bodies, resulting in very exaggerated rumours.[32]

In a broadcast, Bengal's Premier Khwaja Nazimuddin, who replaced Fazlul Huq and went on to become Pakistan's Prime Minister in 1951, said the bombing was a lesson for all those who had been saying there would be no more air raids on Calcutta, hinting that a sense of complacency had set in. He attributed the high rate of casualties to the public's failure to adhere to the necessary precautions after the sirens sounded. A large number of people 'stayed out in the streets or on roof-tops to see what was going on', he said. Regrettably, he added, some of these people were lying in hospital and the more unfortunate ones were dead.[33]

A few months later, Japanese forces, accompanied by Subhash Chandra Bose's INA, would arrive on Indian soil to 'liberate' the country. But this foray from Burma into India's North-east, in March 1944, was a short-lived misadventure. By then, India was better armed and the troops better equipped for jungle and mountainous warfare. They were capable of not only staging a defence but of counter-attack. Lieutenant General William Slim's 14th Army won the battles of Kohima and Imphal, inflicting the first major defeat on the Japanese in the war. Retreating Japanese soldiers were chased into Burma, which was eventually retaken.

6

The Politics of War

On 3 September 1939, Prime Minister Neville Chamberlain went on the BBC's Home Service to declare Britain was at war with Germany. Speaking from the Cabinet room at 10 Downing Street, he said Hitler had failed to heed Britain's demand that troops be withdrawn from Poland, which was invaded a couple of days earlier. Within hours, Linlithgow, some 4000 miles away at his palatial Viceregal Lodge in Simla, echoed Chamberlain on All India Radio. As a British colony, India was at war as well, he said. Linlithgow expressed confidence that Indians would be 'forthcoming without distinction of class, of creed, of race or of political party' to support the war effort.[1]

The idea that all of India would rally behind Britain in its war effort was probably little more than a platitudinous hope. Even though Linlithgow was arguably somewhat removed from political ground realities (Nehru described him famously as 'a rock and with almost a rock's lack of awareness'[2]), he couldn't have been totally unaware of the way India would react. The Congress had already made it clear, even as the war clouds were gathering over Europe, that it would not be a party to an 'imperialist' war. While it had no hesitation in declaring its opposition to the fascist powers, it was averse to letting India be exploited by Britain in the event of another world war. As early as late 1936, it had warned of 'the grave danger of Indian manpower and resources' being utilized for British military ends. 'No credits must be voted for such a war and voluntary subscriptions and war loans must not be supported and all other war preparations resisted,' it declared at its annual session in Faizpur in December 1936.[3]

The uses that Indian soldiers were put to in the past were not lost on Indian nationalists. At different phases of colonial consolidation, these men were utilized to set kingdom against kingdom and establish British control in various parts of India; they were also deployed to maintain order and quell uprisings in various Asian colonies. More recently, and very much in living memory, they were the foundation on which the Allied victory over Germany was built. Over 1.3 million Indian soldiers served in World War I, the majority of them combatants deployed in campaigns in Europe, East Africa, Mesopotamia, Sinai, Gallipoli and elsewhere.

That war effort also required a large number of non-combatants; India was again at the forefront of providing auxiliary support in the form of butchers, sweepers, cobblers, tailors, carpenters and cooks. About 75,000 Indian soldiers were killed, but India's contribution to the war went even further. Enormous quantities of rice, wheat, sugar and other foodstuffs were sent abroad, resulting in a sharp spike in prices at home. Even after disregarding the generous loans given by the Indian government to Britain during the war, India's direct cash contribution was 229 million pounds and another 250 million pounds in overseas materials.[4] There was reason to worry that another world war would be written in the same extractive and aspirating script.

Linlithgow, of course, knew some support would be forthcoming. Geographically, more than a third of India was made up of princely states, over which he enjoyed suzerainty. A large number of these rulers—a royal list that included big-ticket states such as Gwalior, Baroda, Mysore, Cochin, Travancore and

Bhopal—declared they would back Britain in the event of war. Several of them donated tidy sums of money; some offered men and materials. The Maharaja of Travancore, for instance, contributed Rs 6,00,000, placed his entire army at the disposal of the British government and went further by promising to raise a labour corps whenever necessary.[5] This kind of generous support was offered in the hope of consolidating the relationship with Britain at a critical time. One in which republican and democratic values were taking root and princely interests were being threatened by an increasingly uncertain constitutional future.

There have been various interpretations of Linlithgow's unilateralism. It is possible that he was simply too insensitive to bother informing, let alone consulting, the Congress, other political parties, the Central Legislature and provincial governments before making his announcement. He may have believed that this was unnecessary in the circumstances. He was constitutionally empowered to take a unilateral decision and may have felt there was no other option but to quickly harness India for war. Whatever the truth, he clearly miscalculated how much this would upset the Congress and the chain of events it would occasion.

His meeting with Gandhi the day following his announcement couldn't have prepared the Viceroy for what followed. Linlithgow spent almost two hours with an emotional Gandhi, who dropped his head and wept at the thought of German bombs destroying London, where he had arrived in 1888 as a starry-eyed eighteen-year-old in search of a law degree. As visions of a ruinous Westminster Abbey and Parliament building flashed through his mind, Gandhi said he thought of the war 'with an English heart'. While his non-violent support for the British cause was unconditional, he said he couldn't speak on behalf of the Congress.[6]

Quite clearly, Gandhi couldn't. After days of debate at Wardha, the Congress Working Committee (CWC) put out a lengthy and conditional statement on 14 September that had Nehru's hand written all over it. On the one hand, it 'unhesitatingly' condemned the Nazi assault on Poland and recorded its continued 'disapproval of the ideology and practice of Fascism and Nazism and their glorification of war and violence and the suppression of the human spirit'. On the other, it subtly equated the Allied forces and the Axis powers, by blaming the war on the root causes of fascism and imperialism; the true measure of democracy, it suggested, lay in removing both.[7]

Shorn of long-winded political opinion, the CWC's resolution had three significant features. First, it declared that the Congress had taken 'no final decision' on the war. Second, that any such decision would depend on what Britain's war aims were 'in regard to democracy and imperialism'. Third, and by implication, Congress' support for the war would depend on how far Britain would go in transferring power to Indian hands. In effect, the statement discreetly signalled that the Congress' doors were open for negotiation.

Predictably, the resolution disappointed the colonial administration, which peddled the line that the only thing that mattered at this grave hour was to bury all differences and fight the good fight. In short, the war trumped all politics. Reflecting this view, the British-owned the *Times of India* wrote sarcastically of the CWC's meandering resolution: 'To many, it must seem that the Committee has put itself in a position of a body which, when asked to assist a fire brigade to stop a conflagration, sits down first to discuss the sins of the fire brigade and to ask what its intentions are.'[8]

But there was a good reason for the Congress to temporize and dress up the statement with vague generalities. It was an open secret that at Wardha, there were varied opinions among its leadership about the war. Gandhi's sympathies lay with Britain, which he felt deserved unconditional non-violent support in the circumstances. On the other side were those who smarted from the insult of not being consulted by Linlithgow. Subhash Chandra Bose, who had just established the All India Forward Bloc, a left-wing faction within the Congress, was enraged enough to advocate a campaign for mass civil disobedience. But even those unwilling to go as far as Bose in threatening open revolt if independence was not granted were upset with Linlithgow. India, after all, was vital for the worldwide war effort, being as it was a critical arsenal for men and material. Even so, the courtesy of being consulted was denied while it was extended to other dominions. As the *Indian Express* disdainfully noted, the privilege of such consultation was conferred even 'on a country of size and importance as New Zealand'.[9]

But the issue went beyond mere insult. There was also an irrefutable logic in the Congress' position. Why was India being asked to fight a war for the sake of democracy when the very same was being denied to it? Surely, the premise of a just war should be predicated on securing justice? Such logic coexisted with a sense of pragmatism. While the opposition to Nazism was unwavering, Congress leaders such as C. Rajagopalachari were not averse to using the new circumstances to nationalist advantage, holding out support to the British in exchange for a clear timeline towards meaningful self-government.

As we shall see, the differences in the Congress over the war would create fissures within the organization, the cracks widening further after Japan's gambit in South-East Asia. The war seeded the ground for competitive communal rivalries, which spawned the idea that India was not one but two nations—a plank that gained unexpected political support after the Muslim League's demand for Pakistan. War also forced Britain in divergent ways, coercing it to make arguably insincere overtures to secure Indian cooperation on the one hand, and privileging immediate imperial interests over nationalist aspirations on the other.

* * *

But a little background first about the India that Linlithgow arrived to reign over. When he docked in Bombay in 1936, India was on the cusp of change. Prime Minister Stanley Baldwin had narrowed down the choice of Lord Willingdon's successor to two, eventually opting for Linlithgow over the Marquess of Zetland.* The latter had more hands-on experience of India, having served as Governor of Bengal. But Linlithgow, who chaired the Joint Select Committee on Indian Constitutional Reform, was responsible for drafting and seeing through what was then the longest Act, with 321 sections and 10 schedules, passed by the British Parliament—The Government of India Act, 1935. Given this, it is likely that Baldwin felt Linlithgow was better equipped to oversee the implementation of the new constitutional arrangement.

The territory Linlithgow oversaw comprised British India, under the rule of the Crown since 1857, and a few hundred princely states, which numbered 584 before India was partitioned in 1947. Of the 400 million population, about three-fourths lived in British India, administered under The Government of India Act, 1919. The Act, which provided a small measure of self-government to Indians, mandated a Legislative Assembly and a Council of States at the Centre, the Lower and Upper Houses. About 30 per cent of the members in the Assembly and over 40 per cent in the Council were nominated; moreover, the electorate was severely restricted by property and income qualifications.

The real power lay with the Central government, made up of the Governor-General and a seven-member Executive Council. (The Viceroy and the Governor-General were one and the same, the former reflecting the role as Head of State and the latter as

* According to John Glendevon, Linlithgow's son and biographer, his father was asked to choose between Viceroyship and Secretary of State for India. Linlithgow accepted what he regarded as a greater challenge. As a result, he reported to Zetland, who remained Secretary of State until 1940. John Glendevon, *The Viceroy at Bay: Lord Linlithgow in India, 1936–1943* (London: Collins, 1971), p. 21.

Head of Government.) The supremacy of the Governor-General's office lay in such provisions that required his prior assent before bills on certain subjects (for example, armed forces and British citizens) were introduced in the Legislative Assembly and his power to dismiss both legislatures.

At the provincial level, there existed a diarchy or double government. The Governor and an Executive Council appointed by the Crown oversaw subjects on a 'reserved list' (notably, law and order and land revenue). A legislature (or council) was charged with administering a list of subjects on the 'transferred list' (including health, education and agriculture). Once again, the Governor's supremacy was reflected in provisions that allowed him to disregard the Council and the legislature under certain conditions.

There was no common framework for the princely states, which were coerced into recognizing the paramountcy of the Crown by separate treaties, signed in differing circumstances and at varying times. In theory, these states enjoyed internal autonomy, ceding control of external affairs to the Crown. But in practice, the real power lay with a network of residents and agents, essentially British diplomats who could make forceful administrative interventions when required, their orders masquerading as advice. They could replace a troublesome or inconvenient Maharaja with a person of their choosing. A few could be excessively fastidious. As Punjab's Resident, Harold Wilberforce-Bell pored over the princes' coat of arms with a magnifying glass to determine whether there were violations of his strict and exacting code.[10]

As historian Manu Pillai has compellingly argued, there is a persuasive case for revising the received opinion, held with smug assurance by the British, that the Maharajas were no more than lotus-eating imperial stooges.[11] They were capable of strongly resisting the British administration when their perceived interests were threatened. Linlithgow, who was tasked with putting

The Government of India Act, 1935, into operation, discovered this the hard way.

The 1935 Act envisaged an All-India Federation, made up of British provinces and princely states, which could decide one way or another on accession. For the federation to work, Linlithgow needed to bring a sufficient number of princes on board. Some princes initially canvassed for federation, but had a change of heart. Linlithgow believed that their original enthusiasm was the result of a mistaken belief that federation would put an end to political control by the British government and confer full autonomy on their own states. Even so, he seemed confident of making it work, sending emissaries to try and allay princely fears that the Act did not have sufficient safeguards and would reduce them to mere constitutional figureheads.

But the problem didn't lie with the princely states alone. The Act, particularly the federal part, had powerful detractors within the British political establishment and there is some cause to believe, as Linlithgow himself did, that his efforts were undermined from within. Particularly by Zetland, who was worried that the right wing of the Conservative Party would scrutinize anything done to further federation 'with a highly critical and jaundiced eye'.[12]

The Act, and the federation it envisaged, indeed had strong opponents among the Conservatives. When it was finally passed in June 1935, as many as eighty-four of them voted against the government. The most vocal among them was Churchill, who attacked the legislation for creating a federal system before the formation of its units. ('The wall before the bricks are made; the faggots before the stake is cut.') In January 1935, he spared no words in his BBC radio broadcast titled 'The Great Betrayal':

> But what is this India Home Rule Bill? I will tell you. It is a gigantic quilt of jumbled crochet work. There is no theme; there is no pattern; there is no agreement; there is no conviction; there is no simplicity; there is no courage. It is a monstrous monument of shame built by pygmies.[13]

The 1935 Act was an improvement over 1919 in some respects. For instance, it expanded the electorate to about 14 per cent of the adult population and provided a measure of provincial autonomy by putting an end to diarchy, increased ministerial power and made elected governments responsible only to the legislature. On the flip side, subjects such as defence and external affairs were vested with the Governor-General (creating a diarchy at the Centre). Under the Act, the Governor-General continued to enjoy enormous discretionary powers, including that of declaring an emergency, making laws and suspending a part or whole of the Act. Clearly, any semblance of democracy could exist only with the indulgence of his office.

Annoyed among other things by the absence of even a mention of Dominion Status, let alone independence, Nehru panned the Act as a charter of slavery. But the Congress was soon faced with a dilemma. After the Act was notified, the constitutional ground was prepared for holding elections to the provincial legislatures. Should it participate in the provincial elections that were mandated under the 1935 Act? The irony of a party taking part in a constitutional process that was perceived as furthering British rule was apparent to many. But pragmatism, triggered by fears that other parties would capture the legislatures, won the day. Of the eleven provinces in which elections were held, the Congress performed splendidly by winning six major ones emphatically—Bombay, Madras, the United Provinces, the Central Provinces, Bihar and Orissa. It fell short of a majority in the North West Frontier Province (NWFP) but was able to cobble together a ministry. Despite emerging as the largest party in Bengal and Assam, it was unable to do the same. It was only in Punjab and Sind that it really failed. In contrast, the Muslim League fared poorly, unable to secure even 25 per cent of the reserved Muslim seats.

Having won comprehensively, another schism surfaced in the Congress, with some arguing against the assumption of office, advocating instead the undermining of the legislature from within. To accept office is to stand self-condemned and tantamount to negating the party's wholesale opposition to the Act, argued Nehru. Once again, however, pragmatism prevailed. The Congress went on to form ministries, first in provinces where it enjoyed a majority, and then wherever it could. The scale of the Congress victory meant it didn't need the Muslim League. But the failure to share power with Muhammad Ali Jinnah hardened the League's position against the Congress and may, as some have argued, have sown, or at least unintentionally nurtured, the seeds for Pakistan.[14]

Assuming office meant striking a balance between playing government in the provinces and opposition at the Centre. Gandhi urged that the offices be held lightly rather than tightly, while exploring how ministerial power could move India closer to independence. Congress ministers chose to draw only a fourth of their salary, Rs 500 a month, signalling that they didn't regard their offices as rewards but duties.

* * *

The experiment with self-government ended a couple of months after Linlithgow's declaration of war. The Viceroy took more than a month to formally respond to the Congress' Wardha resolution. Meanwhile, the party reiterated that its door was open for negotiation by suggesting it was not demanding immediate constitutional change, but only a commitment to independence after the war. After consulting fifty-two Indian leaders, Linlithgow reacted on 17 October, his lengthy statement influenced by a mix of his own intransigence and the British Cabinet's view that it was unwise to make any firm commitments at this juncture.

In a study in evasion and vagueness, Linlithgow declared that the partnership between the United Kingdom and India would continue 'within our Empire' so that the latter may 'attain its due place among our Dominions'. At the end of the war, Britain would consult representatives of different communities, parties and the Maharajas to frame 'such modifications [of the 1935 Act] as may seem desirable'.[15] Five days later, the CWC panned this as an 'unequivocal reiteration' of the old policy, 'wholly unsatisfactory' and intended to stoke 'resentment' among those seeking independence. At the same time, it called on all Congress ministries in the provinces to resign.[16]

By mid-November, all seven had quit, a decision that was politically counterproductive (even Linlithgow thought it unjustified in terms of 'practical politics'), but arguably unavoidable given the position the party had staked out earlier. If the resignations were aimed at embarrassing the British and undermining their claims of putting India on a path towards democratic self-government, they went only so far. Linlithgow may well have been secretly relieved, sharing the opinion of some British administrators that the resignations helped by freeing them to focus on the war. His discussions with Congress leaders, among the fifty-two he held meetings with, had prepared him for the eventuality.

Not every province reverted to Governor's rule, with governments in populous Muslim-majority provinces such as Bengal and Punjab remaining in power and pledging their support to the Centre. This allowed the British to claim that the experiment with self-government was far from over. A year and a half later, Secretary of State Leo Amery would remind the House of Commons, during a debate on extending Governor's rule in seven provinces, that in four (Bengal, Punjab, Sind and Assam), provincial self-government continued to work. A hundred million people, one-third of the whole population of British India, had enjoyed four years of democratic self-government, he said. 'I think we ought not to under-estimate the significance of this remarkable advance . . . over so large a field.'[17]

The resignations hardened the position of a Congress frustrated by British reluctance to transfer effective power. In March 1940, at Ramgarh, the Congress declared that nothing short of independence was acceptable, adding that Dominion Status or any other arrangement within the 'orbit of imperialism' was 'not in keeping with the dignity of the nation'.[18] Stating it was against the recruitment of men and the drain of material for the war, the party opened the door for civil disobedience, saying that such a campaign, which follows 'naturally' from the decision to quit provincial ministries, would be taken up when the Congress was fit to carry it out. A few days later, Jinnah declared in Lahore that the Muslim League stood for a separate homeland for Muslims: Pakistan. By then, he was already aware that the federation, which he was sharply opposed to, was a non-starter. His qualified support for the war played into Britain's divide-and-rule policy; at the same time, it helped to firm up the government's view that any future constitutional arrangement would have to be acceptable to Muslims (in other words, the League).

* * *

In the run-up to the war, the Congress was already caught in a churn; Linlithgow's declaration, if anything, agitated it even more vigorously. In early 1938, Subhash Chandra Bose became president of the Congress. His politics was marked by three presumably inconsistent traits—a fiery and uncompromising nationalism, an abiding faith in socialism and an admiration for the hard-nosed efficacy of authoritarianism. Having plunged into politics in 1921, after he returned from London having given up a position in the Indian Civil Service (ICS), Bose rose quickly within the party. A vocal member of the Congress' so-called left wing, he was strongly against what he regarded as the right wing's policy of conciliation and compromise.

His disenchantment with Gandhi's political style occurred early. Like many others in the party, he was angry when Gandhi called off the non-cooperation movement in 1921, believing its abrupt termination weakened a struggle that was 'advancing on all fronts'. A decade later, he would continue to be dismayed by what he saw as Gandhi's irresolute ways, upset with his decision to summarily call off the civil disobedience movement in 1931, sign a pact with Viceroy Irwin, and then leave for London to discuss constitutional reforms at the second Round Table Conference. Bose was delighted, however, that Gandhi called on Mussolini in Italy on his way back to India, a visit he described as a great public service.

By this time, his interest in fascism had begun to reveal itself. Addressing the Calcutta Corporation in September 1930, a month after he was elected Mayor, he spoke in praise of a politics that combined the justice and equality of socialism with the efficiency and discipline of fascism.[19] Rejecting Nehru's view that there is no middle ground between communism and fascism, he argued that the two shared common traits, such as party rule, lack of faith in parliamentary democracy, suppression of dissent and planned industrial organization. Predicting that communism and fascism would be fused together in the years to come, he wrote, 'It will be India's task to work out this synthesis.'[20]

Bose became less effusive about fascism before the end of the decade, probably as a result of Mussolini's aggressive conquest of Abyssinia and the demands of impending office (as Congress president, it was important not to alienate colleagues).[21] He told journalists that the manner in which he spoke about fascism earlier was 'not a happy one' and that his ideas were formed at a time when the ideology 'had not started on its imperialist expedition'.[22] At the same time, Bose had a sense that the balance of military power was shifting in Europe. He recognized that Britain's imperial hold was weakening in places such as Ireland, India and the Middle East, and its supremacy was also being challenged from without by countries such as Italy and Japan. In his speech as Congress President at the Haripura session in February 1938, he said Britain's military decline was the result of a new force—the emergence of air power. Adding presciently: 'Distances have been obliterated and despite all anti-aircraft defences, London lies at the mercy of any bombing squadron from a Continental centre. In short, the air force has revolutionized modern warfare, destroyed the insularity of Great Britain . . . The clay feet of a gigantic Empire stand exposed as it was never before.'[23]

Bose had become convinced that war would break out well before September 1939. And he was honest about declaring that India should use the crisis to secure her freedom. Ever since Neville Chamberlain signed the infamous Munich Pact in September 1938, permitting Hitler to annex the Sudetenland, Bose tried to persuade the Congress 'to shape its policy in conformity with the march of events abroad'. He believed his efforts were obstructed by the party's 'Gandhi wing', charging its members with having no clue about international developments and being eager to compromise with Britain.[24]

It was Gandhi who proposed Bose as Congress President in 1938, but their rickety political alliance soon came apart. By the time Bose offered himself up for re-election in 1939, the differences between him and Gandhi had considerably widened. After failing to persuade Bose not to contest again, Gandhi turned to Nehru, and then Maulana Abul Kalam Azad. Both refused and it was down to the somewhat lightweight Pattabhi Sitaramayya to square up with Bose, who went on to win the contest, inflicting what Gandhi regarded as a personal defeat.

Bose's denials that he opposed Gandhi personally failed to prevent matters from coming to a head. In February, a dozen members of the CWC resigned at Gandhi's behest. At the Tripuri session in March, Bose made bold to move a resolution that served an ultimatum on the British government: grant independence within six months or face civil disobedience. It failed and the motion that was eventually adopted was one that constrained his own independence. The 'Pant resolution' that required him to seek Gandhi's approval for constituting a working committee was carried.

Effectively neutralized, Bose resigned and formed the Forward Bloc, a faction of the Congress that aimed at bringing leftists together. His criticism of British rule and what he saw as the Congress' complicity in it became more strident. By June 1940, probably influenced by the situation in France, he was convinced that a German victory was imminent, telling author Nirad Chaudhuri that Britain would surrender by 16 July.[25] Five days after his failed prediction, Bose was arrested for sedition and sent to a Calcutta prison. He spent a few months there before threatening to starve to death. Six days into his fast, the authorities got cold feet and allowed him to return home for a spell of house arrest. Here he grew a beard and fled Calcutta in 1941 disguised as a Pathan, eventually making his way to Germany via Afghanistan and Moscow. Two years later, he was in Japan, from where he travelled to Singapore to take charge of the INA, the army that lay in wait for his leadership.

* * *

The Congress' opposition to the British Raj during the war remained unshaken. This was quite unlike the Muslim League, which was broadly supportive, an approach that led Linlithgow to regard it much more favourably. What the war did to the Congress, however, was to divide it on the question of participation. Bose, whose intense dislike of British rule swept him into the arms of the Axis powers, may have been an outlier. But there were serious differences within the core or inner ring of the Congress on whether to participate and, if so, in what form and under what conditions.

The differences began to manifest as war clouds started gathering over Europe. Gandhi had already decided against India's direct participation in the war under any circumstances, a position forged by an innate sense of pacifism. Congress President Maulana Abul Kalam Azad was unfair, or at the very least much too simplistic in saying that for Gandhi 'the issue was one of pacifism and not of India's freedom', the binary obscuring the difficult moral pulls and pressures produced by his aversion to violence and his desire to set India free.* At the same time, there is no denying that Gandhi's strong commitment to non-violence, which wore the appearance of a pacifist absolutism, created a distance between him and some other senior Congressmen. While leaders such as Nehru and Maulana Azad were also against participating in the war, their opposition was contingent rather than absolute; they were against Indians supporting

---

* Maulana Abul Kalam Azad, *India Wins Freedom* (Hyderabad: Orient Blackswan, 1988), Chapter 3, Kindle. It is pertinent to acknowledge that questions have been raised about the reliability of Azad's *India Wins Freedom*, which was first published in 1958, some months after his death and well after the events it covers. Another controversy relates to the thirty pages of a so-called personal nature that Azad directed should be published later. Based on a narration to Humayun Kabir, academic, Congressman and minister in the Indian government, a number of questions have arisen relating to the inaccuracies, omissions and interpretations in Azad's autobiography. Rajmohan Gandhi in *India Wins Errors: A Scrutiny of Maulana Azad's India Wins Freedom* (New Delhi: Radiant Publishers, 1989) acknowledges Azad's great political contribution, but argues that the disappointment of being politically surpassed by the likes of Nehru and Patel between 1940 and 1946 coloured his views. In citing *India Wins Freedom*, this book has stayed clear of the obvious errors and distortions that Rajmohan Gandhi has painstakingly pointed out; where necessary, it has qualified Azad's observations with he 'claimed' or 'wrote'.

the war effort as a subjugated or enslaved people. A third view emerged, represented by C. Rajagopalachari, who was in favour of supporting the British war effort, while negotiating with the Raj for further constitutional reform. As the war progressed, his views would diverge much more sharply from the first two approaches.

By the middle of 1940, the war assumed a new form and fresh urgency. In May, Hitler invaded Norway, bringing an end to the so-called phoney war, that deceptive lull after the attack on Poland. In June, his panzer divisions hurtled through France, forcing an armistice before the end of the month. In the midst of the raging battle, Gandhi's pacifism came under even sharper scrutiny. The violence wreaked by war and his inability to stop it left him distraught. Azad claimed Gandhi spoke of suicide on many occasions, saying that 'if he was so powerless to stop the suffering caused by the war, he could at least refuse to be a witness to it by putting an end to his life'.[26] At the same time, his attempts to secure greater support for his policy of non-violence were failing. Most Congressmen felt that it was one thing to advocate such a course of action in the internal struggle against British rule and quite another to bat for non-violence in the face of naked external aggression.

In Gandhi's mind, there was no basis for making such a distinction. His appeal to 'every Briton' was of a piece with his belief about the appropriate way to respond in the face of war and oppression. He advised the British to lay down arms and invite Hitler and Mussolini to take possession of the 'beautiful island', the 'beautiful buildings' and 'homes'. Suggesting that the important thing was not to surrender their minds and souls, he wrote: 'If they do not give you free passage out, you will allow yourself, man, woman and child, to be slaughtered, but you will refuse to owe allegiance to them.'[27]

Earlier, he had advocated that the Abyssinians should have adopted a similar approach in the face of Italian aggression, a form of non-violence that can 'break to pieces' but never 'bends', one that tells Mussolini that he was welcome to reduce them to 'dust and ashes'.[28] In his eyes, such non-violent resistance and the willingness to die unarmed was honourable. 'In so doing, I lose my body, but I save my soul . . . my honour,' he wrote of what he would do were he a Czech under German assault.[29] At the same time, he believed that a dignified, peaceful defiance would rob the aggressor of his resolve. If not one Abyssinian cooperated, wouldn't Mussolini have been forced to retire, he asked. After all, 'He did not want a desert.'[30]

Not surprisingly, there were those who regarded such ideas as dangerously misplaced, a result of the naive and credulous belief that violence can be neutralized by arming yourself with the sword of non-violence. But Gandhi was convinced of the persuasive force of the idea of non-violence. He wrote two widely publicized letters to Hitler addressing him as 'Dear Friend', essentially well-meaning appeals to the Fuehrer to end the war. But where he gravely erred was in describing the man. In May 1940, not long after Germany took the Low Countries and invaded France, he confided to his friend Amrit Kaur that he did not 'consider Hitler to be as bad a man as he is depicted'. In his letter to the woman he would fondly address as 'rebel' and 'idiot' (who would go on to become the country's first health minister), Gandhi would add: 'He [Hitler] is showing an ability that is amazing and he seems to be gaining his victories without much bloodshed.'[31] A few days later, he struck a similar note in a letter to Linlithgow, advising him that it was possibly time to sue for peace. 'I do not believe Herr Hitler to be as bad as he is portrayed. He might even have been a friendly power as he may still be. It is due to suffering humanity that this mad slaughter should stop.'[32]

By this time, Gandhi's idea that brave but suffering victims would alter the minds of aggressors, or at least rob them of the rationale for wreaking war and violence, seemed increasingly far-fetched to other Congress leaders. By mid-1940, the schisms in the Congress had widened enough to cause a breach. In June, after five days of deliberation, the CWC concluded it was 'unable to go the full length with Gandhiji'. Recognizing that he should be 'free to pursue his great ideal in his own way', the CWC absolved him of the activities that the party wanted to pursue in the face of 'external aggression and internal disorder'.[33] In distancing himself from Gandhi, Rajagopalachari noted that the Congress was not an organization 'working for non-violence but for a political ideal'. Nehru agreed.[34]

The political breach was complete despite Gandhi saying the differences did not cause any 'break in friendship' and Nehru declaring the Congress would continue to avail of his 'guidance and wise counsel'. 'The Congress of the last twenty years is his [Gandhi's] creation and child and nothing can break this bond,' Nehru said.[35] With the big four—Rajagopalachari, Nehru, Azad and Patel—in alignment, Gandhi was isolated. He continued to push for non-violence in his capacity as an 'individual', advising Linlithgow that Nazi methods to defeat Germany would result in no deliverance from Nazism.

In July, the CWC went further, led by Rajagopalachari, who steered a resolution demanding the immediate grant of independence and the setting up of a national government at the Centre. If these measures were adopted, the Congress would 'throw its full weight in the efforts for the effective organization of the Defence of the country'.[36] A resigned Gandhi, whose draft resolution was rejected, declared: 'We must all act according to our own views. Visualizing the position as it changes from moment to moment we have to find out what part each of us plays in the drama.'[37]

In a month, however, Gandhi would relinquish his bit part and resume his role as lead actor. The Congress rallied around him once again after Linlithgow failed to offer anything of substance in exchange for the party's support of the war effort. The momentous change in Britain, with Churchill replacing Chamberlain as Prime Minister, was responsible for the hardening in Britain's attitude.

Although Secretary of State Leopold Amery was willing to be somewhat accommodative to break the constitutional deadlock, his attempts were frustrated by a staunchly imperialist Churchill, who went on to famously declare that he had 'not become the King's first Minister in order to preside over the liquidation of the British Empire'.[38] Linlithgow, who shared an uneasy relationship with the new Secretary of State, was invested in the status quo. In the Viceroy's mind, the war effort was the real priority; ushering in meaningful constitutional reform at this juncture was an unnecessary distraction, if not a betrayal of British interests.

In truth, Amery's proposal was modest. It contained no definite time frame and was assiduously non-committal about instituting political reform before the end of the war. It offered, among other things, Dominion Status in the near future; the promise that India would be allowed to frame a new Constitution; and the setting up of a Constituent Assembly to ratify it at the end of the war. After going along with Amery, Linlithgow abruptly changed his mind when he learnt the proposal was not approved by Churchill's War Cabinet. The Viceroy followed this up by complaining about the pressure Amery had applied on him and demanded that all future proposals for political reform be initiated in New Delhi.

Amery was rebuked by Churchill. The former complained that the Prime Minister had launched a 'tremendous onslaught' on him, declaring he would have resigned but for the war. In response, Churchill was cold, saying that he would 'rather give up political life than be responsible for a resolution that meant the end of the Imperial Crown in India'.[39] It was the War Cabinet's decision that any resolution must be redrafted by Churchill himself that led to the August Offer—a modification of Linlithgow's draft that was wordy and indistinct about Britain's commitment to reform. The Viceroy said he would invite more Indians to his Executive Council and set up a War Advisory Council. Reiterating his government's view that Dominion Status was its objective for India, he said that any further reform of the 1935 Act should give full weight to minority opinion and that a representative body of 'the principal elements of India's national life' could prepare a framework for a new Constitution after the war.

There were at least two problems with this in the Congress' eyes. First, the offer of a few seats at the high table didn't constitute real reform. Second, the statement made it more or less clear that the Congress could not speak for India regarding its constitutional future—the Muslim League and the princely states would have a say as well. Not surprisingly, the Congress outrightly rejected the August Offer. With this, the party's conditional offer of cooperation in exchange for a promise of independence and the formation of a national government was off the table too.

This was a victory of sorts for Gandhi, and the party reunited itself under his leadership with a sense of 'palpable relief'.[40] Unexpectedly, the crack that had developed between senior Congressmen and Gandhi was filled by Linlithgow. The British government's position had rendered the conflicts over non-violence and participation in the war redundant. Nehru declared that the conditional offer of cooperating in the war effort was dead and past all resurrection.

In essence, the issue now before the Congress was civil disobedience, which the Ramgarh resolution in March 1940 had said the party would 'unhesitatingly resort to' either when the Congress was ready or in the event of a 'crisis'. The open-ended nature of the threat was a result of Gandhi's reluctance to launch mass civil disobedience as it could turn violent. In the run-up to the Ramgarh session, he had already made it clear, 'It will be suicidal to declare it [civil disobedience] when there is so much indiscipline and violence within the Congress itself.'[41] While he admired the zeal of those who questioned him, he warned them not to be impatient. 'Let it be understood that I cannot be hustled into precipitating the struggle.'[42]

After the insubstantial August Offer, the question of whether to launch civil disobedience or do nothing at all assumed a more pressing form. By then Bose, who had called for an all-out campaign to rid India of the British, was in prison. Gandhi, however, remained cautious, settling on an incremental path of individual passive resistance. Specific people were called up to offer satyagraha by making speeches against the war. The first chosen was Vinoba Bhave, the philosopher, who was known as Gandhi's spiritual successor. He was arrested days after the Congress formally launched the individual satyagraha movement. Other leaders such as Azad and Rajagopalachari followed, and the round of arrests and convictions continued well into the following year as members of the Congress rank and file were asked to court arrest and swell the jails. By the middle of March 1941, over 7000 had been arrested and 4400 were serving sentences.[43]

Nehru was among the early leaders to be arrested, but unlike Bhave and the others, he was held under the Defence of India Rules, even before he undertook satyagraha. His sentencing by a district judge to four years of imprisonment evoked consternation in both Britain and India. Even the hard-headed Churchill was moved to direct Amery to write to Linlithgow, expressing the hope that the sentence would be modified and that Nehru would not be treated like a common criminal.[44] The pressure to release the Congress satyagrahis grew as the length of their incarceration progressed and the war assumed an even wider dimension with Hitler's attack on Russia and Japan's creeping influence in Thailand and Indochina.

In December 1941, Nehru was released. A few days later, Japan struck Pearl Harbour and invaded Malaya. By the end of the month, Congress President Azad and many others were set free, a decision he believed was intended to test how the Congress would react to the new war situation. Britain's need to shore up war support within India was greater than ever before. And the entry of Japan would mark a new phase in the process of decolonization and the struggle for independence.

7

The Entry of Japan

Japan's entry into the war caused another convulsion in the Congress. At the end of December 1941, once again at Rajagopalachari's urging, the CWC declared its willingness to support the war in exchange for independence. The Bardoli resolution drafted by a committee of four—Nehru, Azad, Rajagopalachari and Pant—took note of the 'new world situation that has arisen by the development of the war into a world conflict and its approach to India', adding that 'only a free and Independent India can be in a position to undertake the defence of the country. . .'[1] Whether this was a departure from or a mere reiteration of the Congress position became a matter of debate, but a plain reading suggested that the party was holding out *active armed* participation in return for an acceptable timetable for constitutional reform.

Predictably, this did not go down well with Gandhi, who was against the door for participation being kept open in any shape or form. He requested the CWC to relieve him of the responsibility of leading the party's campaign. The CWC did as requested, but assured Gandhi that the policy of non-violence would be adhered to internally, that is, in the struggle for freedom. Gandhi hoped the Bardoli resolution would not be ratified by the All India Congress Committee (AICC) in January, telling his followers that they could either throw it out or modify it suitably to rule out help in the war effort.[2] However, sensing the prevailing mood, Gandhi ended up endorsing the resolution at the AICC session. 'Retrograde' though he thought it was, this was not the time to 'divide the house' or 'canvass support for our groups and seek a vote'.[3] He went on to say that it was (always) Nehru and not Rajagopalachari (or Vallabhbhai Patel) who would succeed him—a declaration that raised the question of whether Rajaji had forsaken his heirship for actively advocating support for the war effort. Nehru, of course, had more charisma and was more widely acceptable. Also, Rajagopalachari may have ruled himself out by failing to master Hindi despite Gandhi's urging. 'One unable to communicate with India's Hindi heartland could not guide it.'[4]

By this time, the force of the Japanese onslaught in South-East Asia and the threat this posed was very much on India's mind. People had already begun to flee coastal towns for the 'safety' of the interior. Hitler's stunning advances in Europe in mid-1940 had seeded doubts about Britain's capacity to win the war. The fall of Hong Kong and the rapid retreat in Malaya created an additional and more fundamental misgiving—about Britain's willingness to stoutly defend India.

While the risk of a Japanese attack emboldened the Congress to press the British to make firm commitments towards self-government, there was a deepening frustration in other political quarters over the constitutional deadlock. In early January 1942, Tej Bahadur Sapru, leader of the so-called moderate and gradualist Liberal Party, wrote directly to Churchill with a set of proposals in an attempt to bypass Linlithgow and Amery. At its heart lay the suggestion that the Viceroy's Executive Council be expanded and converted into a national government; this was to be made up of representatives of political parties responsible to the Crown. In effect, the proposal met the British need for involving India in the war effort, while going some way in providing a measure of self-government. But the idea of enlarging the Council and possibly handing over the defence and finance portfolios to Indians was strongly resisted by Churchill.[5]

However, after the assault on Singapore and its eventual fall, pressure mounted on Britain to break the deadlock. Some of this came from within. The Labour Party, which was pressing for a more accommodative attitude towards India, pitched for another discussion on reform in the face of the new strategic situation. In early February 1942, Clement Attlee challenged the status quoism of Linlithgow and Amery in the War Cabinet, presenting a memorandum that argued Britain could no longer afford to do nothing and continue clinging to a Eurocentric view of the world.[6] Rejecting what he described as Linlithgow's 'crude imperialism', he said it was time for an act of statesmanship. 'To mark time, is to lose India.'

Attlee suggested that someone who was widely acceptable be sent over to India to reach a settlement. Churchill pushed for a limited proposal of his own, but the war situation was driving changes and forcing compromises. The loss of Malaya and the fall of Singapore in mid-February led to a significant restructuring of Churchill's Cabinet. Attlee was made Deputy Prime Minister and Secretary of State for Dominion Affairs while Stafford Cripps, a well-known sympathizer of Indian self-rule, was included in the War Cabinet. By the end of the month, a Cabinet committee, chaired by Attlee and including Cripps, was formed to discuss and prepare a draft on what constitutional reform, if any, was possible at this juncture.

More than one draft declaration was discussed and many amendments were made before the War Cabinet approved a version on 9 March. Essentially, it promised India Dominion Status with the power to secede from the British Commonwealth if it so chose. After the war, a Constitution-making body would be created comprising representatives of British India and the princely states, with the proviso that any province or princely state that did not 'wish to acquiesce in the new Constitution' had the right to opt out and create its own. Meanwhile, Britain would retain control of the defence of India, to which end it would invite the support of the people and their leaders.

The draft declaration offered little until the end of the war. But it went beyond the August Offer in giving India the freedom to secure full independence by seceding from the Commonwealth. One sticking point for the Congress was that it effectively gave the Muslim-majority provinces and the princely states the right to secede from India. The British government felt, and quite correctly, that making the declaration public would risk its outright rejection. But this wasn't really necessary as by then, Cripps had put his hand up to visit India to try and break the constitutional impasse. The declaration would become the basis for his negotiation with Indian leaders. Two days after the Japanese poured into Rangoon on 9 March, Churchill announced in Parliament that his Lord Privy Seal, Stafford Cripps, would be heading to India.

The pressure on Churchill to end the status quo also came from without. In February 1942, Chiang Kai-shek, who led the Chinese resistance against Japan with Allied support, visited India for a fortnight. In his eyes, Japan's entry into the war and the invasion of Burma had made it essential that India throw its weight unreservedly against the Axis powers. He carried messages for both sides. He told the British that it was time they transferred real political power to Indian hands. At the same time, he warned Indians that Japan would bring nothing but savagery and servitude, and that there was no room for neutrality and non-cooperation in a war where the very future of the world was at stake.

On his return to China, Chiang Kai-shek conveyed his sense of shock to Churchill about the political and military situation in India. 'If the Japanese should know of the real situation and attack India, they would be virtually unopposed.' He also told US President Franklin Roosevelt that if Britain didn't change its policy, 'it would be like presenting India to the enemy and inviting them to quickly occupy [it]'.[7]

Roosevelt himself was increasingly concerned about India after Pearl Harbour and the fall of Singapore. His concern was partly strategic, but he was also, in keeping with the prevailing view in the United States, strongly opposed to imperialism on moral grounds.[8] Churchill resented what he saw as US interference in domestic political issues. He noted sardonically:

> Before Pearl Harbour, India had been regarded as a lamentable example of British Imperialism, but as an exclusive British responsibility. Now that the Japanese were advancing towards its frontiers the United States Government began to express views and offer counsel on Indian affairs . . . States which have no overseas colonies or possessions are capable of rising to moods of great elevation and detachment about the affairs of those who have.[9]

The two leaders had wrangled about India during Churchill's visit to Washington DC in December 1941, after Roosevelt suggested, in a private conversation, that the abolition of colonialism in India be treated as a war aim. Churchill recorded that he 'reacted so strongly at such length that the President never raised it verbally again'.[10] Even so, the pressure on Churchill continued. At the end of February 1942, Roosevelt's special representative Averell Harriman met Churchill in London to explore the possibility of a settlement. On 11 March, Roosevelt wrote a private letter to Churchill suggesting that a temporary government be set up in India 'covering different castes, occupations, religions and geographies' until a permanent one could be put in place after the war.[11] By then, however, Churchill had already decided to send Cripps to India.

* * *

The failure of the Cripps Mission and the negotiations that took place in India have been the subject of much academic study. Was it hardwired to fail given the limited bargaining power the War Cabinet had conferred on the Lord Privy Seal? Were the proposals hopelessly insubstantial? Did Churchill merely use Cripps to temporarily appease Roosevelt and fend off the pressures from within his Cabinet? Was Britain's unwillingness to hand over the defence portfolio to an Indian the main sticking point? An analysis of such questions is beyond the purview of this book. More germane for its purposes is a limited examination of the impact the Japanese threat had on the Mission and beyond.

The swift and dramatic victories in South-East Asia triggered a train of thought in India. There were people who believed that Japan was truly working towards a Greater East Asia Co-Prosperity Sphere, interested less in expanding its territorial footprint and more in restoring a colonized continent to its people. In this calculus, the entry of Japan was a threat to British rule and an assist for the freedom struggle. 'There was therefore in the country a section of opinion which grew more and more sympathetic to Japan,' noted Maulana Azad.[12]

Gandhi thought as much too. As Japan is 'knocking at our gates', there are four 'parties' in India, he noted. Three of them comprised the British (and their army), the 'neutrals' (who wouldn't help either Britain or Japan) and the non-violent resisters who were prepared to die (which admittedly were but a few). The last 'party', which made up a sizeable constituency, believed Japan entertained no territorial designs and was aggrieved only with the British. 'It is difficult to guess how many, but there must be a fairly large number who believe in the declaration of the Japanese and think that they will deliver the country from the British yoke and retire.' But even if the Japanese failed to leave India alone, Indians of this persuasion were so fatigued by the British yoke that they would 'even welcome the Japanese yoke for a change'.[13]

Britain watched the developments closely, perplexed that a Japanese invasion could excite more sympathy than animosity. 'A tone of defeatism and indifference mixed with some jubilation with regard to the Japanese menace dominated many of the speeches,' read a fortnightly report from Bombay, while referring to a political meeting. It added that the Deputy Inspector General of Police (Intelligence) saw this as a pointer of what lay in store if the Japanese attacked. In that event, the police official thought 'there will be a nucleus of political agitators whose hatred of the British is such that they will welcome the Japanese on any terms and actively assist them as fifth columnists'.[14]

At the Legislative Assembly, Sir Reginald Maxwell, Home Member and a representative of Linlithgow's Executive Council, controversially implied that Indian politics was an assembly line for the production of fifth columnists. Opposing a resolution for the release of political prisoners (mainly communists and revolutionary socialists, who were not freed along with satyagrahis), he said:

> Political movements in this country tend to advocate disaffection almost as if it was an end in itself. Many political parties regard it as their duty to act as factories for the manufacture of defeatists and Fifth Columnists. It is a small step from that kind of attitude to active collaboration with the enemy and that is what the enemy depends on.[15]

This evoked a stinging response from many, including Akhil Chandra Datta, the Deputy President of the House and the resolution's mover. It was Maxwell who was helping Germany and Japan, he suggested. After all, in whose interest but the enemy's was it to learn that 'India is seething with disaffection and honeycombed by Fifth Columnists'? Anyone who says something like this must surely be 'the arch Fifth Columnist of Fifth Columnists'.[16]

Propaganda against colonial rule in India gained in intensity, rattling the British and adding to their anxieties about fifth columnists. Some of this emanated from Germany, where Bose was sheltered. By November 1941, the Special India Bureau, a creation of the German foreign office, set up the Free India Centre. It recruited a couple of dozen Indians, including journalists, doctors and academics, from across German-occupied Europe.[17] Free India currency notes and stamps were designed and printed and 'Jana Gana Mana' was adopted as the national anthem. By January 1942, Free India Radio was up on the air, making daily broadcasts to India in six languages, interspersing its news bulletins with Indian classical music and proving 'a more reliable and entertaining alternative' to British-controlled radio stations.[18]

An elated Bose watched the advance of the Japanese in South-East Asia. Some days after Singapore fell, he made his first broadcast to the world. 'This is Subhash Chandra Bose speaking to you over Azad Hind Radio,' he began. 'For about a year I have waited in silence and patience for the march of events and now that the hour has struck, I come forward to speak.' Equating the fall of Singapore with the collapse of the British Empire, he said the 'hour of India's salvation is at hand' and that no 'manoeuvre, intrigue or conspiracy on the part of the agents of Anglo-American Imperialism' can prevent the chains of servitude from being broken.[19] By this time, Bose had already begun to think of moving back to Asia and using Burma as the base to launch a military campaign to free India. He was more confident than before that Japan's aims and his own were aligned after Prime Minister Hideki Tojo said that Singapore's surrender was a great opportunity for Indians to free themselves and that Tokyo would assist in this goal.

Parallelly, the Japanese amped up their propaganda. Their swift victories and promises of liberation resonated in India, convincing a number of people that the Allies would be bested. Azad claimed that Gandhi was one among them, 'inclined more and more to the view that the Allies could not win the war'. Although Gandhi did not make public statements about the war's probable outcome,

Azad recalled that, in personal discussions, Gandhi feared that 'it might end in the triumph of Germany and Japan or at best there might be a stalemate'.[20] Others such as Archibald Wavell, then Commander-in-Chief of India, and Maurice Garnier Hallett, Governor of the United Provinces, were also convinced that Gandhi believed that Japan would be victorious.[21]

Azad was struck by another change in Gandhi's 'outlook': his attitude to Bose. Gandhi, whose disapproval of Bose's views was no secret, had begun to admire him for his 'courage and resourcefulness', demonstrated in his escape from India. Gandhi's praise of Bose after hearing the false news of his death in an air crash didn't go unnoticed. In a telegram to Bose's mother, Gandhi wrote, 'The whole nation mourns with you the death of your and her brave son.'* Louis Fischer, Gandhi's biographer, expressed shock that the Mahatma had regretted the passing of a man who went to 'Fascist Germany and identified himself with it'. Gandhi replied that misguided though Bose was, he was still a 'patriot of patriots'. He then hinted at what he probably regarded as Fischer's double standards: 'But suppose he [Bose] had gone to Russia and America to ask aid for India. Would that have made it better?'[22] Cripps would also complain that he never expected a man like Gandhi to speak glowingly about Bose.[23]

Did Gandhi's view of the war situation have a significant bearing on nationalist politics in 1942? And if so, how? Congress President Azad wrote that Gandhi's 'admiration for Subhash Bose unconsciously coloured his view about the war situation'. More significantly, that it 'clouded the discussions' during the Cripps Mission to India. The Cripps Mission has been parsed minutely—day by day, meeting by meeting, through twist and turn, by proposal and counter-proposal. It is, at the very least, worth asking

* CWMG, Vol. 75, p. 443. This could explain the scepticism about reports of his death in an air crash in Taipei three years later.

if the focus on examining the substantive contents of the proposal, its drawbacks and limitations, has diverted some attention from the timing of the Mission and the prevailing perceptions at home about the war situation. There are historians who believe that Churchill set up Cripps to fail or at least deliberately refrained from backing him while he was in India. However, there has been less attention on corresponding Indian attitudes, shaped as they were by the looming threat of invasion and assessments about the war situation.

By and large, the threat of a Japanese invasion has been pushed to the margins in recounting the two momentous political events of 1942—the Cripps Mission and the Quit India Movement. The fact that the invasion never occurred and that there was no clarity about Japan's actual political and military designs don't imply that they played no role in shaping historical outcomes. As Indivar Kamtekar suggests, the prospect of a Japanese invasion doesn't get its due in nationalist and imperialist histories, focused as they are on independence and the end of Empire. The Japanese threat is not easily slotted into either of the two grand narratives of British decolonization and the Indian freedom struggle.[24]

The Cripps Mission may have been crystallized by the fall of Rangoon, but the Japanese had advanced much further by the time he landed in Delhi on 23 March. Earlier that month, the Dutch had surrendered the East Indies. And while he was in India, the Japanese took over the Andaman Islands, bombed Vizagapatam and Cocanada, downed planes and ships in Colombo and Trincomalee, and submitted American and Filipino troops to a bloody and humiliating surrender in Bataan in the Philippines. The talks were held against the backdrop of an irrepressible Japan that seemed as if it was readying to invade India.

Interestingly, Gandhi had no desire to meet Cripps, telling Fischer as much. When Cripps suggested they meet, Gandhi said the Congress had chosen Nehru and Azad for the job. 'You know all my anti-war views. If despite that you still want to see me, I shall be glad to see you,' he responded somewhat reluctantly. Gandhi was clear anything Cripps offered would be in exchange for rallying the Congress in support of the war effort, something he was firmly opposed to. He also appeared to believe that Japan was likely to win the war. In Wavell's view, both considerations played a role in his rejection of the Cripps offer.[25]

Did Gandhi play a role in the eventual repudiation of the Cripps offer by the CWC? There are sharp differences in Indian and British accounts in addressing this question. Nehru dismissed the idea that the rejection was due to Gandhi's uncompromising attitude. 'There was no question of non-violence involved and no mention of this was made at any stage,' he wrote. He did admit though that the war was uppermost in Indian minds given that an invasion seemed imminent. Yet, it was 'not the war that came in the way of agreement . . .'

> The real question was the transfer of power to the National Government. It was the old issue of Indian nationalism versus British imperialism, and on that issue, war or no war, the British governing class in England and in India was determined to hold on to what it had. Behind them stood the imposing figure of Mr. Winston Churchill.[26]

Nehru's biographer Sarvepalli Gopal also flatly rejected that the Cripps Mission was 'beaten' by Gandhi to prevent the readying of India for war. Hadn't the Congress, after all, despite Gandhi, offered its cooperation in the defence of India? Like most other Indian historians, he attributes the Mission's failure to the problematic nature of the post-war arrangements and the British government's unwillingness to transfer meaningful control over defence to Indian hands, which turned out to be a major sticking point before the discussions broke down. In other words, Nehru's hands were not bound by Gandhi or the Working Committee, but by the limitations of the Cripps proposals.[27]

Limited they certainly were, comprising no more than a promise in the future and a minor concession in the present. After the war, the British promised that India could frame its own Constitution, enjoy the same status as other Dominions and have the right to secede from the Commonwealth. As for now, the Viceroy's Executive Council would be restructured, giving India power over most departments, but (critically) no control of defence.

Gandhi's acute aversion to the Mission may not have been sufficient to seal its fate. But unlike other Congress leaders such as Nehru, Azad and Rajagopalachari, his opposition to the proposals manifested early, emerging 'from the very first day'.[28] Nehru, in contrast, had an open-minded stance, even if he was 'profoundly depressed' on learning about how inadequate the package Cripps brought with him was.

At the same time, Nehru's opposition to Nazism and fascism ran deep. He was proud that his views were reflected in the positions staked out by the Congress about the goings-on in Europe and Asia—whether it was Japan's aggression in China, Italy's savagery in Abyssinia or the cowardly sacrifice of Czechoslovakia. Given that Nehru's natural sympathies lay with the Allies, Azad noted that he 'was therefore inclined to consider the proposals favourably'.[29] This was somewhat mildly phrased in comparison with another assessment, which suggested Nehru had 'desperately sought a settlement' to mobilize Indian support for an anti-fascist war in the face of Gandhi's alleged apathy and cynicism.[30]

But if anything, it was Rajagopalachari who was even more positively inclined to reach a settlement. Since the turn of the year, he had been holding a series of meetings, urging resistance against a Japanese invasion. At the same time, he thought the terrifying nature of the times would bring the Raj around to confer a good measure of self-rule, if not freedom. The announcement of the Cripps Mission seemed like an endorsement of his belief, leading Rajagopalachari to express pleasure when it was announced.

The British government had at last realized the gravity of the situation, he said. In contrast, Nehru reserved his comments, not allowing his friendship with Cripps (whose large country home in Gloucestershire he had stayed in) to prompt a reaction.[31]

Rajagopalachari was in favour of the Cripps proposals even before he was fully acquainted with the details. During his meeting with Cripps, he advanced suggestions that would make the British offer more acceptable to the Congress (for instance, replacing the word 'Dominion' with 'Free Member State' and handing over the defence portfolio to an Indian minister). Declaring his acceptance, he said if Cripps brought Nehru on board, they would see it through the CWC.[32]

The Raj administration noted the differences among the Congress leadership to the Cripps Mission. But a section of it laid the blame for the failure squarely at Gandhi's door. Wavell was not the only one who suggested that the Mission was scuppered by Gandhi's beliefs in non-violence and a likely Japanese victory. After a meeting with Nehru at the end of March, Cripps noted that he got a sense (even if Nehru did not 'say so precisely') that it was the influence of Gandhi that created the difficulty in accepting the proposals. He was left with the impression that the 'decisive factor' in the way of Congress acceptance wouldn't be the package itself, but Gandhi's opposition to the war effort.[33] Later, Amery would claim that it was a two-hour telephone conversation between Gandhi and the Working Committee that turned possible approval into rejection, information that came his way from police intelligence via probable phone tapping.[34]

* * *

The failure of the Mission generated a feeling of despondency in India, fuelled by resentment about the continuance of the status quo and insecurities about a murky, uncertain future. Feelings against the British ran high. The *Statesman* went as far as complaining that India had become 'a country of bitterness', adding that in this climate, 'A public word of friendliness to Britain is as rare as a mango in December.'[35]

The growing worry about the possibility of a full-scale Japanese attack put other things into motion. It stirred Rajagopalachari to come up with a new and audacious plan. Essentially, it was an attempt to knit together the three principal antagonists—the Raj, the Congress and the Muslim League—in the face of the invasion threat. It also involved his return to the Madras Presidency as Premier, a post he had reluctantly relinquished in 1939. Madras was a special source of concern since, according to prevailing wisdom, the Japanese would make landfall somewhere along the Presidency's coastline. Weeks after Cripps' departure, Rajagopalachari prevailed on the Madras Congress Legislature Party to pass what became known as the Madras Resolution. There were two resolutions, in fact. The first conceded the separation of certain areas for Pakistan in exchange for the Muslim League's support for a national government. The second sought permission to form a government in Madras with the Muslim League as a coalition partner. Not surprisingly, the Madras Resolution was panned by the Congress leadership. Rajagopalachari, who acknowledged that it should have first been discussed with his senior party colleagues, resigned from the Working Committee.

While Rajagopalachari's views on reaching out to the League were no secret to his colleagues, what came as a big surprise was a much more significant change: Gandhi's attitude. Ever since September 1939, Gandhi was averse to 'embarrassing' the government at a time when Britain was caught up in waging a war. This limited the Congress to conducting symbolic individual protests rather than engaging in mass action. But post-Cripps, a visible change came over Gandhi. His demand that Britain withdraw from India in an orderly fashion now had a firm resolve about it. Slowly but surely, he was gearing up for mass struggle, leading him to unequivocally ask Britain to up and go.

Some of his colleagues, including Nehru, were initially worried, even disturbed by his approach, fearing that any effective action would interfere with the war effort at a time when India risked invasion.

In Nehru's words, Gandhi gave 'a new direction' and invested a 'new urgency and passion in his speech and writing'. Significantly, this time 'there was the hint of action'.[36] Azad put it far more directly. He noted that Gandhi had shifted far away from the position that he had adopted during the outbreak of war. His mind was 'moving from one extreme of complete inactivity to the other of organized mass effort'.[37]

That Gandhi was in a 'strange and uniquely militant mood' in the summer of 1942 was obvious.[38] The change was dramatic enough to demand a rewrite of the traditional labels within the Congress. Gandhi and his die-hard Congress followers now made up the hardline of the party; radicals such as Nehru occupied the space of the moderates. But what exactly brought about this change is something that has rarely, if ever, been fully explained. Perhaps, there is not enough evidence to completely understand Gandhi's sudden transformation. The question is whether one can totally reject the notion that his belief in a probable Japanese victory played a role in the change.

At the same time, it is likely that there was a personal dimension to his pressing for freedom with a new urgency. Could it have had to do with his advanced years? Nehru threw a hint in this direction:

> Gandhiji was getting on in years, he was in the seventies, and a long life of ceaseless activity, of hard toil, both physical and mental, had enfeebled his body; but he was still vigorous enough, and he felt that all his life work would be in vain if he submitted to circumstances then and took no action to vindicate what he prized most.[39]

In his magisterial biography of Gandhi, Ramachandra Guha also suggests that Gandhi's post-Cripps demand, that Britain leave India to Indians, owed to the recognition that his time was running out. And that the deaths of three people he was close to—C.F. Andrews, Rabindranath Tagore and industrialist Jamnalal Bajaj—reminded Gandhi of his own mortality.

> For some time, Gandhi had been planning another mass struggle against colonialism. He had kept that on hold so long as there was any hope of compromise with the British. Now that hope had disappeared, with the failure of the Cripps Mission. Hence his demand that the British leave India to the Indians.[40]

Gandhi's threat of launching mass action to hasten a British departure while opposing the armed defence of India didn't go down well initially with Nehru, Rajagopalachari and some other Congress leaders. Such a policy seemed to forgo any sympathy for the larger Allied cause; worse, it could be read as an open invitation to the Japanese. At the end of April, Gandhi prepared a draft resolution for the AICC (which was to meet in Allahabad) that clearly spelt out his approach. The draft called for the immediate withdrawal of the British, stating they were incapable of defending India. It declared that Japan's quarrel was not with India (but with Britain). Assuring Tokyo that India bore no enmity towards Japan, it controversially stated that a free India's first step would probably be to negotiate with it. While it hoped that Japan would not attack a free India, the draft said that any aggression would be met by non-violent resistance.[41]

The draft was debated at length by a deeply divided CWC. The 'whole thought and background to the draft is one of favouring Japan', Nehru is said to have complained. 'It is Gandhiji's feeling that Japan and Germany will win. This feeling unconsciously governs his decision.'[42] A slightly modified draft was prepared, but eventually, it was Nehru who prevailed, coming up with an alternative that was more even-handed and stripped of any tilt towards the Japanese. While it called on Britain to abandon its hold on India (though not immediately), it rejected the notion that

India could achieve freedom through 'interference or invasion by any foreign nation'. However, there was no getting around Gandhi's insistence that any resistance to invasion would only take the form of non-violent non-cooperation. This was probably no surprise. Post-Cripps, Gandhi's hand was considerably strengthened within the Congress. His differences with Nehru, who continued urging that the Axis powers and Bose be strongly resisted, were no secret. Only earlier that month, Gandhi had pressured Nehru into taking back his recommendation that Indians resort to guerrilla warfare if the Japanese invade.

Inevitably, Gandhi was forced to defend himself from the charge that he held a pro-Japanese stance (something that even Nehru's biographer Gopal believed he adopted before abandoning it).[43] Gandhi argued it was the British presence that was the inducement for a Japanese attack. As a result, a quick withdrawal was in the interests of both Britain and India. 'If the British wisely decided to withdraw and leave India to manage her own affairs in the best way she could, the Japanese would be bound to reconsider their plans . . . Japan's quarrel is not with India. It is with the British Empire,' he argued.[44] The idea that Japan would leave an Independent India alone was arguably fanciful or, at the very least, by no means certain. (A British MP described it as 'one of the most pathetic things said in the world . . .')[45] But right or wrong, naive or otherwise, Gandhi did believe that non-violence was an effective way of defusing violence, of disarming the aggressor. Wouldn't Mussolini have simply retired if the Abyssinians met him with non-violent resistance, he had asked four years earlier.

As someone who opposed returning violence with violence (to answer brutality with brutality can only beget a vicious circle, he believed), Gandhi drew a certain moral equivalence between aggression and counter-aggression.* The fact of violence mattered

* Rajmohan Gandhi pans Azad for 'suggesting' or implying that Gandhi was morally neutral between the Allies and the Axis powers (*India Wins*

so much to him that the reasons for its commission risked being ignored. As an abstract philosophical position, this was one thing. But at a time when India seemed at risk of attack, it was perhaps inevitable that viewing the Allies and the Axis powers through the same moral prism would add fuel to the charge he was pro-Japanese. But Gandhi was firm. '. . . I won't be moved from my position by being told that the Jap or the Nazi is not the same man as the Englishman. I draw no such fundamental distinction between man and man.'[46] Articulating his difference with Rajagopalachari, who thought that Britain was better than Japan, he said: 'For me, an exploiter of other nations is an exploiter, whether he be imperialist or totalitarian. Names do not matter. Besides, who says the British are better?'[47] This kind of non-violent absolutism blurred ideological differences and deflected attention from the significance of happenings abroad. America is a partner in Britain's guilt, Gandhi told a group of visiting American journalists. 'The Allies have no right to call their cause to be morally superior to the Nazi cause so long as they hold in custody the fairest part and one of the most ancient nations of the earth.'[48] Nehru would lament that this approach was 'based on a narrow view of nationalism'.[49]

But Gandhi would alter his position in a crucial way, bridging the gap between himself and Nehru. The change would assuage Congress' fears that a British withdrawal, coupled with a policy of unarmed resistance, would leave India at the mercy of Japan and the Axis powers. Clear signs of Gandhi's course correction were visible by early June, when he told journalist and biographer Louis Fischer that 'Britain and America, and other countries too, can keep their armies here and use Indian territory as a base for military operations'. He added significantly and by way of explanation:

Errors: A Scrutiny of Maulana Azad's India Wins Freedom, p. 26). But this is not the same as stating that Gandhi saw a certain equivalence between aggression and aggressive response, which is reflected in a number of passages in his writings.

'I do not wish Japan to win the war. I do not want the Axis to win.' To further questions, Gandhi said the Allied forces could use the railways and ports, and the terms of such cooperation could be laid out in a written agreement. But why hadn't he communicated this with the Viceroy, persisted an astonished Fischer. Shouldn't Linlithgow be told that 'you [Gandhi] had no objection to India's use as a base for Allied military operations'? To this, Gandhi flatly replied: 'No one has asked me.'[50]

Later that month, Gandhi wrote to Chiang Kai-shek, assuring him that asking the British to go was never meant to weaken India's defence or embarrass China in its struggle against Japanese forces. Allied forces could use India for operations against a Japanese attack, he promised the Chinese leader who had left India only a few months earlier, extremely disappointed with Gandhi's unwillingness to support the war effort. A relieved Soong Mei-ling, Chiang Kai-shek's wife and an active member of the Chinese resistance, wrote to Nehru saying she knew how hard he must have worked on Gandhi to change his attitude towards a possible Japanese invasion. She described Gandhi's nod for India resisting Japan as 'a great step forward'.[51]

Gandhi himself was aware that his U-turn on the presence of troops (which he had strongly opposed only a month earlier) was likely to bewilder people. Having 'drawn up an entrancing picture of a free India without a single British soldier', he admitted that people were 'confounded' by his acceptance of their presence. His defence of the change lay in pointing out that foreign troops would remain, under treaty with a free India, and be used only for the purpose of repelling Japanese attacks and helping China. However, what this explanation did was to effectively turn the position he had maintained earlier (in the face of some opposition, even incredulity) on its head. He had argued all along that Japan's quarrel was with Britain and that the former was less likely to attack India if the latter withdrew. Now, he was suggesting that the absence of troops could be an incentive for Japanese aggression.

It wasn't easy for Gandhi to commit to allowing foreign troops, 'but he swallowed the bitter pill', wrote Nehru.[52] In his estimation, Gandhi changed course because his love for India's freedom eventually 'overcame even his strong adherence to non-violence'. Nehru also suggested that 'mutual discussion' led Gandhi to undergo a more general change, one that took note of 'international considerations and looked at India's problem in a wider perspective'.

Gandhi's new resolve to end the status quo and free India irrespective of whatever course the war took continued to influence his outlook. As expected, he had his way with the Congress. The AICC ratified the resolution calling for the British to Quit India, with Gandhi urging a short new mantra be imprinted in Indian hearts and expressed in every breath: 'Do or Die'.

The abandonment of Gandhi's so-called pro-Japanese stance and his gradual shift in favour of the Allies were paralleled by decisive events in the war. The immediate threat of invasion from the sea receded in mid-April, after it became apparent that Nagumo's Indian Ocean strike force had sailed eastwards for deployment in the Pacific. In May, a series of naval engagements in the Battle of the Coral Sea led to the sinking of some ships and the destruction of dozens of US and Japanese aircraft. While the US suffered greater damage, it was a strategic victory for the Allies, which turned back a Japanese invasion force for the first time in the war. In early June, the US scored a decisive victory in the Battle of Midway, devastating Japan's carrier force and marking what is regarded as a turning point in the war.

There is no evidence that the Congress took serious note of these developments; even less, that they influenced its approach. But by the middle of 1942, there was a practical case for weighing in with the Allies and being open to having their troops defend India, even as it asked Britain to up and go.

This is exactly what Gandhi's Congress did.

8

The Premonition of Danger

In April 1937, Nazi bombers devastated a Basque town, killing a third or more of its population, according to some estimates. A couple of months later, Pablo Picasso completed what is easily his most dramatic and moving painting. *Guernica*, with its mix of tormented humans and animals, was a powerful visual statement against totalitarianism and brutality. But it was also a reminder of how vulnerable civilians had become with the ascendancy of air power, thanks to the radical technological upgrades to bombers and fighters.

In the same year, thousands of miles away, China was also subject to indiscriminate aerial bombardment. Such events reinforced the truth that modern warfare had begun to pose as much of a risk to civilians as armed forces. Spain and China were very much on the minds of British lawmakers when the Air Raid Precautions Bill was discussed in the House of Commons towards the end of 1937. The Secretary of State for Home, Sir Samuel Hoare, who was earlier Secretary of State for India, pointed out that during World War I, 300 tonnes of bombs were dropped on Britain. Now, he estimated, a greater tonnage could be dropped in twenty-four hours. What's more, this scale of attack could continue for days.[1] Civil defence measures to mitigate the impact of air assaults existed earlier. But the new legislation, which came

Courtesy of the *Hindustan Times*

Sir Arthur Hope
As Governor of the Madras Presidency, Hope ordered almost all government departments to move to the interior, fearing a Japanese attack.

Courtesy of the *Hindustan Times*

Lord Linlithgow

Linlithgow wanted 'useless mouths' to be encouraged to leave threatened areas; at the same time, he didn't want the exodus to sweep away labour engaged in war production.

War Production

The British rulers were worried about the possible impact of the exodus from large Indian cities on the production of military equipment.

Courtesy of the *Hindustan Times*

Fujiwara Iwaichi Greets Mohan Singh
It was the friendship between these two men that saw the founding of the Indian National Army.

Bose in Germany
From Germany, Subhash Chandra Bose watched the advance of the Japanese Army in South-east Asia with excitement.

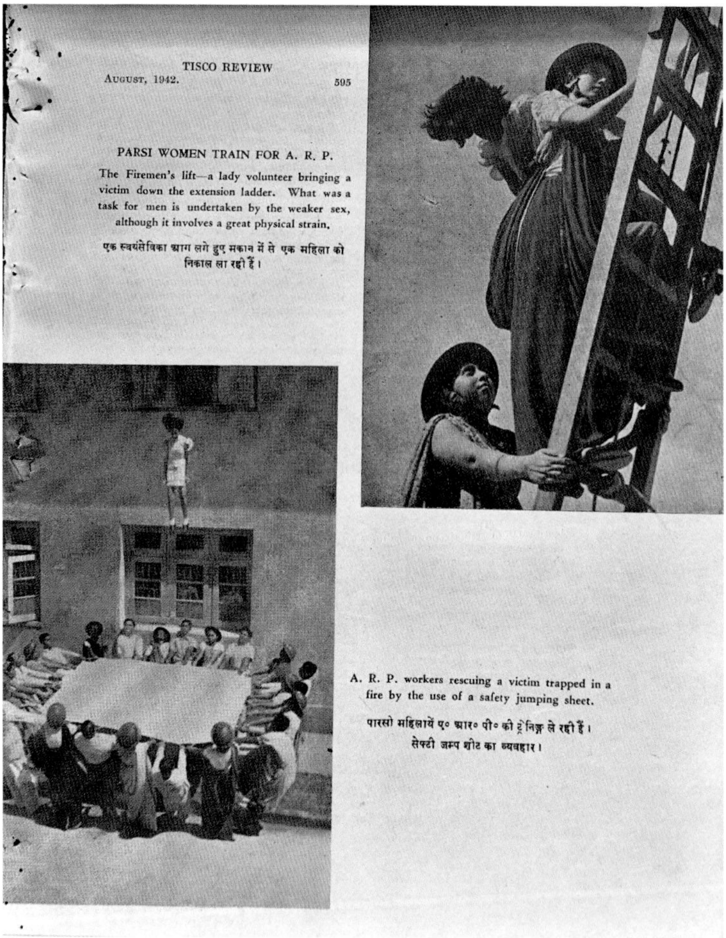

TISCO REVIEW

AUGUST, 1942. 595

PARSI WOMEN TRAIN FOR A. R. P.

The Firemen's lift—a lady volunteer bringing a victim down the extension ladder. What was a task for men is undertaken by the weaker sex, although it involves a great physical strain.

एक स्वयंसेविका आग लगे हुए मकान में से एक महिला को निकाल ला रही हैं।

A. R. P. workers rescuing a victim trapped in a fire by the use of a safety jumping sheet.

पारसी महिलायें ए० आर० पी० की ट्रेनिङ्ग ले रही हैं।
सेफ्टी जम्प शीट का व्यवहार।

Courtesy of Tata Archives, Jamshedpur

Air Raid Precautions (ARP)

A page from *TISCO REVIEW,* an in-house publication of the Tata Iron and Steel Co., depicting ARP drills.

Bombay War Week

Military displays were a part of Bombay War Week in March 1941, a fundraiser for the war effort, which included sports, parades, music and other forms of entertainment.

Screen grabs from the video 'Bombay's War Weapons Week' by British Movietone, YouTube

The Cripps Mission

Courtesy of the *Hindustan Times*

Nehru and Azad were deputed by the Congress to meet with Stafford Cripps and discuss his devolution proposals.

Courtesy of the *Hindustan Times*

Aware that Cripps was seeking Congress support for the war effort, the Mahatma met Cripps, but reluctantly.

Foreign Troops

American GIs shopping for merchandise in Calcutta. By 1943, there were 1,20,000 American soldiers in India.

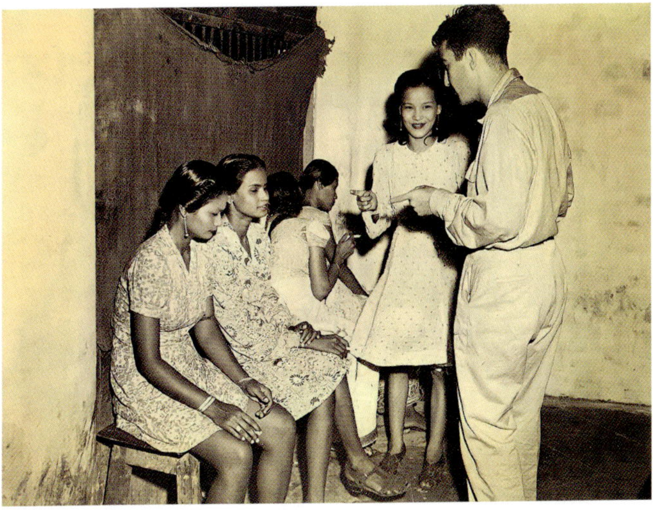

An American GI with sex workers in Calcutta. There was a surge in prostitution as foreign troops arrived in India.

Leonard Birchall

The Canadian pilot spotted Nagumo's fleet steaming towards Ceylon. Churchill would call him the 'Saviour of Ceylon' and applaud him for making 'one of the most important single contributions to victory'.

The *Akagi*

Aircraft prepare to launch from Japan's aircraft carrier, which took part in the Indian Ocean raid.

Chuichi Nagumo
The hero of Pearl Harbour, Vice Admiral Nagumo led the strike force that attacked Ceylon and bombed Colombo and Trincomalee.

Jisaburo Ozawa
Tasked with disrupting shipping in the Bay of Bengal, Vice Admiral Ozawa led the Malay Force, which sank twenty merchant ships in early April 1942.

HMS *Hermes*

The ageing aircraft carrier was sunk by the Japanese off Ceylon's eastern coast. Here, aflame moments before it went down.

HMS *Warspite*

The flagship of Vice Admiral James Somerville which, along with most other ships in his Eastern Fleet, had left for Addu Atoll in the Maldives when Japan attacked Ceylon.

Vizagapatam Bombed
Japanese planes struck Vizagapatam harbour on 6 April 1942. A picture taken from one of the aircraft.

The *Ryujo*
The Japanese light carrier was responsible for much of the damage to merchant ships in the Bay of Bengal.

A Remnant of the Bombing
An unexploded shell on display at the Vishaka Museum in Vizagapatam, which was bombed on 6 April 1942.

Courtesy of the *Hindustan Times*

Archibald Wavell
As Commander-in-Chief, he acknowledged it was difficult to defend India's vast coastline from a Japanese invasion.

The Zero
The Japanese used the speedy Mitsubishi-made fighter aircraft to menacing effect.

Madras Must Not Burn

Front-page advertisement in the *Mail* (5 April 1942) of a film that combined thrilling visuals of air raids on Madras with ARP messaging.

The Indian Ocean Raid

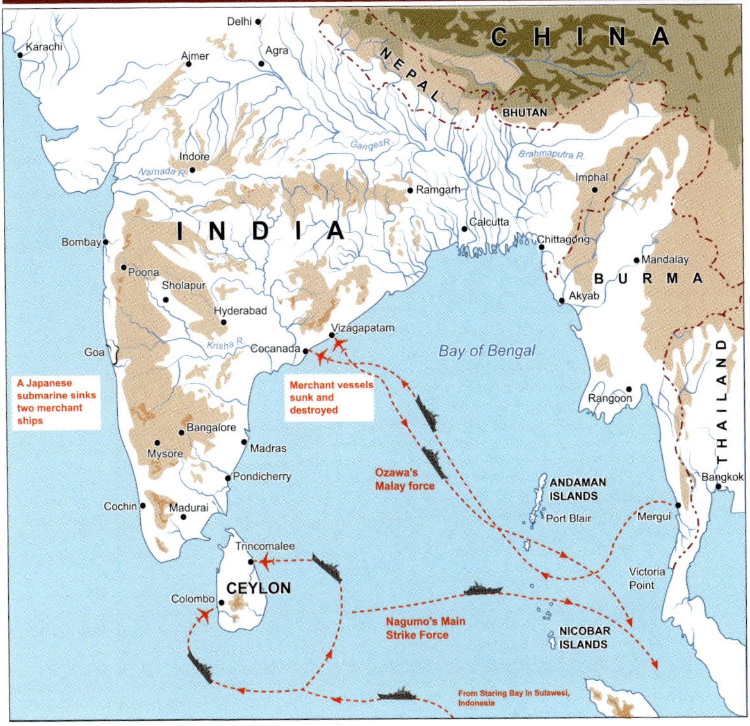

K.G. Rangarajan

In early April 1942, Vice Admiral Chuichi Nagumo, the hero of the Pearl Harbour attack, arrived in the Indian Ocean with a large fleet that had a nucleus of five aircraft carriers. Colombo and Trincomalee were bombed and Britain's ageing aircraft carrier, the HMS *Hermes*, was sunk off the island's eastern coast. In parallel, the Malay Force, led by Jisaburo Ozawa, bombed Vizagapatam and Cocanada and attacked numerous merchant ships off the coast of the Madras Presidency and Orissa.

(This map is based on the one titled 'Pacific War - Southern Asia 1942' in westpoint.edu/sites/default/files/inline-images/academics/academic_departments/history/WWII%20Asia/ww2%2520asia%2520map%252011.jpg)

The Bay of Bengal Raids

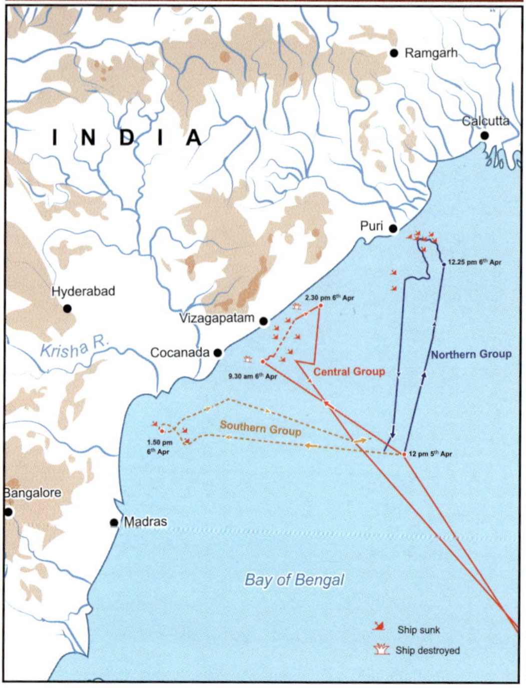

K.G. Rangarajan

On 1 April 1942, Vice Admiral Jisaburo Ozawa's Malay Force—which comprised a light aircraft carrier (*Ryujo*), six cruisers and four destroyers—set sail from Mergui in Burma. Tasked with disrupting shipping in the Bay of Bengal, Ozawa's fleet divided themselves into three groups—the northern, central and southern—as it approached the Indian coastline. The map depicts the positions of most of the twenty-three merchant ships that were either sunk or damaged on 5 and 6 April.

(This map is based on the one titled 'Pacific War - Southern Asia 1942' in westpoint.edu/sites/default/files/inline-images/academics/academic_departments/history/WWII%20Asia/ww2%2520asia%2520map%252011.jpg)

Images that have not been credited have been sourced from Wikimedia Commons.

into effect in 1938, specifically tasked local governments with a number of duties, including building shelters, rescuing affected people and making the necessary arrangements for casualties. At the same time, the idea was to broaden the involvement of civilians and civilian organizations—in Hoare's words, that 'of the householder, of the father of a family, of the local council, and of the local Red Cross and other local organizations'.

Air Raid Precaution (ARP) measures were introduced and zealously expanded in India following the outbreak of hostilities. Given that the war in Europe seemed very remote, there were diverse reactions among the public, from baffled amusement (at the seemingly pointless activity) to irritation (at blackouts and other restrictions) and resistance (to involving Indian people in the interests of Britain).

In Bombay, the ARP set-up comprised one officer and one assistant in July 1939. By June 1941, the city boasted 3000 air raid wardens, 200 first-aid posts, 2000 doctors and an auxiliary firefighting corps. Operation Barbarossa, Germany's invasion of the Soviet Union in June that year, seems to have lent ARP activities a further fillip (or made it 'a live issue' in the words of a British bureaucrat).[2] Complementing ARP services was the Civic Guard organization, made up of civilians trained by the police to deal with emergencies. In June 1941, it was 4400 strong in the Bombay Presidency. A telephonic device was installed in Bombay to inform 500 key people simultaneously of an expected air raid and the position of the raiders.[3] Initially, the Central government bore the entire cost of ARP measures. But this increased so sharply that a sharing agreement with the provinces was put into effect. From 1 July 1941, the Centre met only all non-recurring ARP costs; recurring costs approved by the Centre were shared under a formula. Apart from engaging air raid wardens, ARP measures included setting up air warning systems, construction of shelters, provision of first aid and medical care, firefighting services, lighting services, bomb disposal and much more.[4]

By the end of 1941, over 1,15,000 people were employed in ARP services; the largest number (43,642) in the United Provinces.[5] By February that year, 60,000 had already been enlisted in the Civic Guard. ARP measures took root unevenly, more firmly in some places than others. For instance, Madras was something of a relative laggard, the organizers there finding it difficult to 'arouse public interest and attract suitable recruits'.[6] In July 1941, there were less than 2000 recruits, a fraction of the 13,000 that the authorities had hoped to enlist.

Many of the precautionary measures were enforced well before there was a perceived threat. In Madras, for instance, lighting restrictions were already in force by the time Governor Hope arrived to take charge in March 1940. He decided to do away with them a couple of months later as they were unpopular and 'a perfect farce'. The entry of Italy into the war, however, held up the order to dispense with blackouts.[7] Lighting restrictions were implemented in Bombay and other coastal towns in early 1941; the city was also witness to a string of air raid exercises.

The distinction between a real threat and taking precautionary steps in the event of a full-fledged war was often lost on the public. Air raid sirens, for instance, caused confusion and panic, due to the lack of clarity about what constituted a drill and what signalled an attack. Not surprisingly, ARP measures were the subject of ridicule. There were legitimate concerns about the contribution of blackouts to road accidents. Drawing attention to the tendency of Madras motorists to drive at dangerous speeds and pedestrians to walk on the crown of roads, *The Hindu* acidly observed that 'it is easy to see what we are in for' unless there is a drive to eliminate the road hog and the jaywalker. As for the police vans warning errant drivers on loudspeakers, the newspaper felt it would be useful if the voice sounded human instead of 'ghostly and incoherent'.[8]

In theory, India could be militarily threatened in one of two ways at the time—via Afghanistan on the north-western frontier and from the north-east in the event of further Japanese expansion in China. Both prospects seemed remote. But after Japan's invasion of South-East Asia, there was a palpable sense of official disquiet about possible air attacks. There was a feeling of unease in the coastal areas; the interior was also affected by alarm as revealed by a bizarre experiment conducted in New Delhi. Two men came up with what they believed was a cheap method of protecting important buildings from being bombed by producing profuse clouds of smoke that would obscure them. Although Delhi was well outside the range of enemy bombers at the time, they were granted permission to carry out a trial around the iconic colonnaded South Block, where the defence forces were headquartered. One was John Bicknell Auden, the elder brother of the celebrated poet W.H. Auden and an official with the Geological Survey of India. The other was S.S. Bhatnagar, a former chemistry professor who was appointed Director of the recently constituted Board of Scientific and Industrial Research.* The two enlisted the help of Geoffrey Lamarque, an ICS officer posted in Delhi, in setting up a number of braziers around South Block and filling them with the 'black tarry substance concocted by Auden'. The 'whole thing was a monumental flop', recalled Lamarque of 'the embarrassing experiment'. He wondered 'what officers looking out of their windows must have thought of our little party, or what would have happened had the experiment succeeded and the whole place became submerged in dense smoke'.[9]

ARP activities went into overdrive after Japan's invasion of South-East Asia. The lack of ARP legislation didn't obstruct the speedy implementation of new measures; they could be decreed under the Defence of India Rules 'at the drop of a hat to meet

* After Independence, Bhatnagar would go on to play a major role in developing the country's industrial and technological infrastructure.

any contingency'.[10] Some ARP measures were plagued by a lack of clarity. In Calcutta, the Lighting Order demanded that shades or curtains be opaque or very nearly so. 'In no case must they pass light that will penetrate more than six pieces of newspaper,' it read. This led a resident to engage in a 'friendly argument' with an air raid warden about the vagueness of the order. Surely, 'the opacity of six pieces of newspaper depends on the intensity of light behind them', he argued, appealing for a clarification from the authorities.[11] In Madras, a parent complained that female students at a school were asked to return home immediately after an ARP alarm signal was sounded, resulting in one going missing and being traced only after great difficulty. Schools need to be clearly instructed on what to do in contingencies, the parent demanded.[12] In Bombay, an air raid alarm exercise created panic, leading a few thousand to flee the city.[13]

The outbreak of hostilities in South-East Asia precipitated a rush to construct slit trenches in coastal towns. By the first week of February 1942, the Government of Bengal had dug a staggering 114 miles of slit trenches in Calcutta and its suburbs alone. Such trenches had also been constructed in Chittagong as well as in interior towns such as Mymensingh and Asansol.[14] In the previous month, the government had empowered itself to use any open land to make slit trenches and shelters.

In Madras' expansive People's Park, the Corporation planned slit trenches extending 40,000 ft (7.5 miles) that could accommodate 20,000 people in the event of an air attack. In January 1942, the Corporation approved the construction of 84,000 feet (almost 16 miles) of slit trenches that could accommodate 56,000 people. This did not include the slit trenches built by the provincial government on the land it owned and occupied. In the following month, a communiqué declared that land in Madras city belonging to the government and the Corporation was inadequate to build the required number of slit trenches and air raid shelters. An order was issued under the Defence of India Rules permitting any land to be used for this purpose; those obstructing the construction and maintenance of trenches and shelters would be liable to imprisonment for six months or fines or both.[15] Similar orders were passed in Calcutta.

To many Indians, the British enthusiasm for passive defence measures was a stark contrast to their corresponding lack of interest in strengthening India's capacity to repel an invasion or an aerial attack. Already, there was a feeling that Britain was using Indian troops to fight its war in Europe, Africa and South-East Asia while neglecting the subcontinent. With the focus on protecting people from bombing and strafing, ARP measures only sharpened the question: What about India's internal defence?*

Questions about ARP versus the 'real' defence of India emerged. In Madras, fourteen councillors of the city's Corporation moved a resolution asking the government to abolish the Indian Arms Act to enable people to organize themselves with weapons to defend the country. (Under the Act, Indians were not allowed to carry arms without a licence.) During the discussion, ARP measures came in for some ridicule. One of the resolution's main proponents, G. Rajamannar Chetty, a follower of Subhash Chandra Bose, said he had noticed an ARP van with a couple of Europeans inspecting and checking the pressure on every water hydrant. Surely, this was a 'waste of material and physical energy' when the country faced an external threat, he suggested. A waste of petrol as well, chipped in a fellow councillor. Yet another took potshots at trenches, claiming that the one dug in front of the zoo

* The typical British answer was that in the context of a world war, it was a mistake to speak about internal and external defence as if they were two different things. For instance, Cripps argued it was impossible to dissociate the movement of troops from 'the general strategy and tactics of the war'. 'British Proposals for India', the *Statesman*, 30 March 1942, p. 6.

looked like a well. 'At the time of bombing, we are asked to jump into this well. This is what the gentlemen who profess to do ARP work keep harping on night and day. (Laughter). Apart from this, they have not described any other measure of security to date.'[16]

Doubts about the necessity and usefulness of ARP measures played a role in setting off rumours. In Assam, there were dark fears that the real purpose of digging slit trenches was to bury the dead.[17] ARP recruitment itself was suspected of being a devious means of getting people to sign on for military service, prompting a clarification.[18] And ARP activities in Bihar, coupled with an impending visit by Linlithgow, were enough to get tongues wagging that the capital would be shifted from Delhi to Patna.[19]

That frenzied ARP activity occurred in the absence of a comprehensive strategy to defend India was one source of disaffection. Added to this was the feeling that ARP measures were an underhand method to involve India in the war. As early as March 1938, the Haripura session of the Congress disapproved of the 'large scale manoeuvres and air-raid precautions by which it has been sought to spread an atmosphere of approaching war in India'.[20]

The Congress' opposition, led by Gandhi, who believed that participation in ARP was equivalent to taking part in hostilities, continued well into the war. He and other Congress leaders were alive to the charge that such opposition could be construed as an unwillingness to help victims of an air attack. There were efforts to clarify that non-participation did not imply that Congressmen 'will render no help in caring for those who may be injured by bombs or otherwise'.[21] The idea that ARP measures were something of a 'political stunt', as Nehru described them, was reflected in debates about the measures. In Madras, for instance, the need for slit trenches was questioned. There were misgivings about where they were located. There were accusations that they were unsafe, claims that they would become slushy and unusable when it rained, and arguments about who should bear the cost of digging them.

Meanwhile, the Congress as well as other organizations, such as the Muslim League and the Hindu Mahasabha, had begun enrolling their own protection committees. In the Madras Presidency, Oorkappu Sangams (safety associations) were formed in various towns. In Madras city, different localities had their own Sangams, which the safety committee of the Madras Corporation promised to coordinate with. These parallel organizations were regarded by British administrators as more of a hindrance than a help. For instance, in Bombay, the ARP controller made it clear that there was no question of his organization's functions being duplicated by others.[22] From Delhi, Linlithgow watched the formation of independent civil defence organizations with 'a good deal of anxiety'.[23]

As fears about a Japanese invasion intensified, there were reports from some provinces of 'satisfactory cooperation' between ARP officials and the public, which probably regarded them with a seriousness lacking earlier. In March 1942, the Congress said it had no objection to its organizations taking part in official ARP activities, provided that this work was directed by a board that had non-officials. Meanwhile, Rajagopalachari was telling people that there was nothing wrong in assisting ARP organizations in times of emergency. One official communication noted the Congress' 'somewhat altered attitude' and went as far as claiming that Nehru admitted the necessity for having an official ARP organization.[24]

But for all the publicity and emphasis on the importance of ARP measures, it is far from clear how prepared India was to cope with a serious aerial assault. During his visit to India, a time when the war seemed to be closing in, Cripps shot off a telegram to Churchill saying the situation regarding ARP and firefighting was serious, that urgent requests for help from Delhi to the India Office had fetched no results, and that it was time the 'peace-time tempo' was altered. Regular fire brigades and firefighting equipment were available only in some large towns and a mere 13 million people were covered by rudimentary ARP measures. India was still awaiting delivery of such material as trailer pumps and the 1 million feet of hose it had ordered, he wrote.[25]

Meanwhile, a fierce controversy had broken out over the government's plan to implement a 'scorched earth' policy to deny the Japanese access to key infrastructure such as plants making equipment for war production, oil refineries, harbour facilities, bridges and so on. The military had recommended scorching earth, particularly in Bengal, where it felt that an invasion was bound to involve the loss of parts of the province. Commander-in-Chief Archibald Wavell was clear that it was impossible to defend India along its vast coastline. The strategy in the event of invasion would be based on remaining within striking distance of threatened points and using 'mobile reserves which can move to meet and attack the enemy'.[26] In Bengal, the local military was of the view that a landing may result in the 'temporary loss of Calcutta and the surrounding industrial area'.

The large-scale destruction of equipment and infrastructure before the British fled Rangoon led to the fear that they would scorch the earth in India as well. The lack of clarity over whether they would do so fuelled wild rumours and led Indians, including Gandhi, to demand an unequivocal declaration that a scorched earth policy would not apply to India.[27] He was appalled to receive news that boats were destroyed in Bengal where, by the end of 1942, 'more than 20,000 of these country craft had been sunk, burned, requisitioned for military use or taken to "reception" stations where many decayed and fell into disrepair'.[28] In Orissa, on the advice of military authorities, cars, bicycles and boats were immobilized, the last causing great discomfort to people in the deltaic region.[29]

All in all, the preparations for a war-that-never-happened did one thing. They generated wild rumours, which created a sense of panic, which in turn triggered an exodus from the coastline—the escaping people setting off new rumours and new cycles of panic and flight.

As we shall see, the British administration played no small role in this recurring cycle—thanks to mixed and confusing messaging about the genuineness of the Japanese threat and an unfeeling policy that encouraged people to leave threatened areas. The Great Flap of 1942 wasn't only a term coined by the British. They were instrumental in its making.

9

The Tongue of Rumour

In mid-February 1942, Calcutta's Commissioner of Police, C.E.S. Fairweather, was pushed to clarify that he had not been arrested. There was a loud buzz in the city that he, a Scotsman, had been put away by the Chief Minister for being an Irish retarder of the war effort. In a press statement, Fairweather threatened to deal with rumour-mongering fifth columnists in the same way as he did with the 'hostile and "budmash" elements of the City, whom he felt may have received some temporary encouragement from the rumour'.[1]

'Calcutta has become a jungle of rumour,' lamented the *Statesman*, noting it had become the sinful occupation of just about everyone. 'It is practiced not only by the simple and illiterate but also by many of the sophisticated who wear stiff shirts or backless dresses for dinner . . .' The newspaper was understandably not so exercised by Fairweather's arrest, which it dismissed as a 'most entertaining' piece of gossip. Its concern was directed at the virulent rash of rumours that swept through the city.[2]

Of course, by this time, the eruption had broken out all over the country. This was not surprising as wartime is an ideal breeding ground for rumours, which take root and grow in a climate of fear and anxiety. But the British hadn't anticipated the scale and spread of the 'menace' which, in their eyes, seeded doubts about their ability to defend India, undermining the war effort. Only some of the rumours were a result of Axis propaganda, but the administration regarded every rumour as an enemy bullet.

The Nazi victories in the West, the introduction of ARP measures and the lack of real military preparedness were early sources of the outbreak, but after Japan's entry into the war, rumours went into full play. While they assumed different forms, most rumours were what Robert H. Knapp, the American psychologist, called the 'wedge-driving' kind, essentially those that have 'the effect of dividing groups and destroying loyalties'.[3] The retreat in Malaya and the surrender in Singapore provided a persuasive backdrop for such rumours, many of them tall tales about Japanese prowess and British cowardice.

There was a story in the United Provinces that a Japanese man had parachuted to a mela, addressed the gathering and 'returned to the skies by the same means'. Around the same time, a train dacoity in Gorakhpur was attributed to the Japanese.[4] There were recurring rumours about Japanese attacks at specific times on specific places such as Calcutta, Jamshedpur and the Kumbh Mela at Allahabad.[5] In Dehradun, guns were to be dropped into a PoW camp to empower those incarcerated to capture the town. The official report on the Dehradun rumour made a wry note of another making the rounds: 'The arrest of the Superintendent of Police Cawnpore as a spy has been improved by the addition of the information that he was subsequently shot dead in Allahabad Fort.'[6] Even the 'wildest rumours' are believed by people, complained another official, citing one about the Maharaja of Darbhanga having been detained in Delhi because he had refused to part with all his gold.[7]

There was considerable frustration about the inability to stem the tide of tattle. Stories that the British were in a state of frightful panic particularly annoyed the administration. Rumours about Europeans being spirited away to safety from the coastal areas—a suspicion that was not entirely fanciful given the ignominy in Penang and the selective and racially motivated evacuation from Burma—were among them. In Cuttack, gossip about Europeans being sent away provoked a communiqué that warned rumour-mongers of prosecution under the Defence of India Rules. In Madras city, rumours that European women and children were being rapidly evacuated by special trains were denied in a detailed press note. The government clarified that the extra traffic was no more than that which routinely occurs during the Christmas and New Year holidays.[8]

But what worried administrators most were the rumours that implied that Japan looked kindly on India and Indians and vice versa. The most 'insidious form of rumour' are those about Japanese racial discrimination against Europeans and in favour of Asiatics, read one official communication.* Such stories were hardly surprising in the prevailing climate. Many Indians believed, as did Gandhi at one time, that Japan's war was really against the British. Others, led by Bose, regarded the Axis powers as a force of liberation, an idea that was spread tirelessly by Japanese propaganda.

Given this, it is probably no surprise that rumours of Japanese benevolence made the rounds. In Assam, gossip had it that the British deliberately raided a Buddhist temple in order to blame the Japanese, who had refrained from bombing it. There were stories about Indians appointed to important posts. A Nattukottai Chettiar was said to have been appointed the High Commissioner to Japan after Malaya was overrun. A Bengali was said to have been made the Governor of Singapore; another account had him as a 'Madrasi Muslim'.[9]

---

* Fortnightly Report from Bengal, first half of March 1942, Home Dept, NAI. Interestingly, it also recorded a 'stimulus to the study of Japanese', noting that 'a well known primer of the language is now sold out'.

To counter this, there was a concerted British attempt to alter the narrative by highlighting Japan's record in China and its atrocities in other invaded countries. Deploring 'the false belief that Japan would not attack an Asiatic race', Madras' Governor Hope reminded people that any bombing would perforce be racially indiscriminate. Aircraft flying thousands of feet above cannot distinguish between Englishmen and Indians, he told an audience somewhat condescendingly.[10] But it is doubtful whether the move to highlight Japanese atrocities elsewhere had much success; one official complained of the persistence of the 'marked tendency to indulge in wishful thinking that the Japanese are likely to treat Indians kindly'.[11]

* * *

The day after Pearl Harbour was bombed, a newly constituted Japanese government body, set up to coordinate overseas broadcasting, met to outline a propaganda strategy to be deployed in the war. It agreed that an effort should be made to use propaganda to bring the southern regions and the neutral countries in alignment with Japan.

The Japanese recognized, as Hitler's chief propagandist Joseph Goebbels did, the persuasive power of radio, with its capacity to reach millions of people instantly. The main aim of Japanese broadcasting in Asia was clear: to turn people against their British rulers. The 'radio attack' on India began in Tokyo in December 1941 on the partial advice of Rash Behari Bose.[12] It gathered momentum as Japan gained control over South-East Asia, using stations in Indonesia, Burma and Singapore, the last of which became the nerve centre of India-directed broadcasts. The polyglot transmissions in English, French, Japanese and Arabic included newscasts in Indian languages such as Urdu, Tamil, Bengali and Punjabi.

German radio was already creating ripples before the Japanese opened their radio assault from the East. A 1940 survey conducted by All India Radio in five cities showed that 'more Indians were using the radio for news, and for news hostile to Britain'. Late that year, the Jodhpur Maharaja observed that almost everyone who owned a wireless in the city tuned into the broadcast from Berlin every evening at 8 p.m.[13] There was an official station aimed at Indian PoWs in Germany on which short Hindustani segments were broadcast. But it wasn't until the establishment of Azad Hind Radio (or Free India Radio) in early 1942 that British India was subjected to sustained radio propaganda.

Free India Radio declared it was free from British propaganda and would examine world affairs from a purely nationalist point of view. Its distinguishing feature, its manifesto read, was that broadcasts would be 'by Indians and for Indians'. Subhash Chandra Bose went on its airwaves a month after it was launched, making his first forceful speech not long after the fall of Singapore, and continuing to promise deliverance from the British on the back of successive Japanese victories in South-East Asia. While seeking German recognition for a government in exile and guarantees of independence after the war, Bose brought up the issue of using broadcasts against the British in India. While the Nazi government was reluctant to concede the former requests, Hitler's Minister for Foreign Affairs, Joachim von Ribbentrop, warmed to the idea of using radio propaganda to target India. Ribbentrop appears to have been impressed by the Mussolini-supported Radio Himalaya, which was founded by Mohammad Iqbal Shedai and other Ghadar expatriate activists, who were working to overthrow the Indian government. But the Germans had 'mixed feelings about the more active Italian broadcasting to India'. They looked upon its broadcasts as 'vulgar' in the way they attacked the British.[14] Soon, Azad Hind Radio would eclipse

Himalaya Radio in importance, just as Bose would overshadow Shedai, with whom he had a competitive rivalry.

The British struggled to contend with the influence of Axis broadcasts, complaining about their popularity, highlighting the necessity of containing the propaganda, and lamenting that the increased attention paid to the broadcasts from Tokyo and Berlin resulted in a corresponding lack of faith in British sources. The 'extent and power of the ether war raging in India is difficult to convey', observed a British Broadcasting Corporation official who spent a few months in India in 1942. Against the BBC and All India Radio, there were nine large radio stations battering India every night, offering, among other things, 'good reception and technical proficiency in programming'. Dealers in Bombay told the BBC official that Indians interested in buying wireless sets usually asked: 'Can I hear Germany and Japan on this?'*

Aware that battles are also waged in the mind, Britain responded to Axis propaganda about India with some of its own. The job of countering those advocating the immediate end of British rule and other such 'subversive' ideas fell to the BBC, which was co-opted to join the radio war. Among the professionals the BBC recruited to bolster British propaganda and call out Axis lies about India was the novelist George Orwell. In August 1941, he was hired as a temporary talks producer, which counted as 'essential war work'.[15] Orwell was a somewhat unusual choice, given his profound and unqualified opposition to British imperialism and

---

* *The Transfer of Power 1942–47, Vol. III* (London: Her Majesty's Stationery Office, 1971), p. 196. The BBC official's memorandum was sent to Cripps who passed it on to Amery who, in turn, forwarded it to Linlithgow. The Viceroy described it as 'tripe', but it is possible he was referring not so much to the influence of Axis propaganda, which was a reality, as to the memorandum's other observations—for instance, that bitterness against Britain was never higher and that its prestige was at its lowest.

a strong commitment to Indian independence. 'We like to think of England as a democratic country, but our rule in India, for instance, is just as bad as German Fascism,' he wrote to a friend in September 1939.[16] But as the war progressed, Orwell's views assumed a more pragmatic character. What was important given the circumstances was to defeat fascism; Indian freedom could wait until the Allies won, he now argued.

Orwell wore two propaganda hats at the BBC, one literary and the other political. The former was aimed at Indian intellectuals and Orwell roped in a number of literary heavyweights, including T.S. Eliot and E.M. Forster, to participate in his programmes. The weekly political broadcasts were in the form of news commentaries, which Orwell himself wrote up. Unlike the literary capsules, most of his news broadcasts were read by others. After a while, the BBC, which wanted to cash in on Orwell's popularity, asked him whether he would write and broadcast the news commentaries in his own name. Orwell agreed, but sought assurances on being given a degree of freedom and underlined his preference for commentary that came from an anti-fascist rather than an imperialist standpoint.

Orwell was provided English transcripts of Axis broadcasts every day by the BBC Monitoring Service, which was set up in 1939 and employed hundreds of people to listen in to war-related information from various countries. Churchill, a keen user of the service, who referred to it as 'a modern Tower of Babel', was known to call up in the middle of the night to ask, 'What is that fellow [Hitler] saying?'[17] As for Orwell, his commentaries were routinely censored. As someone who was sympathetic to the Congress, he was unhappy with attacks on Gandhi and Nehru.[18] While he went along with the censorship for the most part, he did chafe at the bit now and then. For instance, he preferred silence over blaming Gandhi for the failure of the Cripps Mission. All the same, he batted earnestly for the success of the Mission, describing Cripps as 'gifted, trustworthy, and self-sacrificing'. This was largely in response to Japanese propaganda, which reminded Indians that Britain had made fools of them earlier and that Cripps' offer of Dominion Status was only a 'sweetener' to create an enemy out of Japan.[19] After Cripps returned empty-handed, Orwell said that only supporters of fascism would be pleased by the Mission's failure.[20]

It is difficult to measure the impact of Orwell's broadcasts or other India-directed propaganda programmes.* An intelligence officer from the BBC's Eastern Service, who visited India for six months in 1942, returned to tell Orwell that the propaganda broadcasts 'were utterly useless because no one listens to them'.† By then, Orwell was already disenchanted with his work and his employer, noting in his diary: 'The thing that strikes one about the BBC—and it is evidently the same in various of the other departments—is not so much the moral squalor and the ultimate futility of what we are doing, as the feeling of frustration, the impossibility of getting anything done, even any successful piece of scoundrelism.'[21] There was an echo of this sentiment in his resignation letter to the Director of the Eastern Service the following year. He wrote that he was quitting not because of any particular grievance, but on account of the realization that 'I have been wasting my own time and the public money on doing work that produces no result'.[22]

Beyond the airwaves, there were Japanese and British propaganda efforts on the ground. The Japanese produced a number of posters and leaflets, some of which were dropped off

---

* At the end of 1939, there were less than 1,00,000 valid wireless set licences, limiting the direct reach of radio propaganda.

† George Orwell, *The Orwell Diaries* (London: Penguin Books, 2010), pp. 355–56. The official, however, did tell Orwell that BBC news was trusted and regarded as more truthful than Axis news broadcasts.

airplanes in South-East Asia in an attempt to persuade people that Japan was fighting for Asia's freedom. Among other things, the posters depicted British racism and discrimination, highlighted the economic exploitation of poor Indians, and expressed the hope that Asians could live in harmony after driving Britain out. 'Each poster evokes a moment of misery under the Empire, and some even attempt to give alternative outcomes, should India free herself from the shackles of the Raj.'[23]

As for the British, processions of defence forces through the streets and displays of military weaponry were a way of signalling strength and resolve. They were also a means to canvass money and drum up popular support for the war effort. In March 1941, Bombay staged 'War Week', an eight-day carnival that was said to have drawn the biggest crowds in many a year. Large columns of troops from the Maratha Regiment, the Royal Indian Navy and the Sappers marched through the city, which witnessed displays of armoured cars, aerobatic fly-pasts and the ear-splitting firing of artillery. In tandem with the displays of military might were a cheery mix of other events. Brabourne Stadium was turned over for athletic competitions, cinema halls were commandeered to screen popular Hindi films, military bands played rousing music, Bombay took on the Rest of India at hockey, children were turned out in fancy dress, and there was cabaret and dancing at the two-day pageant at the Cooperage grounds in Colaba.

The festivities, which were organized under the chairmanship of the Chief Justice of Bombay, Sir John Beaumont, provided a platform to raise money for the war effort. Defence Savings Certificates were championed and sold, which Governor Roger Lumley and his wife 'set a good example' by buying. The Ladies Committee was busy selling 'Win the War' rupee tickets, and the Flags Committee tried to ensure that every car in Bombay sported a 'Defend India' flag, which was sold at Rs 10 a piece, the proceeds earmarked for the Royal Air Force. Among the innovative ways of raising money was a jumble sale to which the most valuable donation was a portrait of Warren Hastings who, as Bengal's first Governor-General, laid the foundations of the Raj. The interest in the painting, and correspondingly its value, was probably that much greater because it was painted by Baron von Imhoff, whose wife Hastings had an affair with and eventually married. At the Cricket Club of India's centre court, a large and enthusiastic crowd paid to watch an early version of a 'Battle of the Sexes' tennis match. Leela Row, the first Indian woman to win a Wimbledon singles match, was pitted against Man Mohan. She lost 4–6, but the report on the match took note of her 'remarkable' performance; only earlier that very day, she had made short work of one of Bombay's leading male players (6–2, 6–0), a Cambridge Blue.[24]

Hearing about the success of Bombay's War Week, Governor Hope tried to imitate it in Madras, but the modest number of troops and the lack of modern weaponry and aircraft were limitations on putting on a grand show of military might and preparedness.[25] But Madras could stage an entertaining money-raising carnival as well as any other city. Months before Bombay's War Week, Madras held its War Fund Fete. The expansive grounds of the stately Government House were turned over for a day of entertainment that included elephant rides, magic gardens, cabaret, American-style diners and saloons, Tamil theatre, two bandstands, an orchestra, coconut shies, raffles and bagatelle. Governor Hope wrote a congratulatory message to the fete's organizing committee in which he said, 'Apart from the financial result, it was a great piece of propoganda (*sic*) which will have its effect.'[26]

There was also outreach of a more modest but sustained kind. Reading circles were formed in rural areas where 'accurate' news of the war was disseminated. Linlithgow felt that the touring propaganda vans, fitted with loudspeakers and film projectors, were most valuable, even if the 'rough mofussil roads' tended to put the 'delicate apparatus' out of order.[27] A Defence Services Exhibition Train made stops at various stations in the country to instil a sense of confidence about defence preparations. When the train arrived in Madras, George Boag, one of Governor Hope's advisers, admitted: 'In some measure, this exhibition is an answer to the criticisms that are sometimes made that the defence of the country has been neglected.'[28]

* * *

The British blamed the torrent of rumours on such things as the gullibility of Indians, scheming fifth columnists, Axis propaganda and the ineffectiveness of their own efforts to counter it. What such explanations ignored was their own contribution to the climate of mistrust and unease in which tales grew tall and tongues wagged fancifully. The attempt to withhold information and even deliberately misinform people about the rapid reverses in South-East Asia were a major cause of the interlocking waves of distrust, anxiety, rumour and panic.

At the beginning of 1942, Japan's dramatic advances in the south-east dwarfed the British success in Libya, where Rommel was forced into temporary retreat. They also appeared to somewhat eclipse the events in the Soviet Union, where weary and overextended German forces ground to a wintry halt. By then, the Japanese forces had already made a mockery of repeated British assurances that Malaya was too protected (geographically and militarily) to breach. Also, by that time, another Japanese attack would reverberate in India—the bombing of Rangoon in Burma.

One of the main targets of the waves of Japanese bombers and fighters was teeming downtown Rangoon, chosen in order to strike terror in people and persuade them that Britain was too weak to safeguard lives and livelihoods. The two attacks on 23 and

25 December killed as many as 2000 people, according to some estimates. The number of dead was markedly greater because, instead of taking cover, people spilled out on to the streets to witness the spectacle. Despite the large number of casualties and the hundreds of homes reduced to smouldering heaps by incendiary bombs, there was little or no publicity about the carnage. The brief newspaper reports in the immediate aftermath focused on exaggerating the number of Japanese aircraft taken down during the raid and glossed over the extent of the destruction. It was only weeks later that the public was given some idea about the extent of the casualties. About half of them were estimated to be Indians.[29]

The delay in putting out statements about the bombings and the military reverses was deliberate. So was the doctoring of or playing down the number of casualties. The justification for lying, or at the very least being very economical with the truth, was to keep morale up and prevent people from getting anxious. But, as historian Devika Sethi points out, there was a 'major contradiction' when it came to the issue of wartime censorship. Allowing the full truth to be told could lead to defeatism and panic. Suppressing the news could lead to alarmist and doom-laden rumours. The tension between these two considerations played out in the twenty-four-page booklet 'Press Instructions for War', the go-to document for censors. It stressed that 'as much accurate news' should be published about the war 'to combat baseless and demoralising conjectures'. At the same time, it laid down a list of things that could not be reported.[30]

This contradiction played out between Governor Hope and Linlithgow in relation to the carnage in Rangoon. In a bold and forthright communication, Hope complained to Linlithgow that the delay and the dissembling were having a 'deplorable effect'. 'I do fervently hope that the truth can be told and told quickly because the rumours being spread both by enemy sources and rumour mongers are doing a great deal of harm.' He said the lag in announcing the number of casualties in Rangoon had resulted in rumours with 'fantastic figures'. But in Hope's view, the lag was not the only problem. 'Why should we announce there were only 600 casualties in the first raid (on 23 December) when we know there were at least 1700?' he made bold to ask.[31]

In April the following year, after the bombing of Vizagapatam and Cocanada in his Presidency, Hope once again urged that the casualty figures from air raids be put out in communiqués as soon as possible. He argued that vague phrases such as 'casualties were slight' only bred rumours. Pointing out that while the casualties from these two raids were indeed 'slight', he said that rumour was placing them much higher.[32]

* * *

Hope's insistence on the importance of 'telling the truth' was commendable but somewhat ironic, caught up as he was in a tawdry financial scandal. In 1944, it came to Whitehall's attention that he had run up huge gambling debts on the racecourse. Among the people he borrowed from were James Doak of Madura Mills (who Hope recommended for a knighthood) and Harry Dunk (a senior official at the Bombay Company Private Limited). Dunk was preparing to sue Hope. Dunk's granddaughter, Pamela Conran-Smith, the daughter of India's Home Secretary, Eric Conran-Smith, turned down her fiancé's suggestion that Hope be invited to their wedding in 1946. She wrote to him: 'One thing, darling—I am sorry but we can't invite Sir Arthur Hope—we are suing him for a considerable sum of money. He borrowed from Pop [Harry Dunk] to the tune of several thousand and never repaid him.'[33]

Probably worse in official eyes was that Hope had also borrowed from wealthy Indians, compromising his office and risking a severely embarrassing public scandal. Remarkably, it was hushed up at the very top—with Viceroy Wavell, Secretary of State Leo Amery, Prime Minister Attlee and King George VI very much in the loop. Pressure was brought on Hope to quit and a doctor's certificate was produced to justify his abrupt resignation in 1946 on health grounds.

Hope was succeeded by Archibald Nye. ('The end of Hope is Nye' went the joke in Madras.)[34] Not long after, Nye discovered that Hope had siphoned off Rs 50,000 meant for the Indian Red Cross in Coimbatore. The money was quietly returned after Whitehall arranged a payment into an Indian account to circumvent questions that would arise if a direct transfer was made. Hope's reputation remained unaffected. After the death of his father in 1949, he became the Second Baron Rankeillour. The scandal remained under wraps for over seven decades, until *The Times* revealed the misconduct that led to Hope's departure from Madras by accessing papers preserved at The National Archives in London.[35]

All the same, as the Governor of a province of 'Madrasis', who made up the 'great majority' of Indians in Malaya and Burma, Hope had a special reason to be worried by lies and half-truths. The two raids in December precipitated an early flight of Indians from Burma, who returned home with a truer picture of what really happened. By this time, Hope was reporting in about a partial exodus from Madras, a general disbelief in official statements and a panicky people anxious about their relatives of whom they had no news. 'I do not agree with Dorman-Smith [Burma's Governor] at all that it is not better to tell the truth,' he wrote.[36]

On Burma, Linlithgow replied that it was up to Governor Reginald Hugh Dorman-Smith to decide what could or could not be revealed. As India's Viceroy, all he could do was put across suggestions for Burma's Governor to consider.[37] Dorman-Smith was against publishing news immediately after the Rangoon raids on three grounds: it would cause undue alarm, prevent those who had fled from returning and risk providing useful information to the Japanese. He was in favour of the 'English practice' of monthly statements. Linlithgow concurred: 'I think this is pretty convincing and I told him I agree.'*

* * *

There were already over a million Indians in Burma according to the 1931 census. Remarkably, at that time, Indians made up over half the population of its capital Rangoon. They covered a wide socio-economic spectrum. There was a small but powerful minority of people (including Chettiars from present-day Tamil Nadu) who formed a business or trading class. There was another minority, predominantly upper caste, that was engaged in professions such as teaching, engineering, medicine and in various roles in the bureaucracy. The majority was made up of lower-caste people who worked as skilled and unskilled labour, many of them from rural areas, lured by the promise of a better life.

Even before the advent of war, there was a feeling of insecurity among all three classes as a result of the constitutional separation of Burma from India and the outbreak of fierce anti-Indian riots. There were apprehensions that the loss of British control would leave Indians vulnerable to hostile elements in the Burmese community. Even though Rangoon, slit-trenched and ARP-compliant, was already prepped for an air attack, the sheer ferocity of the 23 December raid was unexpected. Indians began to flee

* Linlithgow to Hope, 31 December 1941, Linlithgow Papers, F125/69, IOR. (Burma was partitioned from India in 1937 and was no longer under the Viceroy. But by the end of 1941, it was under the operational control of General Archibald Wavell's ABDA [American-British-Dutch-Australian Command].)

Rangoon after the attack, the numbers increasing as the Japanese troops advanced and as the British got to work on their evacuation plans. In what has been called a 'forgotten long march', at least 4,00,000 refugees trekked northwards, trying to make their way back to India via two dangerous and extremely demanding routes, one of them via the mountains into Manipur and the other more easterly into Chittagong. Many thousands, probably somewhere between 10,000 and 50,000, died in the attempt to get home.[38]

Of the two main steamship companies, the British-owned one catered almost wholly to Europeans. The other, the Indian-owned Scindia Steam Navigation Company, abruptly cancelled its services. Even so, in January 1942, arrangements were made to ship 70,000 Indians to Calcutta and Madras. These were the relatively fortunate people. Although they had to leave many possessions behind, they got away unhurt. The uncomfortable six-day sea journey paled in comparison with weeks of trekking through unforgiving tropical terrain, battling diseases such as cholera, dysentery and malaria.[39]

As in Malaya, the British had to cope with allegations of racial discrimination during the evacuation of Burma. In a surcharged atmosphere, it is possible that a few of the allegations were either untrue or exaggerated—at the very least, not corroborated. In the Council of States, a member claimed that Robert Hutchings, the Government of India's Agent in Burma, whipped thirty or forty Indians who had rushed to board a steamer, forcing them out of the vessel. The alleged reason: Hutchings wanted to accommodate thirty more Anglo-Indians.[40] There were other allegations made in both the Central Legislative Assembly and the Council of States based on what members were told by evacuees. Police were said to have beaten up a crowd of Indians that had gathered at Hutchings' office, seeking passes on ships. And there were reports of blatant discrimination in favour of Europeans and Anglo-Indians in the evacuation process by both sea and air.

In both Houses, the government took the position that specific allegations were in want of substantiation. Moreover, it reiterated that it was not government policy to racially discriminate in matters of evacuation. But there was no satisfactory explanation for a couple of things. One of the escape routes leading out of the Burmese border town of Tamu into Manipur was fenced off for Indians, but left open for Europeans and Anglo-Indians. Queried about this, Geoffrey Stephen Bozman, Secretary for Indians Overseas, said he was not in a position to state what the exact facts were. However, he admitted there may have been 'military restrictions' that could have led to discrimination. If this was true, then 'we shall do our utmost to remove that effect', he declared.[41] European refugees received higher allowances, paid directly by Churchill's government, than the Indians who fled. Linlithgow thought there was sufficient evidence of racial discrimination in such practices, refusing to endorse Amery's denial that nothing of the sort existed.[42]

The issue of discrimination played out at a relatively lofty political level. On the ground, the administration was much more concerned by the impact of the stories the Indian refugees carried back with them. Those who walked hundreds of miles, a fair bit of it through perilous forested terrain, came back broken and exhausted. Ambujammal, Congresswoman and author, wept on hearing their accounts of pain, suffering and death: 'The horror stories we heard were of a kind that we had not even read in fiction.' A part of a joint initiative of citizens and the Madras Corporation to receive, house and treat refugees, Ambujammal and her co-volunteers were told stories of husbands separated from wives, of children from parents, of people surviving on grass and thieves making off with money and jewellery.[43]

In Madras city, a number of refugees were temporarily accommodated in a large bungalow on Spurtank Road and then sent on their way to smaller towns and villages once they were able and willing to make the journey. For many, it was a difficult homecoming, a return to poverty and unemployment. In Vizagapatam district alone, there were about 15,000 unemployed evacuees from Burma. The distress was acute enough for the Madras government to consider providing them work under the Indian Famine Code of 1883.[44]

The refugees who found their way home via Calcutta, Chittagong and Madras to villages and smaller towns in different parts of the country took their stories back with them. These were harrowing first-hand accounts of what they saw and experienced. But the stories were also, at least by implication, about a Raj in retreat. This strengthened the conviction in India that Britain was losing its hold on the Empire, a sentiment that British administrators decried as defeatism. But most of those who returned had witnessed the flight of Europeans, Anglo-Indians and the Allied armed forces.

> For the refugees, the outcome of the war was not in doubt, a Japanese victory was certain. They had witnessed the Allied defeat; they knew the empire was to end.[45]

By the end of January 1942, the port city of Moulmein was captured; so were a few vital airstrips. Japan was already close to its objective of taking Rangoon, cutting off the Burma Road and choking off Allied supplies to Chinese nationalist forces via sea and land. On 20 February, the Burmese government advised all non-essential citizens to leave. People, of course, had begun fleeing Rangoon even before this, but it quickly turned into a ghost town. As the Japanese advanced, the British Army scorched earth, destroying vehicles and oil installations before escaping northwards. On 9 March, the Rangoon that the Japanese Army marched into was an empty ruinous shell.

10

The Fog of Confusion

On 14 January 1942, Governor Hope took to All India Radio in an attempt to allay the fear that had gripped Madras and other parts of the Presidency. It is not clear whether he intentionally chose Pongal, the auspicious day the annual harvest festival is celebrated by the Tamil community, to make what was intended to be a reassuring broadcast. By then, people had begun fleeing coastal towns in the Presidency for the interior; as for Madras city, somewhere between 20 and 30 per cent of residents, mainly women and children, had left.[1] Malaya already seemed like a lost cause and the arrival of air raid victims from Rangoon only added to the sense of alarm.

It was a well-intentioned speech, aimed at calming what Hope himself described as a 'panicky atmosphere'. But like other administrators did, Hope erred in linking Singapore's fate with that of India. Ruling out the threat of any serious Japanese invasion of India via sea or over land, he added: 'While Singapore is in the hands of Britain, the question of invasion does not really arise at all.'[2] The thought that the so-called fortress would crumble a month later seemed unimaginable at the time. But when it did, it was hardly surprising that British assurances that there was still no danger to India, no reason to feel despondent, rang very hollow.

Hope did not believe there was an imminent threat of Rangoon-style raids on Madras, pointing out that the city was outside the raiding range of Japanese aircraft. The nearest aerodrome under Japanese control was some 1300 miles away in Thailand, too far away for bombers to fly to Madras and return to base without refuelling. Hope did not rule out a stray Japanese vessel sneaking into the Bay of Bengal and sending a couple of planes over Madras. Of course, what sailed into the Indian Ocean and the Bay of Bengal barely three months later were two full-fledged fleets bearing over 300 aircraft.

Overall, government messaging at both the central and provincial levels about the extent of the Japanese threat was extremely confusing; it was also far from helpful in staunching the surge of alarm. The first communiqué put out by the Madras government which took note of the panic was issued only after the start of the exodus, in late December 1941. It declared that the threat to Madras city, as things stood, was not grave enough to warrant evacuation, 'voluntary or compulsory'. At the same time, it stated that if evacuation was necessary, people would be notified well in time. This implied that things could get much worse, a gloomy possibility that hung heavily in the air. On 21 December, Linlithgow issued a terse ordinance in light of the 'emergency' that had arisen. The decree prohibited people engaged in essential defence work from leaving the places where they worked.[3] A couple of days later, the province of Bengal announced its own state of emergency. The proclamation gave immediate effect to a number of earlier orders and instructions that had been readied in case an emergency needed to be declared.[4] 'The official notifications relating to the declaration of emergency are as cryptic as they are brief, unaccompanied by any sort of explanation as to their real import,' complained *The Hindu*. It said, given the lack of information about the threat, one could hardly blame common folk for concluding that they would be in danger if they did not leave at once.[5]

Two days after the fall of Singapore, the Madras government issued another press statement about the level of the Japanese threat. It acknowledged 'some increase'. Yet, it reckoned that this increase was not great enough to require anyone to leave the city. At the same time, the communiqué recommended that those who have no business in the city and who intend to leave if the danger becomes acute should do so as conveniently as they can. This, it explained, was to avoid 'rush and confusion' in the event of an attack.[6]

Unsurprisingly, this convoluted chain of reasoning triggered another exodus. If the communiqué was meant to reassure, it was undermined by the suggestion that the danger could become acute—in other words, that there was a real possibility of attack. Rajagopalachari squarely blamed Hope for heightening the fear in Madras. He said the Governor had erred in suggesting that there was no danger to Madras as long as Singapore held. An examination of the situation in Malaya should have made it clear that this could not have been forestalled. While he didn't have an issue with those who had no business in the city leaving voluntarily, there was a problem with the wording of the communiqué. The majority of people couldn't distinguish between 'little' danger and 'great' danger and couldn't be faulted for thinking that the government was urging them to leave.[7]

Elsewhere too, people were led to believe that there were imminent plans for mass evacuation. For instance, the duly elected Bengal government appointed a Director of Civil Evacuation, even as it reassured people that there were no plans for mass evacuation. Around the same time, there was a railway announcement that arrangements for special trains had been made to ferry 80,000 people out of Howrah station in Calcutta every day. Given that lakhs of people had already fled, many by rail, the *Statesman* estimated that under this arrangement, Calcutta could be totally emptied, by rail and other means, in a 'few days'. In a stinging editorial, the British-owned newspaper confrontationally asked:

> In what world do we live? Do we dream? Or are we awake amongst the mad? Since when did Governments take it upon themselves to provide for mass panic and universal cowardice in advance? Is this to be Calcutta's answer to some Japanese bombs?[8]

In contrast, Indian-owned publications in Calcutta such as the *Hindustan Standard* and *Amrita Bazar Patrika* were broadly supportive of the evacuation schemes. They felt that there were few options for a people whom the British refused to arm and involve in the defence of the country but to leave areas of danger. This was broadly in keeping with the nationalist view that a defenceless people could not be ordered to stay put and risk their lives. The *Statesman*'s reply to this was that Calcutta was only threatened from the air and that arming the civilian population would hardly deter raiding aircraft.[9] But invasion was considered a real possibility in Chittagong, which lies on the coastline unlike Calcutta, accessible via river. At the end of February 1942, the military ordered some 30,000 people in four villages near Chittagong to evacuate. The operation was completed in a little over a week.[10]

From a military perspective, cities that were more or less emptied of non-essentials would be easier to manage in case of an indiscriminate air attack or defend in the event of invasion. The provincial administrations were aligned with this view. Gandhi, who was in favour of orderly evacuation, arrived at a similar position, though from a somewhat different path. He felt it was wrong to prevent people unwilling to remain from leaving. At the same time, he favoured cooperation with the authorities on evacuation, stating that those who were unwanted should leave as well.

> Those who must remain in the cities whether for business or otherwise should carry out instructions that may be issued by the authorities from time to time. Those who will not, for any reason whatsoever, should clear out in good time. If this simple precaution is taken, we may face the future without perturbation.[11]

This, he clarified, did not compromise his position as a war-resister; 'up to a point military necessity and duty of war-resisters demand the same action'.[12]

* * *

As ARP measures were being put into place and plans for evacuation were being drawn up, India was being readied in another way: for active defence. For the better part of a year after Britain declared war in September 1939, there was no major increase in the numbers of the Indian Army. But from mid-1940, around the end of the phoney war, a change in British policy saw recruitment go into overdrive. At the end of the war in 1945, the army had grown more than tenfold, to 2.5 million men from 2,00,000 in 1939.

As the Japanese threat emerged, British and American soldiers started arriving in large numbers in India. The influx would continue all through 1942, 'a great wave of incoming soldiers, fresh to the country, unfamiliar with local languages, conscripted and sent to Asia not of their own free choice, often resenting their posting and longing to be fighting the Nazis instead'.[13] Many Indians viewed the increasing presence of soldiers with resentment and fear, wishing likewise that they were elsewhere. Apart from the bombs that frightened people, Hope grumbled to Linlithgow about the 'genuine feeling that the troops, both Indian and British, would rape any women they can get hold of'.

Curiously, Hope blamed an incident (rape?) in Calcutta, which was followed by a leader in *The Hindu,* for the climate of alarm. '. . . I have told [Kasturi] Srinivasan [the newspaper's Editor] that he is largely to blame for the fear.'[14] All the 'offending' editorial did was criticize one of Hope's advisers, T.G. Rutherford, for talking about people 'grumbling' about the presence of troops in Madras. Rutherford was blamed for showing a 'poor understanding of the genuine fears of the public' and for injecting a racial character into the issue by hinting that the misbehaving troops were Indian ('their own people'). 'It is a mistake to suppose that the civilian population resent objectionable behaviour only when European soldiers are guilty of it. If an Indian soldier misbehaves, they would far from condoning it, deplore it all the more.'[15]

However, it was the growing numbers of white soldiers that caught public attention. 'They were seen everywhere in the city,' recalled journalist and travel writer A.K. Chettiar, adding they were on trams, buses, trains and rickshaws. They were in 'the nine anna ticket section' in cinema halls, eating masala dosas in restaurants, marvelling at the spherical shape of karaboondhi (spicy gram flour snack), and looking curiously at the custom of people drinking water without letting the glass touch their lips. 'But when the soldier catches sight of an Anglo-Indian girl or a dark Christian girl, his behaviour turns different. The rich and the high-class people of Chennai [Madras] become nervous and start sweating profusely when they see a soldier.' White soldiers wanted to mingle with common folk but were not allowed to. They never understood why, Chettiar wryly noted.[16]

Incidents of actual army misbehaviour, fears about how troops would behave and unfounded rumours about what they allegedly did came in from different parts of the country. The Bombay Corporation unanimously adopted a resolution drawing the government's attention to public anxiety as a result of several reports alleging that women were being molested and that combatant forces were misbehaving as they moved around the city.[17] In the Central Legislative Assembly, leave was not granted for an adjournment motion moved by Deputy President Akhil Chandra Datta to discuss reports that soldiers in Poona Cantonment molested women, injured a watchman and a *tonga* driver, and caused heavy damage to shops and a restaurant.[18] There were a number of other accounts of army misbehaviour that echoed through the Assembly. These included a graphic account of troops on special trains running amok as they passed through Bengal, chasing hawkers, damaging property and stealing foodstuffs. 'The railway officers are proving helpless. The military officers attached with troops also don't interfere nor the railway police.'[19]

Akhil Chandra Datta recalled asking a young girl in Calcutta whether she wanted to leave due to apprehensions about the city being bombed. 'Her answer was: "No, I am not afraid of bombing, not a bit, but what I am afraid of is the goondaism of soldiers."'[20] He drew attention to what he saw as the irony of routine British warnings about Japanese misbehaviour in lands they had conquered. 'We are told: "Look how women were ill-treated in Hong Kong." But here, no. Unless Hong Kongs happen everywhere in every province in India, I suppose no notice will be taken of such "molestation".'[21] In response, the government admitted there had been 'a number of incidents in different parts of India in which some soldiers, Indian and non-Indian, have been offenders'. Gurunath Venkatesh Bewoor, the government-nominated civil servant who would go on to serve on Viceroy Archibald Wavell's Executive Council, expressed regret and promised not to be indifferent or ignore such incidents on the ground that 'Boys will be Boys'.[22]

Other adjournment motions regarding troop misbehaviour were moved in the Central Legislative Assembly around the same time. One was based on a newspaper report which stated that drunken soldiers had attacked pedestrians and a policeman, creating a severe disturbance in Bareilly.[23] The matter was dropped after it was confirmed that the incident had taken place and action taken against the offending soldiers.[24] Another motion on the alleged 'delinquency' of European soldiers, who were said to have killed two students and injured some others at Sarnath, was disallowed for lack of definite information.[25]

Official reports of troop misbehaviour—real, alleged and imagined—came in from different provinces. In Nagpur, there was agitation over the rowdiness of troops, resulting in a press conference being called to explain the steps taken to enforce discipline. Three soldiers from the hospital corps were hospitalized after a fight broke out with the local community at a bazaar near Nagpur.[26] The arrival of a medical unit was said to have triggered rumours of maltreatment of women by British troops in Lucknow; in nearby Allahabad, molestation rumours were said to have originated after members of the Special Armed Constabulary, who were in 'rather high spirits', were mistaken for soldiers.[27]

Despite the general admission that there were indisputable instances of troop misbehaviour, the government was prickly about this being highlighted in the press. In Bihar, the *Yogi* ran an editorial titled 'Terror of White Soldiers', leading the administration to demand that its Editor (and editors of other newspapers) say nothing on such matters without previous consent. This occurred shortly after five soldiers from the Northamptonshire Regiment based in the Dinapur Cantonment attacked two people, killing one of them.[28] The well-known Malayalam daily *Mathrubhumi* was pulled up for carrying a fairly bland news report about Australian soldiers in the princely state of Cochin. It reported a press meet held by the Diwan, in which he referred to the 'unnecessary uneasiness' about the presence of Australian soldiers. Noting the differences in customs, he suggested that had these soldiers landed in England, 'young women would have accompanied them to dances and movies'. Saying they did not know the cultural practices here, the Diwan urged people not to be harsh on the soldiers. At the same time, he acknowledged that there were complaints about these Australian soldiers in Bombay and Egypt, and revealed that he had demanded that the Commander of the Port Trust rein them in if they behaved in an unruly manner.[29] This was sufficient for the Madras government to ban the further publication of the *Mathrubhumi.* It was allowed to resume printing after the submission of a bond for Rs 1000 as surety, a decision that the government felt served to allay an agitation over the imposition of the ban.[30]

As for Gandhi, soldier misconduct, which kept pace with their growing numbers, may well have reinforced his conviction that there should be no participation in the war. 'The behaviour of troops, white or brown, has become a public scandal. Even respectable and well-known women are not free from danger,' he wrote to the multifaceted Desmond Young, variously a British Army officer, author and Editor of the Allahabad-based the *Pioneer*. Gandhi narrated a specific incident about an Indian official's wife who was 'ravished' by (Indian) troops on a train. The official lodged a complaint but withdrew it at the instance of his superiors, said Gandhi as he reminded Young of the mistake in presuming that 'absence of complaint means absence of guilt'.

> Full-blooded soldiers not on duty find vent for their exuberant physical energy by taking liberties which cannot be allowed in a society not used to such conduct.[31]

The increase in sexual molestation went hand in hand with a surge in prostitution as foreign troops poured into India. There were white British soldiers and Africans who had fought in the campaign in Africa. And there were American troops, of which about 15 per cent were black. There were a large number of Chinese soldiers as well. Some had crossed over after the defeat in

Burma; the rest had come over to be trained to strengthen China's capacity to resist the Japanese.

As against 43,000 British troops in 1939, there were as many as 2,40,000 by the end of the war; by 1943, there were an estimated 1,20,000 American soldiers in India.[32] Better paid and with more cash to spare, foreign soldiers spawned a network of pimps, sex workers and middlemen who operated in cantonments. 'Indian prostitution became the mainstay of military "rest and rehabilitation" during the 1940s,' says historian Yasmin Khan. Although brothels were off-limits to the army, the British were resigned to the inevitability of prostitution. 'Education, warnings and some determined provision of prophylaxis ("Defeat the Axis, Use Prophylaxis")' coexisted with a 'military blind eye'.[33]

Molestation was bad enough. The increase in prostitution was another reason for Indians to be wary of troops and, more generally, be doubtful about the war effort. British missionaries and devout Christians were as horrified by the proliferation of brothels. The *Calcutta Diocesan Magazine* alleged that police accompanied by prostitutes were turning up at residences between downtown Marquis Street and Ripon Street, telling occupants that their homes were required 'for brothels for the military'. Complaints had no effect and more homes were being converted into houses of assignation. Would such a thing happen in England, the publication asked.

> When our troops are quartered in their own country, are brothels multiplied on their behalf? In Chester, in Bristol, in Plymouth, in Bath, in York—in a dozen other lovely old English towns, do the benevolent authorities go around clearing decent folk from their homes in order to plant brothels in the heart of town?[34]

In Madras, the *Guardian*, a Christian weekly, had no hesitation in condemning such practices with bell, book and candle. It worried about the impact these would have on the evangelical work of converting Hindus and Muslims. Wouldn't many of them mistakenly assume that what was patronized by Christian soldiers represented Christian standards, it wondered.[35]

* * *

In an attempt to control troop misconduct and allay public anxieties, the Indian government set up a corps of military police to serve in places where large numbers of troops were stationed or passing through. In the Central Legislative Assembly, Bewoor spelt out how the government perceived the issue. He made three main points. First, that the problem was not so serious given the large number of troops. Second, given the difficult nature of their work, troops do allow themselves [maybe deserve?] some relaxation and pleasure. Third, despite strict enforcement, some 'incidents' are bound to occur.

> We have coming into this country or passing through its main ports, thousands of British and Dominion troops. We have, in addition, in our main ports, literally thousands of sailors of different allied and neutral countries who are bringing to us and taking from this country most essential and vital supplies. All these are working under very hard and trying conditions . . . They get a little rest, relaxation and pleasure when they are in ports or in towns or cities. Many of them are complete strangers to the East and to the ideas, feelings, habits and customs, and very few know the local language. They may do somethings most innocently but these might hurt our public. And yet considering the large number of troops and the period since the outbreak of the war, I am sure everyone will admit that the number of serious incidents has been extremely small. In the vastly expanded army of today it is inevitable that there would be some bad characters but how few and exceptional they are! However strict the discipline and however careful the supervision, it is impossible to prevent the occurrence of some incidents. No one regrets these incidents more than the soldiers themselves.[36]

Provinces took their own measures to thwart possible rowdy troop behaviour. For instance, in Bombay, a major point of entry for foreign soldiers, troops were not allowed north of an imaginary line that ran from the docks along Carnac Road and Marine Lines. Off-licence liquor shops were asked to close when large numbers of troops were on shore leave, and the hours during which public bars served alcohol were curtailed. Soldiers on ships were issued warnings that failure to behave would entail cancellation of shore leave.[37] It was reported that Ernakulam, Cochin's twin city, was declared out of bounds for troops unless they were escorted or visiting specific cinema halls and hotels.[38]

In early 1942, it wasn't the fear of Japanese bombing alone that led people to flee cities. The specific fear of troops and general worries about lawlessness were major causes. Around the time Singapore surrendered, about one-third of the population of Madras had already taken flight. Largely responsible for the exodus, in Chief Secretary S.V. Ramamurthy's view, were the preparations made for the defence of the city (which had been fortified with more and more troops), the rumours of molestation of women (which he described as 'unfounded') and the looting by petty criminals.[39]

Elsewhere too, people chose to flee rather than be near troops. Some of those who left Calcutta for Ranchi chose to return home. The reason: the arrival of troops in Ranchi. And in Jamshedpur, the entry of British troops added to the number of those who had already left; the new departures were made up 'mainly of families from the area where the troops are encamped for fear of molestation'.[40]

The anxiety about troop misbehaviour may well have been excessive or exaggerated, but it was real. Moreover, it was an important trigger for a phenomenon that occurred in more than one Indian city: exodus.

11

The Madness in Madras

On the evening of Saturday, 11 April 1942, Sir Sidney Wadsworth, a senior judge of the Madras High Court, received an urgent phone call from Chief Justice Lionel Leach.* Could Wadsworth come over to Brodie's Castle (Sir Lionel's expansive home on the banks of the Adyar river) to discuss a matter of great importance? On arrival, Wadsworth was told of a message from Army Headquarters. It said a Japanese fleet 'with transports' was heading towards the coast of the Madras Presidency. It was expected to land somewhere between Madras city and the extreme south not later than the following Wednesday. Leach told Wadsworth that the civil government was being evacuated and the Madras High Court would have to pack up and leave by Tuesday. The message was loud and clear: the Japanese were on the verge of launching a major invasion.

---

* 'The Wadsworth Papers', Chapter 19, Centre for South Asian Studies, Cambridge. This chapter was made available to the author by Caroline Keen, author of *A Judge in Madras*, who used the papers to write an account of Wadsworth's life in India. Wadsworth mistakenly wrote he was called to Leach's home on Saturday, 13 April. Saturday fell on 11 April in 1942 and the other references in the memoir corroborate that he was summoned by the Chief Justice on this day.

The military 'intelligence' about the imminent invasion may have surprised Wadsworth, but he was already prepared with a plan to evacuate the Madras High Court if asked to. Much earlier, when talk of possible air raids made the rounds after Japan's entry into the war, Wadsworth was deputed to ready a scheme to move the court away from the coast. Done in secret to prevent accusations of creating 'despondency and alarm', Wadsworth's visits and inspections revealed there was no place that had a building large enough to house sixteen judges and hundreds of clerks. So, he planned for two sections. The bigger one, with Chief Justice Leach at its head, would be housed in the Forest College at Coimbatore and serve the mainly Tamil-speaking southern and western districts. The other, headed by himself, would move to Anantapur to serve the Telugu-speaking northern part of the Presidency. One 'unfortunate consequence' of the decision was that 'all the clerks and (court) records would have to be divided according to language which complicated matters a great deal'.[1]

Even so, Wadsworth found he had to conduct only some very general supervision when he entered the majestic, red-bricked, onion-domed Indo-Saracenic edifice of the Madras High Court early on Sunday, the morning after Leach ordered the move. The old court records had been shifted earlier and the scheme had already assigned which staff member would go where; only the current records required bundling and labelling. The one thing that the shift 'nearly broke down over' was the transport of material (which included books, stationery and furniture) to the railway station. In a Madras where almost the entire civil government was moving and where a large part of the population had already fled, there wasn't 'a lorry to be had for love or money'. Even 'the humble hand-cart (which ordinarily moves most things in Madras) had ceased to operate for want of coolies', but to Wadsworth's relief, the court's registrar commandeered buses for the job.

At noon on Monday, 13 April, Wadsworth set off for Anantapur in two cars with his wife, driver, butler, cook and three dogs. Mattresses were strapped to the top of their vehicles, which were loaded with a mix of necessities and valuables such as crockery, utensils, clothes, law books and silver lamps. The only problem (or 'adventure') they encountered was when one of the cars got stuck while crossing a shallow river. There was no need to head directly to the 'furnace' that was Anantapur as it would take some days for the records to arrive. So, the Wadsworths travelled up to Horsley Konda, the small cluster of green hills that seem to defiantly thrust out from the flat and barren landscape near Madanapalle. In the cool and peaceful forest, which 'was like heaven after the turmoil of the last few days', they 'did nothing for a fortnight and thoroughly enjoyed the rest'.

When it became clear the invasion would not materialize, the Wadsworths returned in their cars to Madras, which was alive with troops but dead otherwise. There, he found the military had prevented the judiciary from reoccupying the Madras High Court buildings, which were close to the seafront. As a result, the court took over one of the many empty schools, the Holy Angels Convent, which most judges preferred as a workplace as it was closer to their homes.

* * *

For most ordinary Indians in Madras, or for that matter all over the country, the experience of departure and return was very different from Wadsworth's brief and relaxing sojourn in the hills. Some left on foot. Those who left earlier spent months away from home before returning to the city. Some stayed away even longer. A few probably never returned. Many came back to houses that had been stripped and pillaged. Families were separated, livelihoods lost and lives took new and unexpected turns.

In Madras, founded in 1639, the first Indian city established by the British Empire, the exodus happened in phases, triggered by a succession of events. Those who left soon after Japan entered the war, the earliest phase, fell mainly into two categories. There were the wealthy, who took houses in places such as Kancheepuram and Chittoor in the interior but not far from Madras. And then there were the business folk from the North (Marwaris and others) who left for their native places.[2] As news of the reverses in Malaya trickled in a little later, the general population began to stream out of Madras (and other coastal towns in the Presidency). By the middle of January 1942, Chief Secretary Ramamurthy was reporting that about 20 to 30 per cent of residents had fled the city.[3] Women and children made up most of those who left, an arrangement that allowed men to continue earning a living until they felt it was too dangerous to remain.

The exodus resulted in the sharp rise of rents in places near Madras, 'sometimes as much as five to six times what would normally have been charged'. The *Indian Express* demanded an immediate rent control ordinance to prevent exploitation by houseowners.[4] In nearby North Arcot and Chingelpet, district magistrates issued warnings to houseowners against the raising of tariffs. The Collector of Vellore issued a notification threatening landlords that unjust increases in rentals would invite action under the Defence of India Rules. House rents spiralled in many other small towns all over the country. In Chandernagore near Calcutta, a house rent control order prevented landlords from realizing 20 per cent more than what was levied in October 1941. In some places, old tenants were asked to leave to make way for those willing to pay much more.

Pudhumaipithan, the famous Tamil short story writer and essayist, sent his wife away to Ambasamudram in the deep south, where she remained even after the Japanese threat had blown over.

> I am not bringing you back because all the shops are shut and there is black out. The tanks are on the road, after 7.30 pm. There is no bus service. The white soldiers are guarding the city and lots of soldiers in Adyar are moving about.[5]

A.C. Platt, a civil servant who described himself as 'an unrepenting imperialist', sent his wife and children away to Ootacamund (Ooty), where he was agreeably ordered to go when the revenue department shifted. He would stay on as part of the department, take a summer cottage in Lovedale and father a son in the hill station.[6] In other Indian towns as well, it was women and children who were sent to 'safety' first.

The second flight of people was triggered by the fall of Singapore in mid-February and the Madras government's baffling decision to ask those who were planning to leave later to do so right away. This phase of the exodus continued for a while. With the government advancing the annual examinations for all schools and colleges to enable students to leave earlier, it was expected to be particularly heavy in the first week of March. The railway authorities were asked to run special trains to manage the traffic.[7] By the end of March, an anti-aircraft regiment had arrived in a Madras that was already awash with military personnel. The pace of the evacuation had slowed, leading Hope to believe that almost everyone who had planned to leave had already done so. But 'of course there will be a wholesome exodus if and when the first bomb drops'![8]

As it turned out, it didn't require a bomb to create the conditions for a 'wholesome' egression. In early April, Madras was shaken by successive developments that suggested the war was closing in on it. These triggered another major flight. There was the bombing of Colombo on 5 April, followed soon after by the air attack on Trincomalee and the sinking of the *Hermes*. The severity of the attack on Colombo made people worry that this was the first of many more rounds and that Japan was gearing up for invasion. They fled from Colombo in cars, trains, rickshaws and bullock carts. Many chose to come to India, which furthered the anxiety in Madras. 'The ferry to India from Talaimannar was packed that night and many nights afterwards.'[9] By the third week of April, over 33,000 Ceylonese evacuees had arrived in India.[10]

A day after the Colombo raids, Ozawa's planes bombed Vizagapatam and Cocanada, which added to the pressure on people to leave Madras city. Those who lived in the two port towns of the Madras Presidency were aware that they were likely targets in the event of a Japanese air attack. So were the authorities. Some of the twenty-four anti-aircraft guns and aeroplanes dispatched from England were intended for Vizagapatam. There was 'deep resentment' that they were taken elsewhere (in hindsight, a strategic miscalculation) after they arrived in the town.[11] Vizagapatam's Collector Christopher Masterman* was moved to pen a somewhat awkward poem to convey what he ironically referred to as 'the slight confusion in our defence arrangements' as he waited for the anti-aircraft guns to arrive.

> Our Ack gunners hasten to their posts,
> Their guns are somewhere on the way,
> They may arrive here any day. Why fret about the slight Delay?
> Unarmed our gunners will defy th' invading hosts.[12]

The exodus from Vizagapatam began soon after the Japanese attack on Malaya. By 1 January 1942, about 60 per cent of the population, mainly women and children, had left the port town. Reports of Japan's military successes in the East, talk of Vizagapatam being declared an emergency area and the arrival of refugees on steamers from Rangoon contributed to the panic. Many streets were deserted and streams of bullock carts left daily

---

* Masterman went on to become the Chief Secretary of the Madras Presidency and the United Kingdom's Deputy High Commissioner to India.

for the rural hinterland.[13] A practice air raid warning in this nervous town was enough to prompt 10,000 people (more than 10 per cent of the population at the time) to flee.[14]

The actual air attack in April led Vizagapatam to almost empty out. The railways were 'practically paralysed'. The port labour and the coolies engaged to build the new aerodrome fled. The few that remained in the town faced a severe food shortage. The police themselves were 'not completely untouched' by the panic; among those who could not be traced were members of the Special Emergency Force that guarded the harbour. In comparison, the exodus from Cocanada, raided only by a single plane, was much smaller.[15]

* * *

Before daybreak on 7 April, the morning after the Vizagapatam and Cocanada attacks, the undulating wail of a siren unsettled the air in Madras. One of the city's old reconnaissance planes had encountered some Japanese aircraft off the coast.[16] There is no detailed official record of what exactly happened. But it appears that one of Madras' ageing Atalantas—passenger planes that were fitted with a World War I vintage machine gun—spotted three Japanese planes on a recce. In Judge Wadsworth's account, this is what transpired:

> One of these planes used to patrol every evening and was popularly known as the 'Victory Bus'. It was the Victory Bus that gave us our first air raid warning. She was flying over the sea by moonlight when she ran up against three Japanese planes, which studied her intently for some time and then, apparently frightened by her four-engines and huge size, decided she was too dangerous to tackle and sheered off, which was a bit of luck for the crew and also for us.[17]

The story that the Victory Bus scared off the Japanese planes must have done the rounds in Madras. Margaret Hunt, a young lecturer who taught English at the Women's Christian College, knew the Atalanta by a different name but wrote a very similar account in a letter to her parents in England.

> There is a legend (story) that the very ancient bomber which has for months kept watch over Madras (she is called the Lazy Susan by some people, because she moves very slowly) met 3 Japanese planes 40 miles out at sea; & they were so alarmed at her size that they thought she must be some new 'secret weapon' & turned and fled.[18]

There is no agreement, however, on the type of aircraft that spotted the Japanese planes. In his memoirs, Gul Hassan Khan, who went on to become Commander-in-Chief of the Pakistan Army, said the recce was carried out by a Catalina.[19] But this is unlikely, given the multiple references to the age of the aircraft (Hope himself referred to it as one of the city's 'very ancient reconnaissance planes') and other descriptions of its size and the number of engines. Paul M. Jayarajan, a young civil servant at the time, thought it was a Woppitty (Wapiti) that spotted the Japanese planes. In his account, the Japanese aircraft were not fighters but transports taking reinforcements to Rangoon, which had fallen by then.[20] While this may explain why the Japanese planes avoided a skirmish, the balance of evidence suggests that the 'Victory Bus' or 'Lazy Susan' was an Atalanta.

When the air raid alarm sounded, Margaret Hunt and a dozen students, who had remained on campus to finish their exams, headed to the shelter room, where they sang and chattered cheerfully, until the all-clear was sounded an hour and a half later. The alarm, preceded as it was by the bombings of the two port towns, resulted in another rush of people out of Madras.

Three days later, in what was the last phase of a staggered exodus, the city would virtually empty itself out.

* * *

On 10 April, the Brigadier (General Staff) of the Southern Command in Bangalore called Governor Hope and General Telfer Smollett on secraphone (a scrambler-enabled telephone for secure communication). The Brigadier had just heard from General Headquarters in Delhi that ten Japanese divisions had left for southern India. Of these, a spearhead of two would land any day after 14 April (later altered to 15) at a place anywhere between the north of Madras city and the southern extremities of the Presidency's coastline.* The 'intelligence' was startling—India was on the verge of a massive Japanese invasion.

This led Hope to make two decisions. On Sunday, 12 April, his government issued a terse but opaque communiqué, saying that 'the danger threatening Madras is now more serious' and therefore advised all those 'whose presence in the city is not essential, to leave within the next few days'. There was no reference to what the danger was and no clarity about who was non-essential. Those who had no friends or relatives outside the city could opt to stay at any one of the camps established by the government close to nearby railway stations such as Chingelpet (Chengalpattu), Trivellore (Thiruvallur) and Gummudipundi (Gummidipoondi). It was announced that the courts—the Madras High Court, the Court of Small Causes and the city civil courts—would close for summer vacation. On the same day, Hope and General Telfer Smollett flew to Bangalore to confirm that what they had heard on the telephone was true. They were told it indeed was.†

---

* Hope to Linlithgow, 22 April 1942, Linlithgow Papers, MSS Eur F125/70, IOR. It appears that Hope's Chief Secretary S.V. Ramamurthy became aware of this intelligence only on 11 April (Fortnightly Report from Madras, first half of April 1942, Home Dept, NAI).

† Hope to Linlithgow, 22 April 1942, Linlithgow Papers, MSS Eur F125/70, IOR. 22 April 1942. Hope said that in Bangalore he was shown a Southern Command Operation Order that read: 'It is probable that the

The following day, Hope's government announced it was dispersing. Given the 'possible emergencies' and on the 'advice of military authorities', it would now work from different places in the Presidency's interior. The essential sections of the government's Secretariat moved to Madanapalle in present-day Andhra Pradesh (the non-essential part had already been transferred to Ootacamund). The office of the Inspector-General of Police headed out to nearby Vellore; the Board of Revenue to Salem; the Surgeon-General and the Director of Public Instruction to Anantapur; the Inspector-General of Prisons and the Director of Industries to Bellary; the Director of Agriculture, the Chief Conservator of Forests and the Registrar of Cooperative Societies to Coimbatore.[21] A couple of days later, it was announced that the office of the Accountant-General would shift to Bangalore.[22] Hope told Linlithgow that he stayed behind in Madras along with his advisers, a few bureaucrats and a skeleton staff. But Corporation Commissioner Pulla Reddi and ICS officer Jayarajan, both of whom also stayed put, had a very different story. Both claimed that Hope left Madras. According to Jayarajan, he left by a special train; in Reddi's account, he went to Vellore. However, if Hope really did leave Madras, he did not stay away for very long as he was in the city a few days later. Reddi went further, saying that Hope's First Adviser Sir George Boag left in a hurry by train for Ootacamund on 14 April.[23] Having stayed back, and fairly certain he would be arrested by the Japanese, Jayarajan made the most of the next few days. He enjoyed the best wines at the

---

Japanese would capture Ceylone (sic) in the immediate future.' It predicted that this attack would be supported by land-based bombers. The Japanese would attempt to establish aerodromes in southern India for this purpose and Madras had the best facilities for 'maintaining an air force ashore'. In short, Southern Command mistakenly believed that the Japanese wanted to invade Ceylon and that Madras would be used to support such a plan.

Madras Club, courtesy of the Raja of Chettinad who distributed the contents of his cellar to his friends. Together, they poured the surplus down the drain rather than allow the Japanese to enjoy the wines. If scorched earth is a strategy of denying anything of use to the enemy, then this was their roistering contribution.

The Madras port was closed and banks were asked to move out of the Fortress area. Many private companies moved out of adjoining Georgetown, including one of the oldest and most famous ones—Parry and Co. Ltd, which was founded by Welshman Thomas Parry in 1788. The accounts department shifted to Coimbatore, but others went no further than the expansive bungalows of their managers—sugar and spirits to Hodgson's, chemicals to Davis' and sales to Wilkinson's.[24] Prisoners in the city's penitentiary, one of the oldest jails in the country, were moved to the one in Alipuram, near Bellary in today's Karnataka. The Madras Corporation ordered that the dead should be cremated sufficiently early in the afternoon so that smouldering pyres were not visible from the air after dusk. The magnificent Ripon Building, where the Corporation was headquartered, wore a 'pall of grey' instead of the usual glistening white, which would have made 'a picture from the sea' and therefore an easy target for bombers.[25] Among the other 'threatened' buildings painted grey was Queen Mary's College, the first college for women in Madras, located opposite the city's Marina beach.*

In Madras, Hope's government took some steps to reduce the pain of departure. While maintaining normal railway services, special trains were announced to stations within 40 miles of the city at no cost to passengers. The six camps set up near these

* Anna Varki, who stayed on in the hostel after the college was shut, recalls that she and the other girls would scramble to jump into the slit trenches whenever the air raid alarm was sounded, sometimes in the dead of night. Anna Varki, *One Woman's India: From the Gandhian Era to the Cyber Age* (Chennai, Notion Press, 2018), Chapter 3, Kindle.

stations provided food, water and accommodation for a few days or until people made decisions to leave for places of their choosing. However, most people opted to leave for other towns as paying passengers and the camp facilities were availed only to an extent.[26] Banks were urged to stay open on the Tamil New Year holiday, Tuesday, 14 April, for people to cash cheques not exceeding Rs 1000 to 'meet necessary expenses' for leaving the city.

Explaining the reason for his government's sudden scattering, Hope told Linlithgow that the military was anxious to have everyone out of the way. They were particular about clearing Fort St George and the area around it, where the Secretariat and the Madras High Court functioned, before a landing. Moreover, Hope felt he could not risk the whole government being captured. 'Madras is right in the front line and to have the whole administration involved in possible street fighting was unthinkable.'[27] As for the panic, he claimed it was the result of 'an accumulation of events', starting with the 'timidity of the people' and ending with the government communiqué based on false military intelligence. It was this wrong information that was entirely responsible for the evacuation of his government and its advice that non-essentials should leave. 'I would like to hear of military enquiry if possible,' he wrote to Linlithgow. The Viceroy replied that Commander-in-Chief Wavell was said to have ordered an inquiry to 'ascertain facts' and 'fix responsibility'. But it is not clear what, if anything, came of this.

* * *

So how many people fled Madras? Pre-exodus, the city's population was around 8,00,000.* There was no overall official estimate of

---

* The 1941 census recorded a population of 7,77,481. *Census of India 1961*, Vol. IX, Madras, Part X-1.

how many people fled between December 1941 and April 1943. According to Chief Secretary Ramamurthy, 30 per cent of the population (2,40,000 people) left Madras by mid-February 1942. He also noted that in the seven tumultuous days between the air raid alarm and the end of 14 April, another 2,00,000 people fled.[28] (Interestingly, *The Hindu* reported that 3,00,000 left the city during the same period.)[29] Together, the two government estimates suggest there was an exodus of 4,40,000 people (or 55 per cent of the population).

This is, of course, a gross underestimate for at least three reasons. First, by the government's own admission, there was a constant stream of people moving to the interior between February and April. Second, it was probably in the government's interest to play down the number of people who left Madras. And finally, 55 per cent is much smaller than a raft of other assessments about how many who took flight.

According to the *Indian Express*, Madras' population was reduced to about 25 per cent.[30] This was exactly in line with the estimate of Rao Bahadur C. Tadulinga Mudaliar who said, just before becoming the city's Mayor, that a total of 75 per cent of the population had fled—a figure reaffirmed by another councillor.[31] C.R. Srinivasan, Editor of the venerable *Swadesamitran,* among the oldest vernacular newspapers in the country, estimated that five-sixths of the population (over 83 per cent) had left.[32] But even this was smaller than the number ICS officer Paul M. Jayarajan threw up. In his reckoning, 7 lakh (7,00,000) out of the city's population of 8,00,000 took flight—a staggering 87.5 per cent![33]

While this figure may seem incredible, it is far from implausible. Those mandated to stay under the Essential Services (Maintenance) Ordinance issued in late 1941 were people working in specific sectors such as water supply, sanitary services, oil companies, banks and bus services. The others, presumably the non-essentials, made up almost the entire population. Of course, in Madras, from where most of the government dispersed, it raised the obvious but ironic question—did the government regard itself as non-essential?

Moreover, the exodus had its own internal dynamic—the more people left, the more people had to go. The shortage of such things as labour and household help was one thing. But by April, the provision shops had shuttered, the restaurants were closed and there was an acute shortage of food—a situation that left people with no option but to depart. For instance, the family of Radha Padmanabhan (née Prabhu) made the decision to up and go when the milkman stopped coming. 'He probably fled like so many others. That was the day my father declared, "It's time to pack up".'[34] Departures were hasty and unplanned. 'Everyone was prepared to put up with any difficulty to reach a safe place,' observed the author Pudhumaipithan. 'Bullock carts carried children, the old, the sick, utensils, almost everything from one place to another.' Those who had motor vehicles overtook the rows of bullock carts 'like opportunists in politics'.[35]

Technically, the government's April communiqué only advised people to leave, allowing it to maintain the pretence that the evacuation was entirely 'voluntary'. But the sequence of messages about the threats seemed calculated to make people flee. A letter to the Editor of the *Mail* written by an 'Unwilling Voluntary Evacuee' described this aptly: 'This [April] communiqué is the culmination of a series of communiqués all of which, I have been noticing, have had the tendency to scare the people unnecessarily and make them run away.'[36] *Swadesamitran's* Editor Srinivasan accused 'a panicky government' of driving people out, including presidents of town protection councils (Oorkappu Sangams) who had pledged to remain in the city. Radha Krishnamurthy's account of her family's departure from Madras suggests some arms of the government went well beyond advising evacuation. As a twelve-year-old, she was in school when many parents, including her mother, rushed in before noon on a date she cannot exactly recall. 'There were policemen in cars screaming on the road, asking people to quit Madras and go to their native places. We packed in a hurry taking only clothes and valuables and took a train south from Egmore.' The family stayed in Lalgudi, where they rented a house for about five months before returning to Chennai.[37]

When Wadsworth came back from his relaxing break in Horsley Hills, Madras presented itself as a hollow shell, a 'dismal spectacle'. The shops were shut; almost all private homes and offices were vacant. 'The streets were empty and except for the police, the A.R.P. and the troops who were now arriving in considerable numbers, the place seemed dead.' By the time Wadsworth returned to work after the court vacations, Madras was 'bristling with guns'. The Marina—said to be the world's second-longest urban beach—sported a shoreline garlanded with barbed wire (presumably to retard an invasion via the sea) and a 'large dummy fort' (doubtlessly to scare Jap bombers). The Marina was also 'defended' with felled palm trees. Painted black, they were placed horizontally and vertically to fool Japanese pilots into thinking they were anti-aircraft guns.[38]

Did Hope panic too much? Should his government have all but abandoned Madras? He took responsibility for the decision, acknowledging it was a 'grave' one. But in his defence, he argued that the military was 'insistent' and that he could not have allowed the entire administration to run the risk of capture. Linlithgow was in total alignment: 'I need not say that in acting as you did, you acted perfectly correctly, and I support you entirely.'[39]

Of course, not everyone agreed. Rajagopalachari, for instance, squarely blamed Hope's administration and its muddled communiqués for creating the climate of panic. He censured Hope's adviser, T.G. Rutherford, for reportedly saying that 'even educated men who are in the know of things' are fleeing Madras like 'frightened kittens'. Rajagopalachari thought it was a somewhat 'tactless' remark to make following the British evacuation of Penang: 'Hasty use of bad language only invites a retort.'[40]

In early 1942, Rajagopalachari embarked on a long tour of the Madras Presidency, during which he urged people to remain calm and argued that the risk of invasion was small. At the same time, he advocated firmly resisting the Japanese, distancing himself from Gandhi. 'If we go on offering Satyagraha to everybody who comes to us, I don't know where it will end,' he told a meeting of Congressmen in Madras.[41] Although he recognized Indians were ill-equipped and ill-prepared, he saw strength in numbers. Addressing a crowd in Tiruvannamalai, he drew attention to the fact that India had 400 million people while Japan had less than 90 million. If the country rose as 'one man', the 'mere numerical strength is enough to give hell to the enemy'.[42]

Rajagopalachari's view that Hope's government should have risked a little danger to maintain its prestige was forcefully endorsed by the British-owned the *Mail*, which was consistent in demanding that civilians be armed to resist the Japanese and in opposing measures that encouraged people to flee. 'There is no salvation in flight, no protection in hiding places. The strong man armed keepeth his home, not he who flees in craven fear of he knows not what.'[43] On the government evacuating, it declared that not even the most expert assessor could 'accurately compute the real loss in time, efficiency and above all the prestige of this flight from the capital'.[44]

* * *

Madras was the worst affected, but it was not the only town in the Presidency consumed by The Great Flap. People fled from other coastal towns, from northern Vizagapatam to those all the way in the deep south such as the temple town of Rameswaram, where about half the population fled.[45] C.R. Srinivasan maintained that people also ran away from inland towns such as Trichy, Madurai and Dindigul in 'unreasoning fear'.[46] In fact, there was 'a pretty general panic' throughout South India, including the princely states of Hyderabad and Mysore.[47]

Hope wrote as if he was not altogether surprised that people in South India, whom he regarded as 'very jittery', were panicked. What clearly shocked and dismayed him was that Europeans gave way to 'sheer terror'. In certain cases, he wrote, Europeans 'have set a very bad example, which is deplorable'. He was flabbergasted that 'of all places white people were demanding to be evacuated from the remote and sheltered hill station of Ootacamund'.[48] But more than Ooty, it was at another hill station in the Presidency's interiors that things took a really strange and sorry turn.

In small and secluded Kodaikanal, founded by American missionaries in the mid-1800s, there was a sudden and somewhat bizarre exodus of the white population. On 14 and 15 April, some 300 'Europeans' fled, mainly Americans, many of whom were missionaries. Apart from the regular buses, special buses and private cars were used to hasten down the ghats to Kodaikanal Road, the access point in the plains for the hill station. Seats on buses from Kodaikanal were booked out for the next few days, suggesting that many more people, including Indians, got caught up in the scare.

It began with the families of certain leading government officials being hastily evacuated. It is not clear who the British officials were, but the question that obviously came up was why these families fled. Did they simply panic? Or were they privy to confidential information from official sources? The *Mail* was scathing, making no secret of its belief that members of Hope's government were responsible for precipitating the crisis. Officials should be barred from pursuing courses that cause panic, since their actions affect far more than their immediate circle, it declared.

> If they panic, or get the jitters, when things go awry, they are unworthy of holding office. And Britons especially are required to stand firm, however much they may be tempted to take the easy path of flight.[49]

The newspaper held that it is one thing to shift administrative offices from areas of special danger close to the coast. However, there was no wisdom in fleeing from inland towns such as Kodaikanal and Bangalore, which was also panic-affected.

As for the exodus of Americans and their families, it followed a telegram from the US Consul asking them to leave. It is not clear on what information the Consul—who was described by college lecturer Margaret Hunt as a 'somewhat shaken gentleman'—based his evacuation advisory. But it is possible that he went by reports that families of top British officials were evacuating.

Margaret Hunt had a taste of the terror in Kodaikanal. Asked to head out of Madras by her Principal, Hunt took the train to Kodaikanal Road on the evening of 14 April and then the bus to Kodaikanal on the following morning. Her diary records that on her way up, she met with 'bus after bus, car after car, of people and children coming down the ghat road'. She learnt from a conversation between three American men on the bus that all children from the American school in Kodaikanal were being evacuated. On arrival, she found the bus station swarming with departing people and their luggage. An Englishwoman she met expressed surprise that Hunt was arriving at such a time. A Japanese invasion is imminent, the woman said as she reeled off a list of names of those who had already fled Kodaikanal. Among them were the Collector, the head of police and some other English officials. It has been 'a disheartening & saddening business, seeing English officials and American missionaries lose their nerve & flee in terror from a fairly far-off & uncertain danger', Hunt wrote.[50]

The word 'prestige' was used a lot in connection with the Flap. Rajagopalachari thought the British should have tried to maintain it, a sentiment the *Mail* fully endorsed. Hunt felt the Kodaikanal scare meant a real loss of prestige for both the government and missionaries. In civil servant Jayarajan's view, 'The flap was a terrible blow to British prestige. The British were genuinely scared because it was well known that India could not be successfully defended.'

The magnitude of the Flap—its geographical spread, the extent of the dread and the numbers who fled—is not the only thing that has escaped attention. This was never a story about timorous Indians alone.* Everyone—whatever their race, nationality, class or caste—was caught up in The Great Flap. 'Somehow the British are not their best selves in India,' noted Margaret Hunt gloomily.[51]

* * *

The fact that there was so much panic over an invasion that never occurred, in truth not even planned, left some people in Madras bemused. This was aptly captured in a rhyme in a letter to the Editor of the *Mail*.

> M's for Madras where the scare grew and grew,
> But 'what it was all about' nobody knew.[52]

More than a year and a half later, Japan bombed Madras. On 11 October 1943, a lone reconnaissance plane dropped a few bombs in the harbour area. There were a few casualties, little damage and no evidence of panic. Madras took this well in its stride. There was nothing like a flap; at most, a very mild flutter.

---

* The iconic film star-turned-politician MGR is said to have stayed behind 'without any fear of death' while his mother, wife and family members were packed off to their native village, reinforcing the idea that his bravery was not just a cinematic construct but also a part of his life. M.S.S. Pandian, *The Image Trap: M.G. Ramachandran in Film and Politics* (New Delhi: Sage Publications India Pvt. Ltd, 2015), citing a popular biography in Tamil of MGR, Chapter 24.

12

Exodus, Elsewhere

Madras was the only large Indian city where an official advisory was issued asking people to leave. Calcutta, where a similar advisory was seriously contemplated, also witnessed a massive efflux. The former capital of India was a prime target for a number of reasons. It was close to South-East Asia, was an important industrial centre and housed a thriving major port. Also, in the event of a counter-offensive in Burma, it was bound to become a critical launch pad for Allied operations.

Japan's entry into the war triggered an immediate avalanche of rumours in Calcutta. Word was that Chittagong, Digboi and Madras had been bombed, the Andamans occupied, the Calcutta High Court shifted to Patna and government records transported to Murshidabad. There was 'no considerable movement' of people for a week or so. But from 13 December until the end of the month, about 4,00,000 more people left by train than they normally did during this period. This did not account for the people who streamed out via the roads. The fortnightly report to Home Secretary Conran-Smith described almost all of those who left as 'non-effectives', noting in seeming relief that production remained unaffected since there was no large-scale exodus of skilled labour.

Rather than make them feel secure, the official policy in Calcutta was intently focused on getting 'non-essentials' or 'non-effectives' to depart in an orderly way. In keeping with this plan, three railway companies operating in Calcutta came together to draw up a scheme to evacuate 1,00,000 people a day from Howrah and Sealdah stations. Between 13 December 1941 and 20 January 1942, almost 6,00,000 people left on trains operated by the East Indian Railway Company alone—about 3,50,000 more than would usually leave by this railway during this period.[1]

Such numbers were not sufficient in the eyes of Bengal's Governor John Arthur Herbert. Even though 7,00,000 people (or a third of Calcutta's population) had fled by March 1942, Herbert was looking to remove even more. The idea was to avoid the likely panic and disorder if people got caught up in a raid. Herbert noted, almost regretfully, that only 1,40,000 people could leave by road on a single day. 'If the numbers can quietly be reduced, the remainder will be more easily controlled, and less liable to panic.'[2]

Getting 'ineffectives' out of Calcutta ran the risk of losing some labour engaged in war production, Herbert admitted to Linlithgow. The important thing was to ensure that large numbers of panic-stricken ineffectives did not sweep a lot of essential labour out of the city.

> Our policy is quietly to encourage the departure of 'ineffectives': we have arranged for the transfer of certain non-essential departments of the Secretariat to Darjeeling and North Bengal; we have sanctioned separation allowances to officers in certain grades; and we are quietly advising firms to remove the less essential sections of their offices out of Calcutta.[3]

By mid-December 1941, there was talk that a state of emergency would be declared, which contributed considerably to the first wave of departures, again made up largely of women and children. Bengalis headed mainly eastwards by train to Assam and other places in Bengal such as Dacca, Chittagong and Khulna. Marwaris and other 'upcountry' people residing in Calcutta boarded trains to Delhi and beyond.

Calcutta was bombed only in December 1942, inexplicably late given its strategic importance. By then Vizagapatam and Cocanada in the south, Chittagong and Feni in Bengal, and Manipur and Assam in the North-east had already been raided. The air raids on Calcutta, which followed in quick succession after the first one on 20 December, triggered a second exodus, much less orderly than Herbert would have liked. Though he maintained that public morale was high, the Governor privately admitted that there was a 'considerable exodus from Calcutta'. He also acknowledged that labour was affected and had vanished from the dock area.[4]

The attempt by officialdom to claim that the bombings led to no evacuation and that life carried on as usual enraged the *Statesman*'s Ian Stephens. He had personally seen poor people leaving with their scanty belongings on foot soon after the first raid. 'Indian labour . . . is mobile. If it doesn't like its surroundings, it just rolls up its few possessions in a cloth-bundle and walks off.'[5]

From the very beginning, the *Statesman*—edited by the combative Arthur Moore, who would be succeeded by Stephens in August 1942—was very critical of how the administration, particularly at the Centre, handled issues relating to air raid publicity. But it was a press statement issued on the basis of a briefing by A.W. Ibbotson, Director-General of Civil Defence, that really set the *Statesman* off. Ibbotson, who had come to Calcutta to get a sense of the impact of the air raids, reportedly told his boss, Sir Jwala Prasad Srivastava, Member-in-Charge of Civil Defence in Linlithgow's Executive Council, that the Japanese have 'failed woefully to cause any panic'. Alluding to Ibbotson's briefing, Srivastava's press statement on 26 December read: 'There is no truth whatsoever in the reports that Calcutta is emptying out both by road and rail. Yesterday afternoon the people were going about their business as usual and the streets were full of crowds with no thought other than making the most of Christmas festivities.'[6]

Hundreds of thousands of people know this is 'bunkum', roared the *Statesman*, its ire seemingly directed more at Ibbotson for misleading Srivastava, who it held in high regard for his 'abilities' and 'common sense'. On the 'bungling' air raid publicity, it had this to say:

> When authority does not wish (as in war-time it sometimes rightly may not) that truth should be known, the wise policy is to keep silence. Lying as an instrument of policy is a Hitlerian invention, it is among the things that democratic humanity is struggling to smash, and in our judgment it in the long run must always defeat itself.[7]

Herbert wrote to Linlithgow dismissing Srivastava's claim that Calcutta was carrying on as normal. He told the Viceroy that the exodus 'extends' to the full limit of present railway capacity and that although the figures were unreliable, approximately 2,50,000 people may have left by road. He was surprised that very few of those who fled were Bengalis. In his view, a large number were '*atta*-eating', 'up-country' people (presumably Marwaris and other north Indians), who left because of the scarcity of wheat. 'I need not stress the impact of this on a large proportion of *atta*-eating munitions workers in Calcutta area,' he wrote, worrying about the possible effect on war production.[8]

The truth is that people were streaming out of Calcutta by every means of locomotion, including 'their own legs'. Eugenie Fraser was entertaining friends in Barrackpore, on the outskirts of Calcutta, when an air raid siren followed by the thud of bombs forced them into an air raid shelter. The following morning, she went to the city to see what damage the bombing had done. En route, she witnessed a 'great exodus':

> Men, women and children, cars and lorries of all descriptions, donkeys, goats tethered to carts, parrots in cages on top of lorries, one

> solid mass of humanity were moving along the trunk road, all terrified out of their wits trying to reach a place of safety anywhere away from Calcutta.[9]

Later, there was a grudging official acceptance that the number of evacuees over those few days in late December amounted to 3,50,000.[10]

* * *

Madras and Calcutta were not the only towns that saw government departments move to other places. Cuttack, the capital of Orissa, was moved inward to Sambalpur. Orissa's Governor Hawthorne Lewis was anxious that his province—originally split from Bengal (1912) and later separated from Bihar (1936)—was extremely vulnerable in the event of an attack.

Lewis believed that Orissa was especially exposed given its geography and lack of military preparedness. Three coastal districts—Cuttack, Balasore and Puri—were made up of a narrow strip of plains that lay between the sea on one side and forested mountains on the other. The deltaic nature of the coast presented another complication when it came to defence. Lewis kept reminding Linlithgow that his province—sandwiched between the powerful Madras and Bengal presidencies—suffered from a total lack of military preparedness. Orissa, the Governor complained, is 'the only Province where no troops are stationed and where no representative of the army command is present . . . There is no direct contact between Orissa and the military authority.' All it would take was three hours for a 'small landing party', either at Puri or Cuttack, to force the provincial government into surrender 'without even the slightest show of resistance'.[11]

What worried Lewis and the provincial administration was the location of Cuttack, virtually an island between the two arms of the mighty Mahanadi River and its tributaries. The only ways out were the railway bridges to the south of the town, the ferry from the northern tip and the easterly road towards the aerodrome, an hour away. Evacuating Cuttack at short notice was difficult because of this. Linlithgow heard Lewis out. But the Viceroy said that Orissa could not be protected given the overall military position and that he was unwilling to 'squander troops in erecting a mere façade which would crumble if the Japanese landed'.[12]

Towards the end of February 1942, Lewis suggested there were two ways to address the situation. First, issue a warning asking women and children to leave the coastal towns. Second, start making plans to move the government to Sambalpur.

By March, the province was gripped by unease. The abandonment and fall of Rangoon had a 'profound effect' and 'created great alarm'. There was a familiar pattern to the flight from Cuttack. As in other places, the non-local trading communities, in this case, Marwaris and Kutchis, started sending their families away as they prepared to wind down their businesses. In coastal towns, women and children were sent to the interior, the departures quickening when advances were paid to government employees to move their families from the so-called threatened areas. The arrival of military personnel in places that had never seen them before and decision to shift some government records contributed to the exodus.[13] In the midst of this, Lewis, who was mulling over a possible evacuation of Cuttack, dispatched his Chief Secretary, J. Bowstead, to compare notes on the subject with his counterpart in Bengal, where a scheme for abandoning Calcutta had already been prepared.[14]

On 31 March, the Orissa government issued a communiqué advising people in the coastal districts who had no work or business to move further away from the coastline. It announced that the provincial capital would move to Sambalpur if it became impossible to carry on in Cuttack. Preliminary arrangements have already been set in motion, it said.[15] The communiqué was issued barely a week before Lewis received a message from Calcutta about the Japanese sinking a freighter off the coast of Puri. Over the next couple of days, there were sightings of the Japanese fleet as survivors from destroyed merchant ships washed up on the shoreline.

Lewis moved the bulk of office personnel and almost all the records to Sambalpur on 12 April. By then, he admitted the scare in Cuttack was much bigger than he had estimated. 'The pressure of people getting away by train has been maintained and many others continue to leave by road. Middle class families are finding it difficult to keep servants.'[16] Lewis remained in Cuttack with some secretaries and heads of departments who functioned from small camp offices. On the day the establishment and records were shifted, he wrote to Linlithgow: 'Need I add that Sambalpur has renewed hopes of becoming the new capital of Orissa.'[17]

By mid-April, the Japanese threat had receded. Even so, much further south, in the princely state of Cochin, the 'war situation' led the government to move the Secretariat to Trichur, leaving behind a small staff to deal with urgent papers. It was decided that other offices such as that of the Advocate-General, war publicity, the census, income tax and excise would also move. The government high school for boys in Trichur was commandeered for the Secretariat and the girls' school for other offices. The communiqué announcing this shift added that the issue of transferring the treasury and the bank was under examination.[18]

It is not clear how many people fled Cochin, but anecdotally, it emptied out. As a young boy, journalist K.M. Roy left with his grandparents, mother, brother and their hens and chicks on a *kettuvalam* (houseboat) for the village of Pampakuda. His father, who stayed back, being part of the emergency services, spoke of a deserted Cochin, a place where there was hardly anybody left and where even the thieves had fled.[19]

* * *

The colonial administration's attitude to the exodus was pretty much the same all over the country. It underplayed the extent of the panic and understated the numbers that fled. At the same time, it inexcusably encouraged, tacitly or otherwise, those who were 'non-essential'—a euphemism for those not useful for the war effort—to leave areas regarded as threatened. To those in power, exodus presented itself as a challenge and an opportunity. The challenge was to see that war production was unaffected and sufficient labour remained in towns to ensure that commercial interests and emergency services were not compromised. The opportunity lay in finding a way to get non-essentials to leave in a staggered and orderly fashion; it was administratively more convenient to manage fewer people in the event of a raid or an invasion.

Linlithgow, who was in Calcutta in December 1941 when the first wave of people left, summed up the official approach to exodus in this somewhat unfeeling way.

> I think that it is not a bad thing that there should be this exodus . . . one hopes [it does] a little to reduce possible panic if and when bombs are actually dropped. Apart from that it may result in a good many useless mouths whose presence in Calcutta is not really necessary making away. But of course . . . Calcutta is one of our biggest war supply production centres and the interference with supply which any large exodus of workers might mean would be of real significance.[20]

Bombay lay on the so-called less-threatened western seaboard. But Governor Roger Lumley grappled with this very dilemma—of how to get non-essentials to leave and those of value to stay—well before the Japanese scare infected the city. Lumley worried that the island city was particularly vulnerable as it could easily be choked off by blocking its limited access points. The one and a half million residents could quickly be starved of food and water if the Japanese destroyed or took control of two bridges. Given this, there was a case for encouraging non-effectives to leave before a military threat emerged. But this, Lumley feared, would risk 'effectives' leaving as well. 'This is our problem: it needs further study,' he noted ponderously.[21]

The fall of Singapore in mid-February triggered a small movement out of Bombay. The railways estimated that there was an increase in outward traffic of about 800 people a day. Gujarati Banias and Marwaris, the trading communities, made up the early departures; like elsewhere, women and children started being sent away. Lumley decided it was best 'to let the small drift away continue without giving it any encouragement'.

By the middle of March, about 20 per cent of the workers in Bombay's iconic cotton mills had left, their departure leading others to follow suit. Lumley thought it was difficult to accurately estimate how many people had fled but thought it could have been anything between 1,00,000 and 1,50,000, roughly one-twelfth of the population. For a city that was far removed from military threat, this was a significant number.

Eventually, Lumley didn't go ahead with issuing a communiqué asking non-effectives to leave. Neither did Bengal's Governor Herbert after military authorities there advised him against such a course of action. The one his government had prepared was considered too drastic in tone and risked having the same impact as an air raid. Herbert didn't agree with their assessment but dropped the idea anyway.

People kept trickling out through March, but there was a rush of people from Bombay starting 9 April, around the time the war seemed to be closing in on India. By mid-April, an estimated 4,00,000 people—around 25 per cent of the population—had fled to the interior. Given Bombay's cosmopolitan character, they went pretty much everywhere—to Gujarat, the Central and United Provinces, to Poona and other parts of Maharashtra, and to the interior districts of the Madras Presidency.[22] The *Times of India* noted a marked change in the city's social life.

> Tenement houses are becoming vacant on an increasing scale and certain once-crowded localities have almost become deserted. Attendance of children in schools has fallen to such an extent that many schools in the city and suburbs have ceased to function properly. In several schools teachers have been told their services were no longer required . . . The breaking up of hundreds of homes has increased the demand for food in hotels and restaurants, but the latter are experiencing difficulty owing to a dearth of servants. Some eating houses have already closed down; others are just carrying on.[23]

* * *

Quite bizarrely, even landlocked Delhi, which was considered safe and too far away to be raided, witnessed a controversy over an evacuation advisory. The Chief Commissioner of Delhi, the head of the provincial administration, allegedly wrote to the President of the Delhi Municipal Committee in mid-April, saying that non-essential people should leave as soon as the city comes 'within effective bombing range of the Enemy'. These included all those not employed in essential services, engaged in civil defence or the production of war equipment. Once such a stage was reached, the provincial government should tell people that a reduction in the population was in the public interest given the 'inevitable confusion and dislocation which would attend a raid'. The letter estimated that at least 20 per cent of Delhi's non-essential inhabitants would leave on the basis of such advice.[24]

There was a provisional nature to the letter but since it found its way into the press, it appeared like a communiqué. Bengal's Governor Herbert, who had decided against issuing a press statement advising evacuation, was astonished to see 'a similar communiqué' issued by Delhi's Chief Commissioner. 'If it is a fact that the evacuation of Delhi is being seriously considered, one has to ask where this process is going to end,' he wrote to Linlithgow.[25] While Herbert was usually not in agreement with

Editor Arthur Moore, he thought the *Statesman*'s rebuke of Delhi's Chief Commissioner was fully justified. The British-owned newspaper, in keeping with its strong opposition to what it saw as the administration's bungling evacuation policy, was savage:

> If Delhi is getting ready for bombing, and its civil population is to be urged to flee, where is it to flee to? What about all the large cities nearer the coast? Where are their citizens to go? Is the Government of India arranging to withdraw to Tibet? Or are we at last about to scale the Pamirs and reach the roof of the world? And are there no guts left somewhere? We appeal to GENERAL WAVELL to sack whoever may be responsible before lunch tomorrow, and stop this rot. Strictly speaking the culprit should be hanged.[26]

A few days later, there was a muddled clarification that the provincial administration's letter was written in connection with some proposals made by the Delhi Municipal Committee. And that in discussions with the Committee, the Chief Commissioner of Delhi had said those wishing to leave if Delhi came within bombing range should not be obstructed from doing so. 'This does not mean that that stage has been reached in Delhi, where indeed the danger of air raids is still happily remote.'[27] As for Linlithgow, he blamed the municipality for the 'ill-advised experiment' and described the *Statesman*'s comments as 'characteristically irresponsible'.[28]

But even 'happily remote' Delhi witnessed what Chief Commissioner Arthur Vivian Askwith described as an 'exodus'. While he thought the numbers of people who fled were exaggerated in 'popular reports', Askwith said the exodus was mainly made up of poor people who had come to Delhi seeking work and decided 'that safety at home is to be preferred to good wages abroad'. Some wealthy people also fled, but this had less to do with air raids than the fear of 'civil commotion' in the event of an invasion.[29]

In Jamshedpur, the small proprietary town of the Tata Iron and Steel Company (TISCO) in Bihar, about 40,000 people—mainly women, children and unemployed relatives—fled by January 1942 fearing air raids. Their fear was arguably not entirely unfounded as Jamshedpur was a potential Japanese target for an air attack. The Tata-owned company was the largest steel-producing unit in the British Empire. And its special alloy steels were critical for the war effort. S. Modak, who joined TISCO's accounts department in 1918, recalls that steps were taken by the British to protect the steel plant from bombing even before Japan entered the war. Apart from rows of trenches, 'brick ovens were made to burn coal tar to cover the plant and town with smokescreen' and barrage balloons* 'filled with gas' were deployed to 'pull down' attacking aircraft.[30]

Ironically, Linlithgow had addressed the workers at the plant a couple of weeks before the exodus from Jamshedpur began. 'The present safety of India is in your hands,' the Viceroy had told them. 'It is your strength that drives the soldier's sword-arm forward carrying destruction to our enemies.'[31]

By the end of March, there was some disquiet and unrest among the workers at the Tata plant. There were suggestions that the Tatas themselves were fine with the company closing down as this could save the plant from being the target of a possible air raid. Bihar's Governor Thomas Alexander Stewart dismissed this notion as ridiculous. All the same, he dispatched his Chief Information Officer to Jamshedpur to get a 'slant' on the situation.[32] Speaking to workers on the radio, Jehangir Jivaji Ghandy, TISCO's first Indian General Manager, dismissed the prevailing rumours that the anti-aircraft guns unloaded at the plant would either be used on them or deployed to blow

* Tethered barrage balloons were used to protect ground targets. Approaching aircraft risked colliding with them.

up the plant in the event of an emergency. Acknowledging the alarm that the arrival of gunners had triggered in the minds of workers, he assured them that military personnel would be well behaved and neither molest their women nor interfere with their property. 'Get the facts. Trust the Management . . .' he urged.[33] Elsewhere in Bihar, there was an efflux of workers from the coalfields of Jharia, with as much as 40 per cent of the labour fleeing some collieries. One owner was moved to offer a 50 per cent wage increase to induce workers to remain.[34]

There were other places in the interior that had the shivers. We may deduce, for instance, that a sizeable number of people fled Ahmedabad given an official communication that said the exodus from the city had 'further decreased'.[35] Much further to the east lay Assam, which emerged as a strategic buffer zone after the Japanese conquest of Burma. At the same time, the province was a potential economic target, a source of oil and coal, not to mention the tea estates that contributed to many a British cuppa. There were many European families that lived in Assam's extensive tea gardens. The military recommended an evacuation, mainly of European women and children. Assam's Governor Andrew Clow resisted the proposal on the grounds that an open evacuation of Europeans would lead to a general exodus on a large scale.[36] However, in the event of an invasion, he believed those who would be of value to the enemy should be evacuated first. In his view, these 'valuable people' fell into three categories—(all) Europeans, technical staff and supervisory staff. After this, the evacuation of as many 'superfluous mouths' as possible could be taken up.

The three May 1942 bombings—two in Imphal and the third in a tea estate near Silchar—reverberated all over the province. It wasn't just bomb-scarred Imphal that suffered an exodus. Clow reported that Gauhati lost 75 per cent of its civil population. There was a big exodus from Silchar as the people in the town believed, and not unreasonably, that the air raid on Derby Tea Estate was intended for them. In Shillong, Assam's capital at the time, Clow recorded that 40 per cent of the civil population fled.[37]

* * *

One of the many myths about The Great Flap is that it was brief and, therefore, somewhat painless. The Japanese threat of invasion emerged in December 1941 and more or less vanished, despite official fears of recurrence, by mid-April the following year. But to regard this as a brief and troubled interregnum before order was restored and life returned to normal is to underplay what really happened.

In Bengal and the north-eastern areas, the bombing-induced panic continued into 1943 (Calcutta witnessed its most savage air attack in December that year). But even in Madras, where Hope's government dispersed in mid-April only to announce on 23 April that the essential part of the Secretariat and most other offices would return to the city, the disruption was huge. (The offices needed some time to come back, inviting the snark that while evacuation took but a day or two, the return consumed almost a whole month.)[38]

The majority of those who fled Madras left in the first two waves of the exodus—in December 1941 and February 1942—and so were away for at least a few months. Not everyone returned to the city the moment the crisis blew over. The family of Radha Padmanabhan spent almost a year in Coimbatore before returning to Madras. Like others who returned, they came back to find their home completely stripped. Only the bare walls remained of their home on Brodie's Road; thieves had made off with everything including doors, windows and utensils. The watchman they had hired to keep an eye on the home had fled. 'The house was a bare shell. Anything made of metal—down to nails—was removed.'[39]

As for the family of Radha Krishnamurthy (no relation to the former), they spent almost six months in Lalgudi before returning. She recalls that a number of people who headed to the south along with them never came back. The family returned to a Madras with many empty houses. Landlords were ready to rent for a song, and so their old home was given up in favour of a large and spacious house.

The exodus from Burma has come to be known, thanks to Hugh Tinker's evocative phrase, as the 'forgotten long march'. The exodus during The Great Flap has similarly slipped from our memories. Given the number of Indians who fled Burma, Tinker supposed that at least some among them—'teachers, writers, social workers, perhaps'—would have recorded their memories. As we know, few such personal accounts exist. The same is true about the Flap. There are hardly any detailed Indian accounts about the atmosphere of panic, their flight, their time away as 'refugees' and their return. The story has fallen by the wayside largely because of the long-standing failure of Indians to record events and experiences for posterity.*

For the British, exodus did not present itself as a humanitarian problem—one of abandoned homes, separated families and lost livelihoods. They dealt with it as if it were a managerial issue, of finding ways to encourage people they didn't need to leave, while ensuring that those they required remain. Linlithgow spelt out the government's approach plainly and coldly to Assam's Clow: 'The policy is that . . . in threatened areas "useless mouths" should be encouraged to go before an attack takes place . . .'[40]

---

* I suspect that it was the challenge of retrieving unrecorded personal memories that led Raghu Karnad to deploy what he calls 'forensic non-fiction' to reconstruct the lives of three male relatives that served during the war in his clever and absorbing book, *The Farthest Field: An Indian Story of the Second World War* (New Delhi: Fourth Estate, 2015).

Since the Japanese never intended to invade India in 1942, was The Great Flap much ado about nothing? Should the mere threat of an imagined invasion have impacted India so much? Should the administration have gotten so alarmed? Should there have been a countrywide panic? Could the succession of exoduses have been avoided? How much did the Japanese threat change political attitudes and influence the national movement in 1942?

Such questions hang enigmatically over The Great Flap—a story about how something that never happened triggered a number of events that never should have.

Epilogue: Zoo Story

On 14 April 1942, a team of the Malabar Special Police (MSP) suddenly turned up at the Madras Zoo.* The orders were clear: shoot all the 'dangerous' animals dead. Used as a paramilitary force for large operations—for example, to crush the Moplah rebellion in 1921 and put down the Nizam's private militia (the Razakars) in 1947—this was an easy but most unusual assignment. The MSP carried it out with customary efficiency. Itemized animals such as lions, tigers, panthers, bears and venomous snakes were located and shot dead. All it took was a few blood-splattered minutes.

The kill order was carried out to avert the risk of dangerous animals breaking free and preying on Madras residents in the event of Japanese bombs destroying the zoo and its enclosures. It was issued on the day that Madras was in chaos. Almost all the government offices were in the process of shifting to other places in the interior, a decision that triggered widespread panic and a big exodus.

The murders at the Madras Zoo almost invariably earn a line or two in historical accounts of this period.[1] It's not hard to see why. At one level, it is irresistible as a story of tragic futility. On another, it is a compelling illustration of the extent of the prevailing panic on the eve of a Japanese assault that never occurred. 'Everybody seemed to have lost his head,' wrote Corporation Commissioner

* A version of this epilogue titled 'Murder in the Madras Zoo' appeared in *Open* magazine in their 2022 special new year issue.

O. Pulla Reddi in barely concealed frustration in a passage that suggested his British superiors had taken leave of their senses.[2]

Nine lions, eight tigers, eight leopards, four bears, a hyena and a number of snakes were killed.[3] The idea these 'dangerous' zoo animals could be turned perilously loose on the citizenry seems ludicrous now. But it was a very real fear in those times, not only in Madras but in other war-struck European cities as well. As with the evacuation itself, accounts of the killing at Madras Zoo are written up sometimes as if it was a bizarre idea conceived in alarmist haste by Arthur Hope and his advisers. One that was born in a panicked city headed by a terrified Governor. As we shall see, it was much more than that. There were precedents, striking parallels in other European cities, only considerably grislier. Bombs, zoos and animals: they were very much a part of public deliberation during World War II.

* * *

The impact of an air attack on animals, including those in zoos, played out in other places as well. In Britain, animals were among the first casualties of World War II. The mass slaughter happened before the bombings began and, quite incredibly, these casualties were household pets, mainly cats and dogs. In London alone, a staggering 4,00,000 to 7,50,000 cats and dogs are estimated to have been killed in the first week of the war in early September 1939.[4] Some were euthanized, some shot and others handed over to be killed by gassing. People queued before animal shelters and 'animal welfare charities' with exemplary British patience to have their pets put to sleep. In one shelter in North London, the queue was half a mile long. The wholesale slaughter was fuelled by fears and rumours that mass bombings would follow the outbreak of war. People convinced themselves that there was no choice but to put down their pets. In thousands of homes, 'weeping children, sobbing mothers, stern fathers [were] saying it was the only thing to do. That it was the kindest thing to do.'[5]

The British government, which worried about food shortages and splitting rations with pets, did its bit to advance the Great Pet Massacre. Place your pets with people in the countryside, urged the Ministry of Home Security, in apparent concern. But the announcement came with a dark rider. If you cannot, then 'the kindest thing is to have them destroyed'. After a week, the frenzy of killing died out and people began to question themselves. 'Pet lovers blinked. What have we done? The sky had not darkened with bombers . . . Where now were the faithful Bonzo and little Oo-Oo? Reduced to fertilizer in Sugar House Lane or interred in some cold field in Ilford.'[6]

Given the scale of this extermination at home, it is hardly surprising that zoo animals were also not spared. The London Zoo, founded in 1828 in Regent's Park, was closed on the day war was declared on 3 September 1939. But it had already, an entire year earlier, prepared a blueprint of what to do in the event of war. The precautionary measures drawn up included the immediate killing of all venomous snakes and spiders. Valuable animals would be shifted to the zoo at Whipsnade, north-west of London, and the stock of others gradually reduced.[7]

The zoo's Overseer MacDonald and Keeper Austin got down to brush up their knowledge of the working of a .303 Lee-Enfield rifle to stop the animals dead in their tracks in the event of a breakout. When war seemed inevitable, with news of the German invasion of Poland (1 September), the zoo implemented the plan. The first thing Zoo Director Julian Huxley did was to kill the venomous snakes, which he did regretfully as some of them were so rare and beautiful. The fate of the other snakes, including pythons and anacondas, would be sealed when Britain formally declared war two days later. A black widow spider was beheaded. Saltwater fish were killed, while freshwater species were released in a pond. Later, others would join the death list such as crocodiles from the Nile, alligators from America and two lion cubs.

Pandas, elephants, orangutans, chimpanzees and an ostrich were transferred to Whipsnade for their safety. Here, a young African bull elephant, Jumbo II, was shot dead to make room for the ones dispatched from Regent's Park. The *Daily Telegraph* described the killing rather woodenly as a result of 'housing difficulties'. At the zoo in Southend, all the lions were exterminated. In time, the remaining animals were disposed of and the zoo shut down.

Some of Rangoon's zoo animals met a similar fate. As the Japanese advanced on the city in early 1942, a British civil servant, Leslie Glass, was tasked with snuffing them out. 'One afternoon, I joined in a bizarre and melancholy foray to shoot all dangerous animals in the zoo, as all their keepers had decamped. Tigers, panthers and poisonous snakes were killed and the deer released in the park, except for one which we shot for fresh meat. When we had gutted the poor beast, we threw its entrails into the lake and great fish thrashed and swirled in the course of their unusual meal.'[8]

In distant Australia, ARP measures resulted in the shooting of three lions, a leopard and a tiger that belonged to a circus in Sydney. It appears that the circus owner was unable to move the animals, valued at 500 pounds, further inland because of petrol restrictions.[9]

* * *

Killing zoo animals was not a peculiarly British predilection. Within the first week of the German invasion of Poland, the Warsaw Zoological Garden was bombed. One bomb destroyed the moats and barriers of the polar bear enclosure. A Polish platoon discovered the freed animals, bloodied and circling their old haunt. They were swiftly shot. Afraid that lions, tigers and other dangerous animals might escape, the soldiers went on to kill the more aggressive ones. Some were slaughtered for meat and others were put down with bullets.[10]

The worst came a couple of weeks later, on 25 September or 'Bloody Monday', two days before the city fell into Nazi hands. The Luftwaffe flew about 1150 sorties, dropping unimaginably large quantities of high explosives and incendiary bombs, turning Warsaw into a seething furnace. The zoo was devastated. 'Glass and metal shards mutilated skin, feathers, hooves, and scales indiscriminately as wounded zebras ran, ribboned with blood, terrified howler monkeys and orangutans dashed caterwauling into the trees and bushes, snakes slithered loose, and crocodiles pushed onto their toes and trotted at speed.' As 'parrots spiraled upwards like Aztec Gods and then plummeted straight down', two giraffes lay dead on the ground, their legs twisted, while other animals in cages were 'engulfed in rolling waves of flame'.*

As people watched from their windows, seals slipped into the Vistula River. Camels, llamas, ostriches, wolves, foxes and anteaters wandered around aimlessly or looked for places to hide. The zoo favourite, the infant Tuzinka, the first elephant born in Poland, survived and was carted off to the Reich.[11] Her father, however, did not escape. He was one of the animals shot by Polish Army men during the first wave of the air attacks some three weeks earlier.

Two years later, in September 1941, the Berlin Zoo was struck by British bombers, setting fire to the cattle stables and damaging the surroundings. Earlier, the Nazi authorities had drawn up

* Diana Ackerman, *The Zookeeper's Wife: A True Story of an Unlikely Heroine* (London: Headline Publishing Group, 2007). An account of how zookeeper Jon Zabinski and his wife Antonia sheltered persecuted Jews within the zoo.

'nebulous plans' to evacuate the animals. But they were not followed through.[12] The real damage to the zoo occurred a couple of years later, when on 22 and 23 November 1943, the RAF conducted a massive air raid on the western part of Berlin. Other raids followed soon after and there was 'not a single habitable house' in the streets surrounding the zoo. A number of animals had been temporarily removed from Berlin to other zoos in places such as Frankfurt, Halle and Cologne. But the remaining ones didn't escape the blitz.[13]

In fifteen minutes on the evening of 22 November, 30 per cent of the zoo's animals were killed. Four crocodiles were found dead on the street, possibly flung out as a result of the explosions. 'Some of the larger and potentially dangerous animals, such as jaguars, panthers, or gorillas that managed to escape their bombed out and burning enclosures were chased down the street and shot dead.' There were wild rumours about stampeding elephants among the rubble and tigers mauling everyone they came across. But almost all the animals that escaped their enclosures were killed within the zoo. Among those that broke free were a dingo that was recaptured, some monkeys and a few birds.[14]

Ursula Gebel, who lived nearby, was at the zoo's elephant enclosure, watching six females and a juvenile doing tricks with the keeper.

> That same night, all seven were burnt alive. The entire zoo was destroyed by bombing. The hippopotamus bull survived in his basin [but] all the bears, polar bears, camels, ostriches, birds of prey and other birds were burnt. Every enclosure, except the animal hospital, was destroyed. The tanks in the aquarium all ran dry, the crocodiles escaped, but like the snakes they froze in the cold November air.[15]

Many other animals died, including a black rhino, a sea elephant, two hippos, a couple of giraffes and about half the antelopes and deer. A lot of them found their way to the dining table. Crocodile tails were all the rage; bear ham and sausage became delicacies;

and deer, antelope and buffalo provided hundreds of meals. 'We had meat coming out of our ears,' recalled Lutz Heck, who grew up in the Berlin Zoo, and succeeded his father as Director.[16]

In the elephant enclosure that Ursula Gebel visited, only one animal survived. It was the bull Siam. His entire harem had been annihilated.

* * *

But back to Madras. Its zoo was the country's oldest, founded in 1855, less than three decades after the London Zoo and just eleven years after the one in Berlin. The Madras Zoo came to life with a gift. The Director of the recently founded Madras Museum, Edward Green Balfour, persuaded the Nawab of Arcot to donate his private menagerie. Balfour became convinced about the need for a zoo on discovering that the number of visitors to the museum rose sharply after a tiger cub and a leopard were kept on display as an experiment in the gardens.

The zoo was temporarily housed in the gardens of the museum complex at Egmore. It moved to the sprawling People's Park in 1863, an expansive and ambitious recreational facility, conceived by Sir Charles Trevelyan and opened to the public after his dismissal as Governor in 1860. The Park spanned 112 acres and housed twelve lakes and a boating facility. Over the years, the area slowly gave way to a cluster of development. All that remains now is My Ladye's Garden, a tiny splash of green surrounded by a rash of unprepossessing buildings.

The zoo was shifted to the outskirts of the city in 1979. But at the time it was centrally located and could well have been hit during an aerial assault. The red-bricked, arcaded Madras Railway Station, with its imposing central clock tower, lay just across the narrow Cooum River. And Ripon Building, the seat of the Madras Corporation, full of Greek pretensions and shining in Ionic white, lay just in front of it. There was reason to believe the zoo was located in a place that would be targeted by the Japanese. Also, that it would be very vulnerable if Japanese bombers repeated the kind of destruction they wreaked on Rangoon or Singapore.

Worries about bombs creating the conditions for zoo animals to break free existed from the beginning of 1942, more than three months before the evacuation order. Some of these animals were regarded as dangerous and others as valuable. Since the beginning of the year, Commissioner O. Pulla Reddi had been trying to have both these categories of zoo animals shifted to other 'safer' towns. Letters were sent to places as far-flung as Mysore, Hyderabad, Bhopal and Calcutta requesting these animals be accommodated. But the municipalities and zoos in these towns stalled him, either failing to reply to his letters or saying—in the time-honoured bureaucratic tradition—that his request was under consideration.*

By the first week of April, it was more or less definite that other zoos would not receive the animals. By then, the panic had grown considerably and most people had fled Madras. Having drawn a blank outside the Presidency, Reddi looked within. He packed off the zoo superintendent to Erode, about 400 km away, where he had heard the animals could be housed.[17]

Indeed, they could. But there was a problem. The railways could not make the wagons available for immediate transport to Erode. Reddi recorded that this was for 'obvious reasons' without spelling out what they were. It is likely that by then the railways were too caught up with transporting people fleeing the city to bother with making special arrangements for animals. With no solution in sight, the 'dangerous' animals remained where they were.

---

* The issue of shifting dangerous animals also cropped up in Alipore Zoo in Calcutta. The decision affected those animals classified either as 'carnivorous' or 'poisonous'. The bigger carnivores were shifted to other zoos in the province. Venomous reptiles were killed, but it was reported that a similar group of ferocious animals (crocodiles?) were also destroyed. 'Precautions in the Zoo', the *Statesman*, 8 April 1942, p. 3.

In April, the events that seemed to portend an imminent attack followed thick and fast: the bombings of Colombo, Trincomalee, Vizagapatam and Cocanada; Ozawa's ship-sinking spree in the Bay of Bengal; the spotting of Japanese planes off the Madras coast; the false intelligence that a Japanese fleet would make landfall; and the decision to evacuate the government. As the government dispersed, Reddi went to the Secretariat on 14 April on municipal work, where he was shown a note by one of Governor Hope's advisers. The instruction was to destroy all the dangerous animals in the zoo immediately. 'I returned to the office, thought over the matter and considerably regretted I had to make a decision of that kind,' he said. In retrospect, he admitted that the 'danger that was then apprehended blew off'. But what if it were otherwise, he asked? 'If an emergency had happened and the wild animals had got loose and the reptiles had got into our trenches, then the people would have demanded my head on a charger.'[18]

Reddi's reluctance to order the killings shines through his comments; he seemed to think it was both heartless and unnecessary. But the good bureaucrat that he was, he defended his decision before the Corporation's councillors. He had no choice but to obey the order, he declared, something that Mayor Chakkarai Chetty concurred with. At the same time, and somewhat contradictorily, Reddi took responsibility for what he did, saying he acted on his discretion and in the interest of the city.

In his autobiography, written well after he retired, Reddi was more candid and much more critical about the way the British handled the evacuation as well as the shooting of animals. On 14 April, he recalled that judges ran helter-skelter and the Secretariat had begun moving en masse to Ooty, hill station and summer capital.[19] He said he was told by Sir George Boag, Governor Hope's First Adviser, that only two senior officers were to remain behind—Police Commissioner Lionel Gasson and Reddi himself. Reddi asked Boag what he should do in the event the Japanese landed the next morning. Sir George replied: 'I have no time to discuss details with you. I have to catch the Blue Mountain Express in a few minutes. You can do what you like.' Then, Sir George proceeded to hop on the train.*

When Police Commissioner Gasson called about the arrangements to shoot the dangerous animals, Reddi cautioned him against it, saying he had a hunch the Japanese would never land. He said it was 'too hasty and premature' and that they could wait. But Gasson chose to call in the Malabar Special Police right away. Reddi recalled to his 'great horror, they ruthlessly did the job in a few minutes'.

The Madras Corporation set the value of the animals shot at Rs 4538, though it is not clear how this number was arrived at. Elephants, giraffes, baboons, ostriches, emus, deer and birds were saved from the carnage. The plan to shift these 'non-dangerous' counterparts to Erode remained in place after the shooting, but railway wagons continued to be an issue. Eventually, they were sent to Erode in May; by this time, the threat had already blown over.

At the Council, there was a small exchange that reflected the politics of the times. Having listened to his defence for having the animals shot, Councillor N. Sivaraj asked him whether this was against the principle of ahimsa (non-violence). Reddi's tart reply was that this question should be put to a *sanyasi* and not him. But Sivaraj went on to answer his own question.

It was indeed against the principle, he declared.

* The Blue Mountain Express continues to ply between Madras and Ooty, the last leg up the hills from Mettupalayam on a slow and achingly beautiful journey on a steep metre-gauge track.

Timeline

1939

1 September: Germany invades Poland.

3 September: Viceroy Linlithgow announces India is at war. He does this hours after Britain declares war on Germany.

October–November: Congress ministries resign in protest against Linlithgow's unilateral declaration.

1940

March: Congress declares at Ramgarh that it will settle for nothing short of independence and is against India being harnessed for war.

8 August: Linlithgow offers to accommodate more Indians in his Executive Council. His 'August Offer' is rejected by the Congress Party.

August: Japan's Foreign Minister announces the creation of a Greater East Asia Co-Prosperity Sphere.

27 September: Germany, Italy and Japan ink a Tripartite Pact in Berlin.

1941

17 January: Subhash Chandra Bose escapes from Calcutta and makes his way to Germany.

7 December: Japan attacks Pearl Harbour; launches synchronous attacks in South-East Asia. Invades Malaya.

8 December: People start fleeing coastal towns such as Madras and Vizagapatam soon after the attack.

10 December: HMS *Repulse* and HMS *Prince of Wales* are sunk north of Singapore.

12 December: Japan overcomes Allied resistance in the Battle of Jitra, forcing a gradual retreat and withdrawal to Singapore.

13 December: Calcutta witnesses an exodus. Seventeen per cent of its population flees between 13 and 30 December. By 1 January 1942, about 60 per cent of Vizagapatam's residents have fled.

Mid-December: Captain Mohan Singh and his men surrender to the Japanese in Malaya after the Jitra loss. Fujiwara Iwaichi urges Singh to raise an Indian National Army (INA).

23 December: Japan bombs Rangoon. Indians flee Burma, many on foot via the north, bringing back tales of Japanese prowess and British failures, compounding the panic in India.

1942

Mid-January: As the Japanese advance in Malaya and launch offensives in other parts of South-East Asia, the British assure Indians that all is well as long as 'Fortress' Singapore is secure.

15 February: Lieutenant General Arthur Percival surrenders to Japan in Singapore.

16 February: News of Singapore's fall is met with alarm all over India. In Madras and other 'threatened' towns, there is a fresh wave of departures.

17 February: Under Japanese eyes, Mohan Singh addresses surrendered Indian troops of the British Army at Singapore's Farrer Park. The INA is born.

22 March: Stafford Cripps arrives in India with a mission to win Indian cooperation for British war efforts in exchange for more devolution.

23 March: Japan occupies Port Blair in the Andaman Islands.

26 March: Vice Admiral Chuichi Nagumo sails with a large fleet from Staring Bay towards Ceylon.

5–9 April: Nagumo's aircraft pound Colombo and Trincomalee. The ageing British aircraft carrier HMS *Hermes* and the destroyer *Vampire* are sunk off the eastern coast near Batticaloa.

5–6 April: A second Japanese fleet under Jisaburo Ozawa sinks twenty merchant ships off the eastern coast with an aim to disrupt Allied shipping.

6 April: Ozawa's aircraft bomb Vizagapatam and Cocanada. This triggers another round of exodus.

7 April: A reconnaissance plane spots three Japanese aircraft off the coast of Madras.

10 April: Arthur Hope, Governor of Madras Presidency, receives 'intelligence' that a Japanese fleet will make landfall soon, south of Madras city.

10 April: The Cripps Mission ends in failure after the Congress Party rejects the proposals. The British blame Mahatma Gandhi for scuppering the Mission.

12 April: Orissa's government moves almost all offices and records from Cuttack to Sambalpur. A few days later, the Secretariat in Cochin is moved to Trichur.

14 April: Hope orders the dispersal of his government to various places in the Madras Presidency's interior. Madras city empties out. Exodus from many other towns.

14–15 April: 'Europeans', mainly Americans, flee the secluded hill station of Kodaikanal fearing a Japanese attack.

Mid-April: By now, Nagumo and Ozawa have sailed eastwards to fight other battles.

May onwards: The Japanese bomb a number of towns starting with Chittagong on 8 May. Other places such as Imphal, Calcutta, Feni, Cox's Bazar, Noakhali, Lakhimpur and Agartala would be raided intermittently over the next twelve months.

April to August: An increasingly assertive Gandhi leads the Congress Party to demand that the British leave India at once, culminating in his 'Do or Die' call on 9 August.

1943

13 October: A lone Japanese plane drops a few bombs in the Madras harbour area. The raid hardly causes a flutter.

Acknowledgements

The first few words of this book were written at a Sangam House writer's residency run by Arshia Sattar, whose warmth and encouragement I am deeply grateful for. My thanks go to many others who discussed the book with me, most of whom accepted my request to read a couple of chapters or more of the manuscript. To Ravi Palat for a lifetime of friendship and fun; to William Dalrymple for his very kind words and also for showing that it is perfectly okay to put the story back into history; to Mukul Kesavan for his Nike-like 'just get it done' exhortations in the face of my periodic bouts of self-doubt; to Gopalkrishna Gandhi and Manu S. Pillai for their generous reviews; to Ramachandra Guha for his immensely valuable feedback and for looking at what was sent to him with a gratifying meticulousness; to Sushila Ravindranath for following the book's progress through every twist and turn; to cousin Raghu Sundaram for reacting so warmly and positively to the chapters he read; to Manasi Subramaniam, early reader, always wise beyond her years; to Karan Thapar for the knowledge that his feedback, critical or otherwise, will always be honest; to Janice Pariat for checking in on the progress of the book; to Nandini Nair of *Open* magazine for commissioning an article on the murders in Madras Zoo, which is further developed in the epilogue; to Andrew Whitehead for going out of his way to help and for his shared interest in narratives that are unusual and quirky; and, of course, to Indivar Kamtekar for showing the way.

A number of others helped in the making of this book in different ways. In India, my thanks to V. Sriram, A.S. Panneerselvam, Roopa Madhav, Sujatha Vijayaraghavan, Venkataraghavan Subha Srinivasan, Anjum Hasan, G.B., K.S. Nair, Rajni Palriwala, J. Anten Edilbert and Sandhya Ravishankar. In Britain, to Christopher and Mary Penn, Rosie Llewellyn-Jones, Caroline Keen, Andrew Wyatt and Deborah Gill and in Australia to John Castellas.

For help in accessing archival material, my thanks to Jayaprabha Ravindran, Anumita Bannerjee and their team at the National Archives of India in Delhi; to Ravi K. Mishra of the Prime Ministers Museum and Library; to Ganesh Puranik at the Bombay Municipal Corporation; to Editors G.S. Vasu and Santwana Bhattacharya and Librarian Natarajan of the *New Indian Express*; to Editor-in-Chief Sukumar Ranganathan and Managing Editor (Integrations) Anup Gupta at the *Hindustan Times*; and to all my wonderful former colleagues at *The Hindu,* particularly Varghese George, Sandeep Phukan, Saraswathy Nagarajan, Sudipta Datta, Lalatendu Mishra, Sumit Bhattacharjee and the immensely helpful people at the Index section, V. Chander, K.R. Naresh Kumar, Vibha Sudarshan and K. Prabhakaran. A special word of thanks to Ravindra Kumar, the *Statesman*'s Editor and Managing Director for almost miraculously (although he doesn't realize this) making many thousands of pages of the newspaper electronically available for my research.

My gratitude to Nirmala Rao, Vice-Chancellor of Krea University, for her consistent support and appreciation, which have made working for the institution a joy. Also, of course, to Sunder Ramaswamy, the university's founding Vice-Chancellor, for having me on the teaching staff and generously making a travel grant available for research.

Thanks to Jayapriya Vasudevan for having heaps of the two most important and endearing attributes of a great agent:

enthusiasm and belief. To Elizabeth Kuruvilla of Penguin Random House for the happily fortuitous reversal of roles. I was her editor at *The Hindu* and she ended up as mine—I have to admit that she made the better boss. Thanks to Milee Ashwarya, Ralph Rebello and the editorial team at Penguin Random House for helping to improve the book.

Finally, a word of gratitude for the three people at the centre of my life—Rajul, Vinaya and Rishabh.

Notes

1. The Conquest of Malaya

1 'Japan's Strategy', *Times of India*, 10 December 1941, p. 6.
2 Harbakhsh Singh, *In the Line of Duty* (New Delhi: Lancer Publishers, 2000), p. 95.
3 See for instance, 'Indians and Far East War', *The Hindu*, 10 December 1941, p. 4.
4 Kaushik Roy, *Battle for Malaya* (Bloomington: Indiana University Press, 2019), p. 45.
5 Harbakhsh Singh, *In the Line of Duty*, p. 87.
6 Kaushik Roy, *Battle for Malaya*, citing Brigadier Jasbir Singh, *Escape from Singapore* (New Delhi: Lancer Publishers, 2010), p. 20.
7 Srinath Raghavan, *India's War: The Making of Modern South Asia 1939–1945* (New Delhi: Penguin Books, 2017), Chapter 4, Kindle.
8 Harbakhsh Singh, *In the Line of Duty*, p. 88.
9 Jawaharlal Nehru, *The Discovery of India* (New Delhi: Penguin Books, 2004), Chapter 7, Kindle.
10 Srinath Raghavan, *India's War*, citing Gautam Sharma, *Nationalisation of the Indian Army, 1885–1947* (New Delhi: Allied Publishers, 1997), p. 184.
11 Kaushik Roy, *Battle for Malaya*, p. 57.
12 Harbakhsh Singh, *In the Line of Duty*, p. 92.
13 Ibid., pp. 92–93.
14 Peter Ward Fay, *The Forgotten Army: India's Armed Struggle for Independence, 1942–45* (New Delhi: Rupa and Co., 2020), p. 56.
15 Kaushik Roy, *Battle for Malaya*, p. 58.

16 Ibid., p. 59.
17 Christopher Bayly and Tim Harper, *Forgotten Armies: Britain's Asian Empire and the War with Japan* (London: Penguin Books, 2005), Prologue, Part II, Kindle.
18 Yoji Akashi, 'Japanese Military Administration in Malaya: Its Formation and Evolution with Reference to the Sultans, the Islamic Religion and Malay Muslims, 1941–45', *Asian Studies*, 7(1), 1969.
19 Hugh Toye, 'The First Indian National Army, 1941–42', *Journal of Southeast Asian Studies*, Vol. 15, September 1984.
20 Mohan Singh reminiscing in Fujiwara Iwaichi, *F. Kikan: Japanese Army Intelligence Operations in Southeast Asia during World War II* (Singapore: Heinemann Asia, 1983), p. 13.
21 Kaushik Roy, *Battle for Malaya*, p. 67, citing K.D. Bhargava and K.N.V. Sastri, *Campaigns in Southeast Asia 1941–1942* in Bisheshwar Prasad (ed.), *Official History of the Indian Armed Forces in the Second World War: 1939–45,* (Combined Inter-Services Historical Section India and Pakistan, Distributors Orient Longman, 1960).
22 Kaushik Roy, *Battle for Malaya*, p. 26, citing Memorandum by the Secretary of State for India, 30 January 1942, WP(42)54, CP, Nehru Memorial Museum and Library.
23 The Council of States Debates, 20 November 1941, Vol. II, p. 272.
24 Ibid., p. 292.
25 'The Evacuation of Penang', *The Hindu*, 21 December 1941, p. 4.
26 Christopher Bayly and Tim Harper, *Forgotten Armies*, Chapter 2, Kindle.
27 Kaushik Roy, *Battle for Malaya*, p. 84.
28 Winston Churchill, *The Grand Alliance* (London: Cassell and Company, 1968), p. 551.
29 'The Evacuation of Penang', *The Hindu,* 21 December 1941, p. 4.
30 Rebecca Kenneison, *Playing for Malaya* (Singapore: National University of Singapore Press, 2013), Chapter 4, Kindle.
31 Christopher Bayly and Tim Harper, *Forgotten Armies*, Chapter 2, Kindle.
32 'Current Comments', *Hindustan Times*, 28 February 1942, p. 4.

33 The Council of States Debates, 31 March 1942, Vol. I, pp. 490–91.
34 'Entire Indian Population Still in Penang', *Indian Express*, 6 January 1942, p. 4.
35 Hope to Linlithgow, 4 January 1942, Linlithgow Papers, MSS Eur F125/70, India Office Records, British Library.
36 Hansard, Vol. 378, 26 February 1942.
37 Manicasothy Saravanamuttu, *The Sara Saga* (Penang: Areca Books, 2010), p. 111.
38 Rebecca Kenneison, *Playing for Malaya,* Chapter 4, Kindle.
39 Manicasothy Saravanamuttu, *The Sara Saga,* p. 113.
40 Fortnightly Report from Bengal, Second half of December 1941, Political Section, Home Dept, National Archives of India.
41 Hope to Linlithgow, 4 January 1942, Linlithgow Papers, MSS Eur F125/70, IOR.
42 Fred Glueckstein, 'Churchill and the Fall of Singapore', winstonchurchill.org/publications/finest-hour/finest-hour-169/churchill-and-the-fall-of-singapore/

2. The Fortress Crumbles

1 James Leasor, *Singapore: The Battle that Changed the World* (London: James Leasor Ltd, 2011), Chapter 8, Kindle.
2 Kaushik Roy, *Sepoys against the Rising Sun: The Indian Army in Far East and South-East Asia, 1941–45* (Leiden: Brill, 2016), p. 127.
3 Winston Churchill, *The Hinge of Fate* (Boston: Houghton Mifflin Company, 1950), p. 49.
4 James Leasor, *Singapore*, Chapter 8, Kindle.
5 Ibid.
6 Bisheshwar Prasad (ed.), *Campaigns in South East Asia, Official History of the Indian Armed Forces in the Second World War 1939–1945* (New Delhi: Pentagon Press, 2012), p. 320.
7 James Leasor, *Singapore*, Chapter 1, Kindle.
8 Peter Ward Fay, *The Forgotten Army*, p. 69.
9 Ibid., p. 70.
10 Ibid., p. 83.

11 Ibid., pp. 92–93.
12 Ibid., p. 94.
13 Hugh Toye, 'The First Indian National Army, 1941–42'.
14 Harbakhsh Singh, *In the Line of Duty*, p. 108.
15 Ibid., p. 109.
16 Peter Ward Fay, *The Forgotten Army*, p. 95.
17 Hugh Toye, 'The First Indian National Army, 1941–42'.
18 Fortnightly Report from Bombay, Second half of February 1942, Home Dept, NAI.
19 Christopher Bayly and Tim Harper, *Forgotten Armies,* p. 106.
20 'No Room for Panic', *Evening Post*, 16 February 1942, p. 6.
21 Fortnightly Reports from Bombay, Orissa, Delhi and Madras, December 1941, Home Dept, NAI.
22 'Orgy of Buying in Madras', *Times of India*, 18 December 1941, p. 5.
23 'Firewood Famine in Madras', *Indian Express*, 12 December 1941, p. 2.
24 Fortnightly Report from Madras, First half of December 1941, Home Dept, NAI.
25 'Japanese Nationals Rounded Up in India', *Times of India*, 9 December 1941, p. 3.
26 Ibid.
27 The Legislative Assembly Debates, 19 February 1942, Vol. I, p. 380.
28 'Planning Now', *Statesman*, 2 March 1942, p. 4.
29 'India Determined to Be Free', *Indian Express*, 19 February 1942, p. 2.
30 Christine de Matos and Rowena Ward, 'Forgotten Forced Migrants of War, Civilian Internment of Japanese in British India, 1941–6', *Journal of Contemporary History*, doi.org/10.1177/0022009421997913.
31 Christopher Bayly and Tim Harper, *Forgotten Armies*, Chapter 2, Kindle.
32 Christine de Matos and Rowena Ward, 'Forgotten Forced Migrants of War'.

3. Before the Fall

1 'Tojo Reading Hirohito's Speech', UPI, 7 December 1941, https://www.upi.com/Archives/1941/12/07/Tojo-reading-Hirohito-speech-Japan-declares-war-on-US-Britain/5103382818544/
2 Irvine H. Anderson Jr., 'The 1941 De Facto Embargo on Oil to Japan: A Bureaucratic Reflex', *Pacific Historical Review,* Vol. 44, 1975.
3 A.J. Grajdanzev, 'Japan's Co-Prosperity Sphere', *Pacific Affairs,* Vol. 16, No. 3, 1943.
4 Jeremy A. Yellen, *The Greater East Asia Co-Prosperity Sphere: When Total Empire Met Total War* (New York: Cornell University Press, 2019), p. 27.
5 A.J. Grajdanzev, 'Japan's Co-Prosperity Sphere'.
6 Jeremy A. Yellen, *The Greater East Asia Co-Prosperity Sphere*, p. 36.
7 Ibid., p. 35.
8 'Correspondence Arising in 1936 over the Possibility of Japanese Aggression in India, Burma, Etc', MSS Eur F125/160, Linlithgow Papers, IOR.
9 John Glendevon, *The Viceroy at Bay: Lord Linlithgow in India, 1936–1943* (London: Collins, 1971), pp. 26–28.
10 Christopher Bayly and Tim Harper, *Forgotten Armies*, Chapter 4, Kindle.
11 Ibid.
12 'Japan's Strategy', *Times of India*, 10 December 1941, p. 6.
13 Proceedings of the Council of the Corporation of Madras, 28 February 1941.
14 Ibid.
15 The Marquess of Linlithgow, *Speeches and Statements* (New Delhi: The Bureau of Public Information, Government of India, 1945), p. 287.
16 Proceedings of the Council of the Corporation of Madras, 28 February 1941.
17 'Protecting Civilian Population: Military Training Urged', *Times of India*, 1 February 1938, p. 8.

18 Priya Satia, *'Guns and the British Empire'*, southasia.stanford.edu/publications/guns-and-british-empire.
19 The Council of States Debates, 21 November 1940, Vol. II, pp. 62–64.
20 Finance Secretary C.E. Jones in the Council of States Debates, 28 February 1942, Vol. I, p. 184.
21 The Council of States Debates, 31 March 1942, Vol. I, p. 517.
22 'Evolving an Army', *Statesman*, 15 February 1942, p. 4.
23 Arthur Moore, 'The Defeatist: Beaverbrook's Great Obsession', *Statesman*, 15 February 1942, p. 1.
24 'Singapore', *Statesman*, 16 February 1942, p. 4.
25 Fortnightly Report from Bengal, First half of February 1942, Home Dept, NAI.

4. Ceylon and the Bay of Bengal

1 Quoted in John Clancy, *The Most Dangerous Moment of the War: Japan's Attack on the Indian Ocean, 1942* (Oxford: Casemate Publishers, 2015), Chapter 4, Kindle.
2 Ibid., Chapter 6, Kindle.
3 'Ceylon's Saviour', sundaytimes.lk/020407/plus.ht.ml.
4 Rob Stuart, 'Leonard Birchall and the Japanese Raid on Colombo', *Canadian Military Journal*, journal.forces.gc.ca/vo7/no4/stuart-eng.asp.
5 Donald McIntyre, *Fighting Admiral: The Life of Admiral of the Fleet Sir James Somerville* (London: Evans Brothers Limited, 1961), p. 181.
6 Michael Simpson, *The Somerville Papers: Selections from the Private and Official Correspondence of Admiral of the Fleet, Sir James Somerville* (United Kingdom: Taylor & Francis, 2020), 14 March 1942, p. 394.
7 Ibid., 28 March 1942, p. 397.
8 Donald McIntyre, *Fighting Admiral*, p. 186.
9 Michael Simpson, *The Somerville Papers*, 2 April 1942, p. 398.
10 Ibid., 3 April 1942, p. 398.
11 Ibid., 4 April 1942, p. 399.
12 John Clancy, *The Most Dangerous Moment of the War*, Chapter 3, Kindle.

13 K.S. Nair, *The Forgotten Few: The Indian Air Force in World War II* (New Delhi: Harper Collins India, 2019), Chapter 4, Kindle.
14 'Second Alert in Colombo', *The Hindu*, 4 April 1942, p. 8.
15 S.K. Narang, *Under the Shadow of Death: Story of Japanese Occupation of Andaman and Nicobar Islands* (Chennai: Notion Press, 2019), Chapter 3, Kindle.
16 Robert Stuart, '20 Ships, not 23: Ozawa's Score 5–6th April, 1942', combinedfleet.com/articles.htm.
17 Ibid.
18 Stanley Salt, 'Sinking of the S.S. Sinkiang' in Joyce Hibbert, *Fragments of War* (Toronto: Dundurn Press, 1985), p. 34.
19 Ibid., p. 36.
20 Lewis to Linlithgow, 8 April 1942, Linlithgow Papers, MSS Eur F125/84, IOR.
21 Fortnightly Report from Bombay, First half of April 1942, Home Dept, NAI and combinedfleet.com/I-6.htm.
22 Ibid., 4 April 1942.

5. The Bombings

1 Flight log of D.S. Small, AIR 27 825, The National Archives, Kew.
2 W.W. Russell, *Forgotten Skies*, p. 35.
3 Fortnightly Report from Madras, First half of April 1942, Home Dept, NAI.
4 Ibid.
5 John Clancy, *The Most Dangerous Moment of the War,* Chapter 9, Kindle.
6 Governor Herbert to Linlithgow, Linlithgow Papers, 21 May 1942, MSS Eur F125/42, IOR.
7 M. Ranjit Singh, 'Japanese Bombing of Manipur—Part I and II', e-pao.net/
8 Geoffrey Evans, *Imphal: Flower on Lofty Heights* (London: Macmillan and Co., 1962), pp. 19–20.
9 Ibid.
10 Fortnightly Report from Assam, First half of May 1942, Home Dept, NAI.
11 M. Ranjit Singh, 'Japanese Bombing of Manipur—Part I and II'.

12 Assam Governor Andrew Clow to Linlithgow, Linlithgow Papers, MSS Eur F125/35, IOR.
13 Fortnightly Report from Assam, Second half of May 1942, Home Dept, NAI.
14 Ibid.
15 'Statement of Recent Air Raids in India', Intelligence Notes, AIR 23/5059, The National Archives, Kew.
16 *The Calcutta Municipal Gazette*, 20 February 1943, p. 346, Town Hall Library, Kolkata.
17 'Chittagong Carries On', *Statesman*, 14 February, 1943, p. 4.
18 Intelligence Note, AIR 23/5059, The National Archives, Kew.
19 'Calcutta's Raid', *Statesman,* 22 December 1942, p. 4.
20 Telegram from Linlithgow to Governor of Bengal John Herbert, 21 December 1942. Linlithgow Papers, MSS Eur F125/42, IOR.
21 Ian Stephens, *Monsoon Morning* (London: Ernest Benn, 1966), p. 80.
22 'Calcutta's Baptism of Fire', *Statesman*, 24 December 1942, p. 5.
23 'Air Raid Casualties in Calcutta', *Statesman*, 24 December 1942, p. 5.
24 'Occasional Notes', *Statesman*, 25 December 1942, p. 4.
25 'Remedy Needed', *Statesman*, 27 December 1942, p. 6.
26 'Exodus after the Raids', Associated Press report in the *Calcutta Municipal Gazette,* 16 January 1943, p. 227.
27 Joydeep Sircar, 'In the Skies of Calcutta', bharat-rakshak.com.
28 Ian Stephens, *Monsoon Morning,* p. 216.
29 '500 Civilian Casualties in Jap Raid on Sunday', *Statesman*, 7 December 1943, p. 1.
30 Ian Stephens, *Monsoon Morning,* p. 216.
31 Janam Mukerjee, *Hungry Bengal: War, Famine, Riots and the End of Empire* (New Delhi: HarperCollins India, 2015), Chapter 5, Kindle.
32 Ibid., quoting from Port A.R.P. Report, Chapter 5, Kindle.
33 'Lesson from the Jap Raid', *Statesman*, 10 December 1943, p. 1.

6. The Politics of War

1 'Viceroy's Message to India', *Statesman*, 4 September 1939, p. 10.
2 Jawaharlal Nehru, *The Discovery of India*, Chapter 9, Kindle.
3 'Resolutions of the Indian National Congress at Faizpur in December 1936', Marxists Internet Archive, marxists.org/history/international/comintern/sections/britain/periodicals/labour_monthly/1938/06/x01.htm.
4 Amiya Kumar Bagchi, 'Indian Economy and Society during World War One', *Social Scientist*, No. 42, 2014.
5 'Policy of Farsighted Wisdom in Travancore', *Times of India*, 14 November 1939, p. 4.
6 John Glendevon, *The Viceroy at Bay*, p. 136.
7 'A Democratic India Will Join in Opposing Aggression', *Times of India*, 15 September 1939, p. 8.
8 'Congress and War', *Times of India*, 16 September 1939, p. 8.
9 'Politics of Retirement', *Indian Express*, 10 December 1941, p. 4.
10 G.J. Douds, 'The Indian Princes: India's Fifth Column?', *Journal of South Asian Studies*, 11:2, 1988, citing E. Wakefield, *Past Imperative* (London: Chatto & Windus, 1966).
11 Manu Pillai, *False Allies* (New Delhi: Juggernaut, 2021).
12 John Glendevon, *The Viceroy at Bay*, p. 43.
13 Martin Gilbert, *Winston S. Churchill: The Prophet of Truth 1922–1939* (Michigan: Rosetta Books, 2015), Chapter 30, Kindle.
14 See for instance, Penderel Moon, *Divide and Quit* (London: Chatto & Windus, 1963).
15 'Viceroy States British War Aims in Regard to India', *Times of India*, 18 October 1939, p. 11.
16 'Britain's Attitude Unfortunate: Wardha Resolution', *Times of India*, 23 October 1939, p. 11.
17 Hansard, Vol. 371, 22 April 1941.
18 'Resolution Adopted by the Indian National Congress at Ramgarh, March 18, 1940', Marxists Internet Archive, marxists.org/history/

international/comintern/sections/britain/periodicals/labour_monthly/1940/04/x02.htm.

19 Romain Hayes, *Bose in Nazi Germany* (New Delhi: Random House India, 2011), Introduction, Kindle.

20 Subhash Chandra Bose, *The Indian Struggle 1920–1942* (Delhi: Oxford University Press, 2007), p. 351.

21 Romain Hayes, *Bose in Nazi Germany*, Introduction, Kindle.

22 Ibid., Introduction, Kindle.

23 'Full Text of Haripura Congress Bose 1938', Marxists Internet Archive, archive.org/stream/HaripuraCongressBose1938/BoseTalk_djvu.txt.

24 Subhash Chandra Bose, *The Indian Struggle*, pp. 375–76.

25 Hugh Toye, *Subhash Chandra Bose: The Springing Tiger* (Mumbai: Jaico Publishing House, 2011), Chapter 3, Kindle.

26 Maulana Azad, *India Wins Freedom*, Chapter 3, Kindle.

27 *Collected Works of Mahatma Gandhi, Vol. 72* (Ahmedabad: Navajivan Trust, 1978), p. 230.

28 CWMG, Vol. 67, p. 76.

29 Ibid., p. 405.

30 Ibid., p. 76.

31 CWMG, Vol. 74, p. 70.

32 Ibid., p. 100.

33 CWMG, Vol. 72, p. 194.

34 Ibid., p. 237.

35 Ibid., p. 197.

36 Ibid., Appendix IV.

37 Ibid., p. 245.

38 'From the Archive: Mr. Churchill on Our Aim', *Guardian*, 11 November 1942, theguardian.com/theguardian/2009/nov/11/churchill-blood-sweat-tears.

39 David Whittington, 'An Imperialist at Bay' (PhD diss., University of Leicester, 2016), citing Amery Diary, 26 July 1940.

40 Srinath Raghavan, *India's War,* Chapter 3, Kindle.

41 CWMG, Vol. 71, p. 305.

42 Ibid., p. 306.

43 Srinath Raghavan, *India's War*, Chapter 3, Kindle.

44 Sarvepalli Gopal, *Jawaharlal Nehru: A Biography, Volume 1: 1889–1947* (New Delhi: Oxford University Press, 2011), Chapter 16, Kindle.

7. The Entry of Japan

1 CWMG, Vol. 75, Appendix 2, p. 452.
2 Sushila Nayar, *Mahatma Gandhi, Vol. VII* (Ahmedabad: Navajivan Publishing House, 1997), p. 250.
3 CWMG, Vol. 75, pp. 221–22.
4 Rajmohan Gandhi, *Rajaji: A Life* (New Delhi: Penguin Books, 2010), Chapter 14, Kindle; *The Good Boatman: A Portrait of Mahatma Gandhi* (New Delhi: Penguin Books, 2018), Chapter 10, Kindle.
5 David Whittington, 'An Imperialist at Bay', p. 137.
6 Trevor Burridge, *Clement Attlee: A Political Biography* (London: Jonathan Cape, 1985), p. 279.
7 Bhim Sen Singh, *The Cripps Mission: A Handiwork of British Imperialism* (New Delhi: Usha Publications, 1979), p. 28.
8 Kenneth S. Davis, *FDR: The War President 1940–1943* (New York: Random House, 2000), p. 465.
9 Winston Churchill, *The Hinge of Fate*, p. 185.
10 Ibid.
11 Ibid., p. 213.
12 Maulana Azad, *India Wins Freedom,* Chapter 3, Kindle.
13 CWMG, Vol. 76, p. 5.
14 Fortnightly Report from Bombay, First half of February 1942, Home Dept, NAI.
15 The Legislative Assembly Debates, Vol. I, 19 February 1942, p. 387.
16 Ibid., Vol. II, 1 April 1942, p. 1652.
17 Romain Hayes, *Bose in Nazi Germany*, Chapter 2, Kindle.
18 Ibid.
19 From 'The Fall of Singapore', in Sisir Kumar Bose and Sugata Bose (eds), *Azad Hind: Writings and Speeches 1941–1943* (Ranikhet: Permanent Black, 2018), Kindle.

20 Maulana Abul Kalam Azad, *India Wins Freedom*, Chapter 3, Kindle.
21 Penderel Moon, *Wavell: A Viceroy's Journal* (London: Oxford University Press, 1973), p. 10.
22 CWMG, Vol. 76, pp. 438–39.
23 Maulana Abul Kalam Azad, *India Wins Freedom*, Chapter 3, Kindle.
24 Indivar Kamtekar, 'The Shiver of 1942', *Studies in History*, 18 (1), 2002.
25 Penderel Moon, *Wavell*, p. 10.
26 Jawaharlal Nehru, *The Discovery of India*, Chapter 9, Kindle.
27 Sarvepalli Gopal, *Jawaharlal Nehru, A Biography Volume 1 1889–1947* (UK: Vintage Digital, 2015), Chapter 17, Kindle.
28 Maulana Abul Kalam Azad, *India Wins Freedom*, Chapter 5, Kindle.
29 Ibid.
30 Sumit Sarkar, *Modern India* (New Delhi: Pearson India, 2014), Chapter 7, Kindle.
31 Telegram from Linlithgow to Amery, 12 March 1942 in Nicolas Mansergh (ed.), *The Transfer of Power 1942–1947, Vol. 1* (London: Her Majesty's Stationery Office, 1970), p. 413.
32 Cripps' interview with Rajagopalachari, 28 March 1942, Ibid., pp. 511–12.
33 Cripps' interview with Nehru, 30 March 1942, Ibid., pp. 557–58.
34 David Whittington, *An Imperialist at Bay*, citing Amery draft memoirs, Chapter VII, p. 26.
35 'No Echo', *Statesman*, 30 April 1942, p. 4.
36 Jawaharlal Nehru, *The Discovery of India,* Chapter 9, Kindle.
37 Maulana Abul Kalam Azad, *India Wins Freedom*, Chapter 6, Kindle.
38 Sumit Sarkar, *Modern India,* p. 332.
39 Jawaharlal Nehru, *The Discovery of India*, Chapter 9, Kindle.
40 Ramachandra Guha, *Gandhi: The Years that Changed the World* (New Delhi: Penguin Books, 2018), p. 651.
41 CWMG, Vol. 76, pp. 63–66.

42 As reported from the secret session of the Congress Working Committee in Allahabad by a British official in the Home Department. Richard Tottenham, *Congress Responsibility for the Disturbances,* Government of India, 1943.
43 Sarvepalli Gopal, *Jawaharlal Nehru, A Biography, Vol. 1*, Chapter 18, Kindle.
44 CWMG, Vol. 76, p. 67.
45 Captain Gammans in The House of Commons, Hansard, 2 August 1942.
46 CWMG, Vol. 76, pp. 107–08.
47 Ibid.
48 Ibid., p. 197.
49 Jawaharlal Nehru, *The Discovery of India*, Chapter 9, Kindle.
50 CWMG, Vol. 76, p. 431.
51 Jawaharlal Nehru, *A Bunch of Old Letters* (New Delhi: Asia Publishing House, 1958), p. 487.
52 Jawaharlal Nehru, *The Discovery of India,* Chapter 9, Kindle.

8. The Premonition of Danger

1 Hansard, Vol. 329, 15 November 1937.
2 Geoffrey Lamarque, 'Memories of India 1937–1947', MSS Eur F 180/54, IOR.
3 'A.R.P. and Civic Guards in Bombay', *Statesman,* 23 June 1941, p. 3.
4 Statement laid before the Central Legislative Assembly on 4 November 1941. The Legislative Assembly Debates, Vol. IV, 1941, p. 337.
5 Statement made by Sir Reginald Maxwell, Minister for Civil Defence, in the Central Legislative Assembly on 18 February 1942. Vol. I, 1942, pp. 304–06.
6 'Madras Organisers' Problems', *Statesman,* 23 June 1942, p. 3.
7 Hope to Linlithgow, May 1940, Linlithgow Papers, MSS Eur F125/68, IOR.
8 'Black Outs and Road Safety', *The Hindu*, 24 December 1941, p. 4.

9 Geoffrey Lamarque, MSS Eur F 180/54, IOR.
10 Ibid.
11 'Letter to the Editor', *Statesman*, 25 June 1941, p. 6.
12 'A.R.P. Signal and School Children', *Indian Express*, 17 January 1942, p. 2.
13 Fortnightly Report from Bombay, First half of March 1942, Home Dept, NAI.
14 '114 Miles of Slit Trenches in Calcutta', *Indian Express*, 9 February 1942, p. 4.
15 'Slit Trenches in Madras City', *Indian Express*, 19 February 1942, p. 2.
16 From Proceedings of the Council of the Corporation of Madras, 18 July 1941.
17 Fortnightly Report from Assam, First half of March 1942, Home Dept, NAI.
18 'Services of A.R.P. Personnel', *Statesman*, 5 February 1942, p. 6.
19 Fortnightly Report from Bihar, Second half of November 1941, Home Dept, NAI.
20 'Resolutions passed at the 51st Session of the Indian National Congress at Vithal Nagar-Haripura March 1938', Marxists Internet Archive, marxists.org/history/international/comintern/sections/britain/periodicals/labour_monthly/1938/06/x01.htm
21 CWMG, Vol. 75, p. 238.
22 Fortnightly Report from Bombay, Second half of February 1942, Home Dept, NAI.
23 Linlithgow to John Herbert, Governor of Bengal, 30 April 1942, Linlithgow Papers, MSS Eur F125/42, IOR.
24 Fortnightly Report from the United Provinces, First half of March 1942, Home Dept, NAI.
25 Cripps to Churchill, 30 March 1942, *The Transfer of Power 1942–47,* Vol. 1, pp. 559–60.
26 'Japanese Threat to India', *Statesman*, 14 March 1942, p. 5.
27 CWMG, Vol. 75, p. 410.
28 Srinath Raghavan, *India's War,* Chapter 14, Kindle.
29 Lewis to Linlithgow, MSS Eur F125/84, IOR.

9. The Tongue of Rumour

1 'Rumour Mongering in Calcutta', *Indian Express,* 16 February 1942, p. 4.
2 'The Tongue of Rumour', *Statesman*, 14 February 1942, p. 4.
3 Robert H. Knapp, 'A Psychology of Rumour', *Public Opinion Quarterly,* Vol. 8, No. 1, 1944.
4 Fortnightly Report from the United Provinces, Second half of March 1942, Home Dept, NAI.
5 'Scare of Jap Air Raids on India', *Indian Express*, 8 January 1942, p. 5.
6 Fortnightly Report from the United Provinces, Second half of February 1942, Home Dept, NAI.
7 Fortnightly Report from Bihar, Second half of February 1942, Home Dept, NAI.
8 'Rumour about Evacuation of Europeans', *Indian Express*, 10 January 1942, p. 2.
9 Fortnightly Reports from Assam and Madras, First and Second half of February 1942 respectively, Home Dept, NAI.
10 'No Possibility of Attack on India', *Indian Express*, 12 February 1942, p. 8.
11 Fortnightly Report from Bihar, Second half of February 1942, Home Dept, NAI.
12 Jane Robbins, 'Freedom under Britain or Freedom under Japan: The Radio Battle for India, December 1941–September 1945', *Japan Forum*, 7:2.
13 D. Gupta, 'The Raj in Radio Wars', *Media History*, 25(4), 2019, citing Partha Sarathy Gupta, *The Radio and the Raj: 1921–1947* (Calcutta: Centre for Studies in Social Sciences, 1995).
14 Milan Hauner, *India in Axis Strategy* (London: Publications of the German Historical Institute, 1981), pp. 246–52.
15 Bernard Crick, *George Orwell: A Life* (London: Secker & Warburg, 1980), p. 281.
16 Letter to Geoffrey Gorer, Ibid., p. 234.
17 bbc.com/historyofbbc.

18 George Orwell, *The War Commentaries* (New York: Pantheon Books, 1985), p. 19.
19 Jane Robbins, 'Tokyo Calling: Japanese Overseas Broadcasting 1937–1945' (PhD Diss., University of Sheffield, 2017).
20 George Orwell, *The War Commentaries*, p. 76.
21 George Orwell, *The Orwell Diaries* (London: Penguin Books, 2010), p. 348.
22 Bernard Crick, *George Orwell*, p. 287.
23 Anchal Malhotra, 'Kill All the British Sucking Blood: The Canny Poster Propaganda Used by Japan in WW2', scroll.in/magazine/912337/kill-all-the-british-sucking-indian-blood-the-canny-poster-propaganda-used-by-japan-in-wwii.
24 These paragraphs on Bombay War Week are sourced from various *Times of India* reports dated 17 to 22 March 1941 and the short film *Bombay's War Weapons' Week,* British Movietone, YouTube.
25 Hope to Linlithgow, 23 June 1941, Linlithgow Papers, MSS Eur F125/69, IOR.
26 Karen Stapley, 'The Great War Fund Fete', blogs.bl.uk/untoldlives/2019/01/the-great-war-fund-fete.html.
27 Fortnightly Report from Madras, Second half of November 1941, Home Dept, NAI.
28 'A View behind Defence Preparations', *Indian Express*, 30 January 1942, p. 2.
29 'Heavy Casualties in Rangoon Raid', *Times of India*, 16 January 1942, p. 7.
30 Devika Sethi, *War over Words: Censorship in India, 1930-1960* (Cambridge: Cambridge University Press, 2019), p. 127.
31 Hope to Linlithgow, 4 January 1942, Linlithgow Papers, MSS Eur F125/70, IOR.
32 Ibid., 7 April 1942.
33 Reference in letter provided by their daughter Deborah Gill to author.
34 Papers of ICS officer C.V. Narasimhan, Eur F 180/56, IOR.
35 'Sir Arthur Hope: Scandal of Governor's Theft Hushed Up', and 'Mischief in Madras: How the Establishment Closed Ranks to

Cover Up One of the Last Scandals of the British Empire', *The Times*, 11 March and 16 March 2019, respectively.

36 Hope to Linlithgow, 4 January 1942, Linlithgow Papers, MSS Eur F125/70, IOR.

37 Linlithgow to Hope, 16 January 1942, Ibid.

38 Hugh Tinker, 'A Forgotten Long March: The Indian Exodus from Burma, 1942', *Journal of Southeast Asian Studies*, Vol. 6, March 1975.

39 Ibid.

40 The Council of States Debates, 18 March 1942, Vol. I, p. 332.

41 Ibid., p. 342.

42 Hugh Tinker, 'A Forgotten Long March'.

43 S. Ambujammal, *Naan Kanda Bharatam* (Madras: Srinivasa Gandhi Nilayam, 1973), pp. 218–28.

44 Fortnightly Report from Madras, First half of May 1942, Home Dept, NAI.

45 Indivar Kamtekar, 'The Shiver of 1942'.

10. The Fog of Confusion

1 Fortnightly Report from Madras, First half of January 1942, Home Dept, NAI.

2 Reported in *Madras War Review*, 16 January 1942.

3 'Emergency Decree in India', *Manchester Guardian*, 22 December 1941, p. 6.

4 'State of Emergency in Bengal', *Times of India*, 25 December 1941, p. 8.

5 'Panic Is Our Worst Enemy', *The Hindu*, 28 December 1941, p. 4.

6 'Risk Not Very Great', *Indian Express*, 18 February 1942, p. 2.

7 'India Determined to Be Free', *Indian Express*, 19 February 1942, p. 2.

8 'Stop It', *Statesman*, 1 February 1942, p. 4.

9 'The Nature of the Danger', *Statesman*, 3 February 1942, p. 4.

10 'Evacuation Nearing Completion', *Statesman*, 4 March 1942, p. 6.

11 CWMG, Vol. 75, p. 326.
12 Ibid., 10 March 1942, p. 401.
13 Yasmin Khan, *The Raj at War: A People's History of India's Second World War* (Vintage Digital, 2015), Chapter 12, Kindle.
14 Hope to Linlithgow, 25 January 1942, Linlithgow Papers, MSS Eur F125/70, IOR.
15 'City's Civil Defence', *The Hindu*, 13 January 1942, p. 4.
16 A.K. Chettiar, 'Chennai Nagaram, 1942', *Kumari Malar*, April 1943.
17 '"Misbehaviour" of Soldiers in the City', *Times of India*, 13 March 1942, p. 6.
18 The Legislative Assembly Debates, 11 March 1942, Vol. II, p. 970.
19 Ibid., 16 March 1942, p. 1156.
20 Ibid., p. 1163.
21 Ibid., 13 March 1942, p. 1125.
22 Ibid., 16 March 1942, p. 1199.
23 Ibid., 20 March 1942, p. 1397.
24 Ibid., 23 March 1942, pp. 1439–40.
25 Ibid., 2 April 1942, pp. 1698–700.
26 Fortnightly Report from Central Provinces and Berar, Second half of March 1942, Home Dept, NAI.
27 Fortnightly Report from United Provinces, Second half of March 1942, Home Dept, NAI.
28 Fortnightly Report from Bihar, Second half of January 1942, Home Dept, NAI.
29 'Behaviour of Australian Soldiers', *Mathrubhumi,* 22 March 1942.
30 Fortnightly Report from Madras, First half of April 1942, Home Dept, NAI.
31 CWMG, Vol. 75, p. 416.
32 Yasmin Khan, 'Sex in an Imperial War Zone: Transnational Encounters in Second World War India', *History Workshop Journal,* Vol. 73, Oxford University Press.
33 Ibid.
34 From an article titled 'Do Our Troops Want More Brothels?' in *Modern Review* reproduced in the *Calcutta Municipal Gazette,* 16 January 1943, p. 232.
35 Ibid.

36 The Legislative Assembly Debates, 17 March 1942, Vol. II, p. 1228.
37 Fortnightly Report from Bombay, First half of March 1942, Home Dept, NAI.
38 'Ernakulam Out of Bounds for Troops?', *Indian Express,* 4 March 1942, p. 8.
39 Fortnightly Report from Madras, First half of February 1942, Home Department, NAI.
40 Fortnightly Report from Bihar, First half of February 1942, Home Dept, NAI.

11. The Madness in Madras

1 'The Wadsworth Papers', Chapter 19. Centre for South Asian Studies, Cambridge.
2 Fortnightly Report from Madras, Second half of December 1941, Home Dept, NAI.
3 Fortnightly Report from Madras, Second half of January 1942, Home Dept, NAI.
4 'Rent and Price Control', *Indian Express*, 31 December 1941, p. 4.
5 Pudhumaipithan in a letter to his wife on 21 April 1942 in *Kanmani Kamlavukku* (Chennai: Shanti Publishers, 1994).
6 A.C. Platt papers, MSS Eur F 180/57, IOR.
7 Fortnightly Report from Madras, Second half of February 1942, Home Dept, NAI.
8 Hope to Linlithgow, 22 March 1942, Linlithgow Papers, MSS Eur F125/70, IOR.
9 Michael Tomlinson, *The Most Dangerous Moment: Japanese Assault on Ceylon, 1942* (London: William Kimber and Co. Ltd, 1976), p. 106.
10 Fortnightly Report from Madras, Second half of April 1942, Home Dept, NAI.
11 Hope to Linlithgow, 22 March and 18 April 1942, Linlithgow Papers, MSS Eur F 125/70, IOR.
12 Christopher Masterman, 'Air Raid Precautions, Vizagapatam, 1942', Centre of South Asian Studies, Cambridge University,

cited by John Castellas, 'CH Mastermind, Waltair Club's Master Bureaucrat', *Waltair Times*, Vol. 27, April 2023.

13 'Exodus from Vizagapatam', *Mail*, 3 January 1942.

14 Fortnightly Report from Madras, Second half of December 1941, Home Dept, NAI.

15 Fortnightly Report from Madras, First half of April 1942, Home Dept, NAI.

16 Hope to Linlithgow, 18 April 1942, Linlithgow Papers, MSS Eur F125/70, IOR.

17 'The Wadsworth Papers', Chapter 19.

18 Papers of Margaret Hunt, MSS Eur 241/20, IOR.

19 Cited in Srinath Raghavan's *India's War*, Chapter 11, Kindle.

20 Paul M. Jayarajan, 'Facets of My Life under the British Raj', MSS Eur C509, IOR.

21 'Removal of Government Offices', *The Hindu*, 15 April 1942, p. 6.

22 'ARP Organisations in the City', *Statesman*, 18 April 1942, p. 6.

23 O. Pulla Reddi, *Autumn Leaves* (Bombay: Bharatiya Vidya Bhavan, 1978) and Paul M. Jayarajan, MSS Eur 509.

24 Hilton Brown, *Parry's of Madras* (Madras: Parry & Co. Ltd, 1954).

25 Proceedings of the Council of the Corporation of Madras, 31 October 1942.

26 Fortnightly Report from Madras, First half of April 1942, Home Dept, NAI.

27 Hope to Linlithgow, 18 April 1942, Linlithgow Papers, MSS Eur F125/70, IOR.

28 Fortnightly Report from Madras, First half of April 1942, Home Dept, NAI.

29 '3 Lakh Leave the City', *The Hindu*, 15 April 1942, p. 3.

30 'Discuss It', *Indian Express*, 22 April 1942, p. 2.

31 Proceedings of the Council of the Corporation of Madras, 31 October 1942, pp. 54–55.

32 'Do Not Yield to Blind Fear', *Mail*, 21 April 1942, p. 6.

33 Paul M. Jayarajan, MSS Eur 509, IOR.

34 Interview with author.

35 A.R. Venkatachalapathy (ed.), 'Padapaddappu', *Pudhumaipithan Kathaigal*, (Nagercoil: Kalachuvadu Pathippagam), 13th edition, 2021, pp. 662–66.

36 'Stop the Rot', *Mail,* 20 April 1942, p. 2.
37 From Radha Krishnamurthy's written notes made available by her daughter Pritham Chakravarthy.
38 Anna Varki, *One Woman's India*, Chapter 3, Kindle.
39 Linlithgow to Hope, 27 April 1942, Linlithgow Papers, MSS Eur F125/70, IOR.
40 'Dispelling Panic', *Indian Express,* 21 January 1942, p. 4.
41 'India Will Fight Not for Her Slavery but Her Freedom', *Indian Express,* 6 January 1942, p. 3.
42 'Lay Down Your Lives to Liberate India', *Indian Express,* 2 March 1942, p. 2.
43 'The Antidote to Panic', *Mail,* 8 March 1942, p. 6.
44 'Either Or', *Mail,* 24 April 1942, p. 4.
45 'Do Not Yield to Blind Fear', *Mail,* 21 April 1942, p. 4.
46 Ibid.
47 Hope to Linlithgow, 22 April 1942, Linlithgow Papers, MSS Eur F125/70, IOR.
48 Hope to Linlithgow, 18 April 1942, Linlithgow Papers, MSS Eur F125/70, IOR.
49 'Fear in the Hills', *Mail,* 19 April 1942, p. 6.
50 Papers of Margaret Hunt, MSS Eur 241/20, India Office Records, British Library.
51 Ibid.
52 Letter to the Editor, the *Mail,* 20 April 1942, p. 2.

12. Exodus, Elsewhere

1 'Calcutta Exodus', *Times of India*, 31 January 1942, p. 12.
2 Herbert to Linlithgow, 8 April 1942, MSS Eur F125/42, IOR.
3 Ibid., 21 April 1942.
4 Herbert to Linlithgow, 23 December 1942, MSS Eur F125/42, IOR.
5 Ian Stephens, *Monsoon Morning*, p. 82.
6 'Sir J.P. Srivastava on the Raids', *Statesman*, 27 December 1942, p. 7.
7 'Bad Bungling', *Statesman*, 28 December 1942, p. 4.
8 Herbert to Linlithgow, 27 December 1942, Linlithgow Papers, MSS Eur F123/42, IOR.

9 Eugenie Fraser, *A Home by the Hooghly: A Jute Wallah's Wife* (Edinburgh: Mainstream Publishing Company, 1989), p. 104.
10 Ian Stephens, *Monsoon Morning*, p. 83.
11 Lewis to Linlithgow, 26 February 1942, MSS Eur F125/84, IOR.
12 Linlithgow to Emery, 17 March 1942, MSS Eur F125/22, Linlithgow Papers, IOR.
13 Fortnightly Report from Orissa, First and Second half of March 1942, Home Dept, NAI.
14 Lewis to Linlithgow, 10 March 1942, MSS Eur F125/84, IOR.
15 'Precautions in Orissa', *The Hindu*, 2 April 1942, p. 3.
16 Lewis to Linlithgow, 12 April 1942, MSS Eur F125/84, IOR.
17 Ibid.
18 'Exodus from Cochin', *The Hindu*, 17 April 1942, p. 6.
19 'When Sirens Blared, Trenches Were Dug', MetroPlus, Kochi Edition, *The Hindu*, 8 April 2003, p. 1.
20 Linlithgow to Governor of Bombay Roger Lumley, 21 December 1941, MSS Eur F125/56, IOR.
21 Lumley to Linlithgow, January 1942, MSS Eur F125/56, IOR.
22 ' Big Exodus from Bombay', *Times of India*, 16 April 1942, p. 5.
23 Ibid.
24 'Evacuation in the Case of Emergency', *Statesman*, 17 April 1942, p. 6.
25 Herbert to Linlithgow, 21 April 1942, Linlithgow Papers, MSS Eur F125/42, IOR.
26 'Delhi', *Statesman*, 18 April 1942, p. 4.
27 'Evacuation Only in Emergency', *Statesman,* 19 April 1942, p. 5.
28 Linlithgow to Herbert, 30 April 1942, Linlithgow Papers, MSS Eur F 125/42, IOR.
29 Fortnightly Report from Delhi, First half of April 1942, Home Dept, NAI.
30 S. Modak, *What I Have Seen in Jamshedpur*, Unpublished, Tata Archives, Jamshedpur.
31 'Tata's War Production Praised', *Statesman*, 13 December 1941, p. 8.

32 Stewart to Linlithgow, 24 March 1942, MSS Eur F125/49, IOR.

33 'Mr. J.J. Ghandy Refutes Rumours', *Searchlight,* 4 April 1942, p. 6.

34 Fortnightly Report from Bihar, Second half of December 1941, Home Dept, NAI.

35 Fortnightly Report from Bombay, First half of April 1942, Home Dept, NAI.

36 Clow to Linlithgow, 8 May 1942, MSS Eur F125/35, IOR.

37 Ibid., 2 June 1942.

38 'Either Or', *Mail,* 24 April 1942, p. 4.

39 Interview with author.

40 Linlithgow to Clow, 30 May 1942, MSS Eur F125/35, IOR.

Epilogue: Zoo Story

1 See for instance, Indivar Kamtekar, 'The Shiver of 1942', Chris Bayly and Tim Harper, *Forgotten Armies,* and Yasmin Khan, *The Raj at War.*

2 O. Pulla Reddi, *Autumn Leaves*, p. 55.

3 Madras Administrative Report, 1942–43, p. 39.

4 Hilda Kean, *The Great Cat and Dog Massacre: The Real Story of World War II's Unknown Tragedy* (Chicago: The University of Chicago Press, 2017), Chapter 3, Kindle.

5 Clare Campbell, *Bonzo's War: Animals under Fire 1939–1945* (London: Corsair, 2013), Author's Note, Kindle.

6 Ibid., Chapter 5.

7 Clelly Johnson, 'Prisoners in War: Zoos and Zoo Animals during Human Conflict 1870–1947', (MA Thesis, Clemson University, 2015), tigerprints.clemson.edu/all_theses/2222/ Also 'A.R.P at the Zoo', *The Times,* 29 September 1938.

8 Cited in Amitav Ghosh's blog, amitavghosh.com/exodus-from-burma-1941-a-personal-account/.

9 'A.R.P. Measures in Sydney', *Statesman*, 7 January 1942, p. 6.

10 Warsaw Zoological Garden website: zoo.waw.pl/en/about-us/zoo-history.

11 Ibid.
12 Khalid Elhassan, 'The Tragic Ordeal of the Berlin Zoo in World War II', historycollection.co/the-tragic-ordeal-of-the-berlin-zoo-in-world-war-ii/
13 Kevin Prenger, *War Zone Zoo: The Berlin Zoo and World War II* (independently published, 2018), Chapter 9, Kindle.
14 Khalid Elhassan, 'The Tragic Ordeal of the Berlin Zoo in World War II'.
15 Roger Moorhouse, *Berlin at War: Life and Death in Hitler's Capital 1939–45* (Vintage Digital, 2011), Chapter 15, Kindle.
16 Ibid., Chapter 4.
17 Proceedings of the Madras Corporation Council, 17 April 1942.
18 Ibid.
19 O. Pulla Reddi, *Autumn Leaves*, pp. 55–56.

Index

D

E

F